TESTING THE TEACHER

TESTING THE TEACHER

HOW URBAN
SCHOOL DISTRICTS
SELECT THEIR
TEACHERS AND SUPERVISORS

Paul L. Tractenberg

With a Foreword by
Eleanor Holmes Norton

AGATHON PRESS, NEW YORK

Distributed by
SCHOCKEN BOOKS, NEW YORK

AGATHON PRESS, INC.
150 Fifth Avenue
New York, N. Y. 10011

Trade distribution by:
SCHOCKEN BOOKS INC.
200 Madison Avenue
New York, N. Y. 10016

Library of Congress Catalog Card Number: 72-95966

ISBN 0-87586-040-0

Printed in the United States

CONTENTS

ACKNOWLEDGMENTS

Without many people this book would not have been possible. My wife and children tolerated my vacation, weekend and evening disappearing acts for a year and a half, and my wife provided constant encouragement, perspective and a literary sense. Eleanor Holmes Norton and Brooke Aronson, and their staffs at the New York City Commission on Human Rights, helped me to conceive and shape this book, and generously gave me the benefit of their reactions and insights. The Fund for the City of New York and members of the Rockefeller Family Fund provided necessary financial support. My research assistants, Marilyn Morheuser and Marsha Greenfield, researched and assisted in a variety of areas with unfailing good cheer. Ms. Morheuser did most of the research and much of the writing for Chapter 1. The faculty secretaries at Rutgers University Law School in Newark, especially Mary Hanlon, Elizabeth Urbanowicz, Belinda Williams and Colleen Duffy, worked diligently in the preparation of several drafts of the manuscript. Finally, Burt Lasky and Alan Liss, my editors and publishers, were everything editors and publishers should be.

P.L.T.
Millburn, New Jersey

FOREWORD

It is one of the great ironies of the struggle for social progress in this nation that just when we have become committed to quality education for *all* children, our schools are found most wanting in their ability to provide such an education. Urban schools have unquestionably failed to meet the challenge that has been thrust upon them by the social transformation of the last decades: the task of educating those who have been traditionally excluded from educational opportunity. This failure is the result of many complex and controversial factors. Among the most important, but too often overlooked, are the inadequate and outmoded methods of training, qualifying and selecting the teaching and supervisory personnel who are most directly involved with the process of education.

Ironically, teachers have too often gotten short shrift in the arguments over problems of education. But anyone concerned about today's children must be interested in improving today's teachers. Teachers face an unprecedented situation when they try to educate youngsters caught in deteriorating urban conditions. Yet few teachers have been prepared to handle this new challenge; teacher training and preparation have not kept pace with the astonishingly rapid transformation of our pupil population in the cities. As our central cities continue to absorb more and more minority and poor people, many of them migrants from rural areas in the South or Puerto Rico or foreign countries, our school systems have had to handle in-

creasingly more children with special problems and needs. Today many who form the bulk of the school population in the
cities come from severely deprived backgrounds; many do not
speak English. These children are making unique and compelling demands on school systems that have not yet changed
to respond to their needs.

To be sure, city schools have always had the task of educating and assimilating immigrant groups and poor people. But
never before has that task been so formidable. Earlier immigrant
groups often did not send their poorest, most deprived children
to school beyond the lowest grades. They were needed to work
to add to meagre family earnings in a period in which unskilled
jobs were plentiful for those with little education. The "dropout" in pre-technological society did not necessarily lack a
future, as he does today. Now that society has accepted the
responsibility of educating *all* children—even the poorest—and
of offering equal opportunity to all, the task is immeasurably
greater. Yet little has been done to prepare teachers for these
changes, to prepare them for this new task. And little has
been done to reexamine the ways we qualify and select those
who must educate our children.

In January 1971, the New York City Commission on Human
Rights held week-long hearings on teacher and supervisor
selection. Originating in an effort to determine reasons for
unusually poor minority representation among New York City
school personnel, our investigation necessarily expanded to
encompass the broader issues of training and selection of
school personnel.

It became clear that we were dealing not alone with a
question of possible discrimination. Rather we found that we
had tackled a matter of great complexity with far-reaching
implications for education in the schools of the nation's cities:
that of how to develop and recruit a corps of teaching personnel
best able to cope with the formidable problems of educating
the children who have inherited our deteriorating cities. The

fact that there were, indeed, so few minority teachers in New York City served as the initial indicator of what turned out to be a larger and more formidable problem. For teaching has traditionally been the most open of all the professions to blacks and other minorities. Originally this was because of the irony that segregated schools assured the need for black teachers. But the teaching tradition among minorities clearly survived legal segregation; it can be seen in their significant inclusion as teachers and supervisors in virtually every large urban school system except, at the time of the hearings, New York. The contrasting situation in New York (only 9 percent of our teachers were black and less than 1 percent Puerto Rican) raised serious questions about the entire system of personnel selection, questions which were illuminated by the testimony at the hearings.

The hearings brought these questions—too often dealt with in terms of unproductive conflict and mutual recrimination—into the realm of reason and objectivity. For five days and evenings the Commission heard testimony of an extraordinarily high quality. Much of this testimony came from people within the system—the Chancellor, other school and union officials, supervisors, teachers, and representatives of community boards—all of whom demonstrated an impressive commitment to improving education in their acknowledgment and analysis of the faults of the system and their willingness to work to remedy them. But the hearings gained national significance from experts and school officials that came from across the nation: from other urban systems, from the Educational Testing Service, and from colleges and universities that train teachers.

After studying the testimony the Commission concluded that the poor minority showing was not due to conscious and deliberate discrimination, but to a *de facto* exclusion of minority groups that was a reflection of the rigidities that infected the entire personnel system. This system was judged, in the words of New York City School Chancellor Harvey Scribner, to be "antiquated, outmoded and inconsistent with both contemporary educational requirements and the concept of decentralized schools." Originally designed to exclude from the educational system those not suited to teach, its effect under current conditions was to exclude not only the traditional minority groups, but anyone who thought differently from those who designed and conducted the licensing examinations. Described by one expert as "so inbred as to be sociological incest," the examination process embodied a cultural and geographic bias hardly consistent with the flexibility and innovation demanded by rapidly changing conditions.

The hearings also raised serious doubts about the validity of the examinations as instruments to ensure selection of those best suited to teach. It could not be shown that the examination process tested those qualities necessary for good teachers, nor that performance on the tests was in any way an indication of future success in teaching. It became clear that the best that could be said about the examination system was that it screened out incompetents. But surely the exigencies of urban education today require more—that ways be found to screen *in* the best potential talent to educate inner-city children now so inadequately served, that ways be found to recruit and select those with the special knowledge, skill, interest and devotion. There was virtually unanimous agreement among the experts who testified that such qualities cannot be easily evaluated by a written examination; that they are best judged by objective observation and evaluation of personnel during training and on the job. Developing such performance-based criteria has already become a major goal of the best school systems throughout the country.

The Commission's recommendations for New York City schools were comprehensive. It suggested the discontinuation of the Board of Examiners in its present form, and the adoption of an alternative method of selection, relying on state certification for initial screening of applicants, with community school boards exercising ultimate responsibility for selection criteria and procedures. To ensure objectivity, it recommended that the central Board of Education develop appropriate policy guidelines to guarantee protection of due process to all applicants and personnel. Such guidelines are necessary to preclude the possibility of reliance on irrelevant criteria such as race, religion, origin, attitude toward unions, political beliefs, and the like. Witnesses testified that thus far bias had not been a factor in teacher selection under New York's decentralized school system. The hearings, in fact, brought forth no concrete evidence to justify fears of inevitable bias, corruption and disorder in the event that the school system changed to another selection system, especially one depending on decentralized selection, which is presumed by some to be vulnerable to local pressures. This Commission will require that the law against discrimination always be adhered to as the school system tries to find and employ those teachers who can do the best job of educating our children, whatever their race, religion, background or beliefs. These hearings convinced us that this could not be done without significant changes in the training and selection of teachers.

Soon after the Commission issued its analysis of the hearings, our findings were in effect confirmed by an independent action by the U.S. District Court for the Southern District of New York. Ruling in the case of *Chance & Mercado v. Board of Examiners et al.,* Federal Judge Walter Mansfield found the examinations used to select supervisory personnel were discriminatory in effect and issued a preliminary injunction forbidding the further administration of exams, the issuance of new eligibility lists and the use of existing lists to fill supervisory posts. At the beginning of the school year, the Board of Education approved a new policy to enable New York's decentralized school districts to fill acting supervisory posts during the period of the injunction. Under the interim system, candidates are eligible for these posts "if they meet eligibility requirements for the most recent appropriate supervisory examination or if they possess appropriate state certification." Other provisions include the formulation by the Board of written guidelines for the selection and assignment of acting supervisory personnel, provisions for the development of performance criteria for evaluation of personnel, and for the periodic evaluation of on-the-job performance of such personnel.

These new provisions coincide with several recommendations made by the Commission in its report on the hearings. The broadening of eligibility requirements, with increased reliance on state standards, is an especially commendable move toward greater flexibility, toward a system that will bring in more qualified candidates rather than serve merely to exclude the totally unqualified. The provisions for the development and use of job performance criteria, too, show a commitment to finding new and better ways to evaluate supervisory candidates and personnel. We commend the Board on taking these first important steps toward changing its recruitment and selection practices. To complete such change requires a great effort, which has now been begun.

The transcript of the hearings, which forms an original and valuable document, has previously been published, together with the Commission's recommendations (Agathon Publication Services, Inc., New York). In this new work Paul Tractenberg has used the New York City experience as the basis for an extraordinarily rich and comprehensive examination of personnel practices and their educational and social implications for the nation's schools. Mr. Tractenberg, a Professor of Law at Rutgers University and a former Special Counsel to the New York Board of Education, served brilliantly as Special Counsel to the Commission for the hearings. He has brought his vast knowledge and incisive understanding to this nationwide study. The Commission is gratified that its work has formed the basis for two such remarkable volumes. We are hopeful that our efforts will stimulate the kind of change—in New York and throughout the nation—that will enable our schools to meet the challenge of providing all our children with the education essential to equal opportunity and rewarding and productive lives.

Eleanor Holmes Norton
Chairman, New York City
Commission on Human Rights
March, 1973

TESTING THE TEACHER

**HOW URBAN
SCHOOL DISTRICTS
SELECT THEIR
TEACHERS AND SUPERVISORS**

To
IRENE, BETH and **JOEL**

INTRODUCTION

This book is about urban teachers and the process by which they ultimately find themselves in urban classrooms. It is a process which usually begins in the teacher training institutions, continues through the certification, recruitment and screening of prospective teachers, and culminates in final selection, employment and assignment. Increasingly, the broad public policy issues, legal questions and educational consequences which flow from the shaping and execution of this process are being recognized and held up for careful scrutiny.

An important example of this scrutiny was the New York City Commission on Human Rights' investigation of teacher and supervisor selection in the city school system. That investigation, and the public hearings which concluded it during the week of January 25, 1971, raised many fundamental questions, not just about technical personnel practices but about many other aspects of education in urban areas.*

The Commission's work in this area provided the inspiration for this book. Much of the factual material in these pages, updated and expanded where necessary, came from the hearings

*The full transcript of the hearings has been published as a companion volume to this one under the title *Selection of Teachers and Supervisors in Urban School Districts* (hereinafter *Selection of Teachers*). The Summary and Recommendations section of a report issued by the Human Rights Commisssion after the hearings is reproduced as Appendix A to *Selection of Teachers.*

and other investigative activities of the commission. Having served as Special Counsel to the commission for the hearings, and as draftsman of its report, provides me with a unique vantage point. But this book is *not* an expanded version of the commission's report. Rather, I have sought to use the New York City experience as a springboard to the national questions which must be considered.

New York City as a Model

Many people assume that New York City, because of its extraordinary size and complexity, is not an apt model for other school districts to consider. However, that is simply not the case. There are many respects in which New York City is the best or even only model. For example, New York City has a historic reputation for being a leader in social progress and enlightenment, yet its school system has the poorest performance record of any large city in the country for attracting minority group professionals. To identify the causes of New York City's poor performance, or the reasons for the better results in other school districts, should give *all* school districts hints about improving their own performances.

There are more specific examples of the New York City school system's relevance to other school districts. The New York City Board of Examiners is an institution with few precise counterparts in other school districts. It has been responsible for creating, administering, and grading examinations in 1200 teaching and supervisory license categories, and for issuing eligible lists of those qualified to be appointed. Yet, what is the Board of Examiners but the "logical" extension of applying the civil service system to school district personnel practices. A careful look at the Board of Examiners may therefore result in important insights into the nature and implications of civil service concepts both generally and as they are applied to school systems.

New York City's experience may be pertinent in another
respect as well. Because of its size and complexity, the New
York City school system has been forced already to face special
problems bearing importantly on professional personnel which
are now just on the horizon for other school districts. Decentralization is an obvious example. In 1969 the New York City school
district was divided into 31 community school districts by
legislative action. Elected community school boards have significant responsibilities for operating the elementary and junior
high school programs in their districts. Personnel powers are
fragmented among the community boards, the chancellor (the
successor to the superintendent of schools), the city board of
education and the Board of Examiners. Is this a procedure
likely to produce the best qualified teachers and supervisors?
An important and difficult question; but, should anyone outside of New York City care? Definitely! Most other large
school districts in the country are already decentralizing in
some form or talking about it. There are Detroit, Los Angeles,
Boston, Washington and Newark for openers. Indeed, many
small school districts are looking into ways to increase community participation in the operation of their schools. So,
considering the consistency of certain personnel procedures
with decentralization has broad relevancy.

Broad Implications of Teacher Selection

Having determined to use the New York City experience as a
starting point, the basic premise I then turn to is that selection
of teachers by urban school districts has two major sets of implications—educational and employment. Both will be treated
in this book but the educational implications are the main
focus. That reflects a bias of mine that, over the long haul,
improving this country's educational system will do more to
help realize our egalitarian goals than any other social or
technological advance. I recognize there are wide differences

of opinion about this but, despite certain recent studies, I continue to believe there is no scientifically conclusive evidence to the contrary.

The development of the commission's investigation and public hearings paralleled my development of this book's basic premise. The investigation began as an inquiry into alleged employment discrimination, a customary type of investigation for a human rights agency. But the case involved two relatively unusual elements: the employer being charged with discrimination was another public agency, and the employer's product was the education of children. Recognizing quickly that this could not be just another employment discrimination case, the commission staff began to extend the concept of the traditional employment process both backward and forward—to teacher training and certification on the one end, and to upgrading and promotion on the other. Moreover, given the incomparably important job school professionals have, the commission's staff began to look not only to whether the selection process affords equal employment opportunity to the professionals, but also to whether it is attracting professionals best equipped to work with and help to educate youngsters of every color, creed and national origin. This broadening of focus is inevitable in any serious study of a school system's personnel practices and it fully characterized the commission's work. This book will take the broadening process even further.

Educational Implications

In looking to the educational implications of teacher selection, one is struck by the scope and number of important public policy issues raised. The starting point for the analysis is, surprisingly perhaps, several matters of broad agreement. Most people would agree that children and their parents must be at the heart of the educational process and that the success of the educational process must ultimately be judged by how

well children are educated. That is hard to remember sometimes as school systems career from crisis to crisis. For ex-
pressions of concern for children seem to be reserved for public
moments when cameras are grinding and reporters are taking
notes. In board of education meetings and negotiating sessions,
when the real decisions about school systems are usually made,
it is budgets, salaries, job security, working conditions, awarding
of contracts and compliance with technical rules and regulations
which dominate the discussions. Of course, these considerations
ultimately affect the children. But they seem to take on a life
and dynamic of their own.

Another area of broad agreement is that nothing affects the
education of children more directly than who their teachers
are, and without good teachers there can be no good education
(although good teachers may not guarantee good education).
For 180 days a year, year after year, teacher and children are
linked in a process which will fall somewhere along the spectrum
between superior education and stagnation or worse. The
success or failure of this process may go far toward determining
the shape of the future urban America.

A final area of broad agreement is that the process by which
teachers are trained, certified, recruited, selected, assigned,
supported and supervised, upgraded and promoted is critically
important to a school system's goal of having the best teachers
for its pupils.

As soon as these broad principles are put to one side, however, any impression of a consensus quickly disappears. This is
to be expected. Whenever the job of translating broad principles
into reality begins, differences of approach, emphasis, and even
style intrude. One of the first serious questions which must be
asked is who is a "good" teacher and how are candidates to be
judged. An approach increasingly suggested is to measure a
teacher's ability through the performance of his or her pupils.
But that approach itself raises a number of perplexing issues.
Is there any way to use pupil performance to judge a candidate

whose only prior classroom experience has been student teaching, perhaps with different kinds of students in a very different kind of school district? Some possibilities will be discussed in Chapter 7. How can pupil performance be fairly and adequately evaluated? Problems with the use of written tests will be explored in Chapter 6 and alternative evaluation methods will be considered in Chapters 7 and 8. Should teachers really be evaluated and held accountable principally on the basis of student performance without taking into account differing student capabilities and incentives?

Many argue that the individual teacher and the school as a whole simply can't be expected to overcome all of society's multi-faceted failures, and that is undeniably true. Teachers and their schools don't function in a vacuum. Their jobs are made immeasurably more difficult when classes are large, facilities are poor, and children bring to school the emotional and physical infirmities which accompany life for many in American cities. To conclude from this that teachers and schools can make *no* difference, or that little should be expected from them, is wrong, however. We must ask much of them; and we must ask more rather than less when many children come to them with educational disadvantages. But we must be prepared to provide our schools with the necessary resources and support to attempt this demanding job. And we must require that they use those resources effectively toward providing all children with maximum educational benefits.

Teachers and prospective teachers cannot be measured then *solely* by the performance of their pupils even if "pupil performance" is viewed as going far beyond scores on standardized reading and mathematics tests. The traditional measuring rod for teachers has been the *teacher's* knowledge, abilities. capacities, and personal characteristics. This is based in part on legal requirements and in part on the state of the art of personnel selection.

The constitutions of many states, including New York, require that teachers and other public employees be hired on the basis of "merit and fitness" to perform their jobs. This is the heart of the civil service concept, a concept by now deeply engrained in the American sense of fairness. Emphasizing the merit and fitness of candidates has tended to focus the selection process on their personal characteristics. And these characteristics have been evaluated largely by reference to the academic and other records of the candidates, their performance on written tests, and oral interviews. Often the process has been *knowledge*-oriented, perhaps because it is easier to be objective about assessing knowledge. But increasingly, critics of the selection process have been urging that knowledge is only a part, and probably a rather small part, of the personal qualities needed in good teachers. Especially is this true in urban school districts where the educational process is often complicated by overriding psychic factors.

The need for a new definition of merit and fitness is not limited to urban schools, however. Teachers everywhere exist in the midst of ferment. Perhaps never before has public education faced problems of such magnitude and variety as now confront it. Many of these problems will be discussed in Chapter 1. Here it is sufficient to say that most of the traditional wisdom about teachers, teaching, and the educational process, is being challenged or overturned. Traditional techniques for training teachers and certifying them as minimally competent have begun to give way already. Similarly, traditional classroom techniques for educating children are giving way before the pressure of new ideas. No more stationary seats in regimented, silent classrooms with all eyes directed to "The Teacher." The open classroom, the open corridor, schools without walls, ungraded programs, individualized instruction, team teaching, modular scheduling—this is where education is moving. And the teacher is being moved with it, but often reluctantly and without adequate preparation or skills. Teachers, like most other people, resist the unknown and different. Particularly is this so where teachers are involved in the educational revolution from many points of view. They are employees of a school system which has to deal with enormous pressures being brought to bear on it. They are professionals who are trying to define and justify their professional roles. They are themselves members of one of the most important power blocs.

All this adds up to a period of great uncertainty for teachers and the schools. Where the process of change, already set in motion, will end no one can say. It may free education to break through long-standing barricades; or it may lead back ultimately to the most traditional approaches. But one thing seems certain —during the period of turmoil teachers will be subjected to different stresses and challenges than before. For them to meet these stresses and challenges forthrightly and with a chance of success, teachers will have to be different from their predecessors. That is where the selection process comes in. It too must adapt. For merit and fitness are not precise, timeless, static notions. Who is most meritorious and fit to teach and to supervise teachers will vary from time to time and from place to place depending upon the particular needs of particular children. Although the merit and fitness of a teacher cannot be judged exclusively by the performance of the pupils, neither can teachers be judged without reference to their pupils and how they serve them. After all, teach exist only for children. While it is all too easy to become engrossed in test scores, percentages, ratios, norms, and course hour requirements in any study of teacher training, selection, and performance they tell only a part of the story. The essential human relationship between teacher and child is the key to the learning process and education. This is especially true during a period of transition in educational philosophy. Specific types of knowledge, techniques, and skills must be regarded as less important, and certain broad personal characteristics must be brought to the heart of the selection process. For, if we cannot predict what knowledge, techniques, and skills will be important to the educational process in the near future, it makes no sense to evaluate new teachers on the basis of their present knowledge, techniques, and skills. In-

stead, we must reshape the selection machinery so that it focuses
on the kinds of fundamental characteristics which we know must
be important—concern and respect for children, sensitivity, openness to new ideas and approaches, creativity and intelligence in
the broadest sense.

All well and good, skeptics will say, virtue and motherhood
are nice ideals too, but can you run an educational system on
them? How can you measure these qualities in prospective
teachers? Isn't this really the end of an *objective* merit system?
Won't we be substituting each selection body's special set
of prejudices?

Much of this book is devoted to trying to find answers to
those questions. My own view is that the surest way to bring
about the demise of the merit system and the civil service
format it has spawned is to adamantly resist all pressures for
reform. The reasons for my view and the adequacy of the
specific reforms which are being urged are discussed later,
but one policy issue must be referred to now. That is the
matter of race or ethnicity. Are all of these reform efforts
really a smoke screen to obscure the effort to create a selection process which favors black and Spanish candidates? Are
we moving inevitably toward a system of "reverse discrimination," "preferential hiring," "benign quotas"? Can only black
teachers teach black pupils? Some of the legal implications
of this possibility are discussed in Chapter 6, but there are,
of course, important educational and public policy aspects, too.

These queries tend to be lumped together but conceptually
that is a mistake. They raise fundamentally different policy
issues, and, for that reason, they form a good bridge between
the educational and employment aspects of this introductory
policy discussion.

From an educational perspective, the effect of vastly increased numbers and percentages of minority group pupils
cannot be ignored. It has enormous educational implications
which must be dealt with in the training and selection of

teachers, as in all other facets of the school system. Teachers who might have been "best qualified" to educate predominantly white, middle-class students are not automatically the "best qualified" to educate other kinds of students.

Is the answer a process that yields more black and Spanish-speaking teachers? That may help. The teacher has always been one of the chief models for youngsters. Seeing more teachers and supervisors of his or her own color or ethnic background undoubtedly helps to improve a child's self-image and raise his or her sights. Moreover, teachers of the same color or ethnic background are more likely to be sensitive to special needs of the child and parents. At the least, these teachers are unlikely to regard a child as having a low potential *because* of the child's color or ethnic background, or to give a child that impression.

Studies of educational performance suggest that two critical factors in the learning process are the student's perception of his or her own capabilities, and the teacher's perception. The two are, of course, intertwined. If a teacher gives the impression that he thinks a student has little potential, it is much harder for the student to have a positive self-image. This is especially true if the student comes from a nonschool environment which does little to reinforce positive feelings about his or her worth.

But this is not to suggest that the problem is a "black problem" or a "Puerto Rican problem." Philip Kaplan, chairman of a community school board in Brooklyn, testified at the Human Rights Commission's hearings that the problem had existed for some time:

> I myself, when I started kindergarten, did not speak a word of English. I just spoke Jewish. When I started elementary school, the fact that there were teachers that understood Yiddish was a tremendous crutch. ... It was a help to me and to my parents, who came to school to find out my progress, to speak to someone who spoke the same language as we did at the time. [*Selection of Teachers,* 1972, p. 201]

Nor is it necessary to suggest that only black teachers are capable of teaching black children, any more than it is true that only Italian teachers can teach Italian pupils, or only Jewish teachers can teach Jewish pupils. Indeed, all children can benefit from having variety in their teachers as in their classmates. And sensitivity to children's feelings, respect for their potential and affection for them does not depend solely on color coordination. Many white teachers have demonstrated these personal qualities in their relationships with children of other racial or ethnic backgrounds, and they have been accepted by the children and their parents (although special problems may exist where there are severe language barriers). Despite this possibility, it would not be fair to minimize the problems that white teachers face in many urban schools. Children are marked early by growing up in the ghettoes of this country and they often bring to school hostility which cannot be immediately dissipated by a kind word or an expression of genuine interest. At best it may be a long and trying process, so tenacity is likely to be another essential personal quality for the urban teacher.

Let's assume we can agree on the kinds of qualities and strengths that urban teachers should have. The test of a selection process is how well it has been selecting *in* candidates with those strengths. For, if it has been failing to do so, for whatever reason, education and the children are the big losers. If it has been failing, for whatever reason, it is not a "merit and fitness" system. If it has been failing, for whatever reason, it must be restored to a true and current conception of "merit and fitness" or "merit and fitness" will become a meaningless shibboleth.

The thesis of this book is that, as quickly as possible, the process by which urban teachers are selected must be converted to a contemporary merit and fitness system. The ability to understand and reach all kinds of children, and to devise or apply new approaches to that end when necessary, must be vigorously sought. The ability to score well on academically oriented written tests must be relegated to a lesser place in the selection process, replaced by other techniques becoming available to evaluate the more essential qualities of applicants. What is at stake may be nothing less than the future of urban education in this country.

I reject the arguments of some that present selection techniques will serve us well in the long run and we must simply wait patiently for them to bear fruit. According to Albert Shanker, president of the United Federation of Teachers, for example:

> . . . [It] has almost always been that the teachers in urban school systems represented predominantly the immigrants of the previous generation who were teaching the children of the newer immigrants. So, when the Irish came into the system, they were taught by WASP's; and the Irish then taught the Jews; and the Jews, the Italians; and I suppose the next group of Black and Puerto Rican teachers and administrators will be teaching the newly affluent grape-pickers, represented by Cesar Chavez, moving up from the lowest to the next rung. [*Selection of Teachers*, 1972, p. 342].

This is presented as a kind of natural law. Black and Puerto Rican teachers have only to wait their turn. But should they have to wait? For what? If it is the *employment* implications that are the focus, there may be some justification for the statement. The school system as employer may have built up a certain debt to each immigrant wave as it supplied the personnel to staff the schools. No one ought to suggest that individuals already employed by the schools should be discharged because they represent an earlier rather than the present ethnic group. Indeed, it could be argued that some expectancy has been created even about future jobs.

But *educational* implications, rather than employment ones, should be the focus. The real question is whether the ethnic categorization of Mr. Shanker obscures rather than clarifies the educational issue. If we come back to the goal of the school system as getting the teachers who are best qualified to teach the particular students populating the schools at the particular time, is there any justification for asking any group of prospective teachers to bide their time because waiting is how the system functions? Not unless the reason they have to wait is so that children can have the best qualified teachers in their classrooms at every moment. But even Mr. Shanker implies that that may not be the effect of his "natural law." Are black and Puerto Rican teachers really being asked to wait because they will be the best teachers for Cesar Chavez' "affluent grape-pickers"?

We must get back to the basic issues. If selecting teachers in a way which will produce teachers better qualified to reach urban youngsters will result in far more black and Puerto Rican teachers, then that should happen as soon as possible. If it would not have such a result, now or in the future, then it would be *educationally* mischievous to turn the jobs over to blacks and Puerto Ricans just because an appropriate waiting period has elapsed. A *true* merit and fitness system for selecting urban teachers, one which really tested qualifications for the actual job, could and should be color and ethnicity blind. Anything less would cheat the children. From the *educational* point of view, compensatory employment by any name may prove to be self-defeating. On the other hand, if many selection processes continue to be only questionably related to the real job and continue to screen out disproportionately high numbers of minority applicants, then color and ethnicity will justifiably remain in the forefront.

Even if selection processes can be suitably reformed to reflect merit and fitness, an important educational *and* employment problem will remain. Many teachers already selected by inappropriate methods or criteria, or many senior teachers selected when the methods and criteria might have been more appropriate to the times, are employed in urban school districts. Whether or not it would make *educational* sense to replace them quickly, legal, practical and perhaps moral considerations make that impossible. So, many teachers who have been serving in school systems throughout periods of marked change in racial and socioeconomic make-up will be in urban schools, and they pose one of the most perplexing problems in urban education. Do they have the strength, flexibility, and will to bridge the gap? Will they be helped to do so by their school systems?

Regrettably, the frustration, confusion, and fear felt by many of these teachers about having to deal with dramatically changed circumstances often is manifested in their attitudes toward children. Many of us educated in urban public schools who have former teachers still active there can attest to the problem. They hang on grimly until retirement age, pining for the "good old days" when so many of their students were "serious and nice and interested in their studies." The lack of understanding, respect, and affection for their current students is appallingly obvious even to a casual listener. Surely the students who have to witness it 180 days a year can't be unaffected by it.

But the older teachers can't be made out as the villains of this piece. Typically, they are being thrust into situations which *are* alien to them. They were trained and all their experience prepared them to cope with certain kinds of children who no longer populate urban schools in the same numbers. These teachers have received little, if any, assistance from their school systems in handling the new challenges. In a sense, they are captives of their own job security and retirement benefits. They are confused, frightened and embittered. Hardly a frame of mind for being open to new ideas and approaches.

The school systems must do more with and for these senior teachers. A genuine effort has to be made to understand their problems, to work with them in the development of new perceptions and skills, and to support their attempts to change in the classroom. Some senior teachers will simply not be able to make the transition even with adequate support, and the school system will have to make some difficult decisions about their future in the district. Hopefully, the school authorities and teachers' organizations will be prepared to discuss this problem candidly and to work out a program consistent with both the educational needs of the children in the district and the personal and professional needs of the teachers. Failure to do so will consign many urban schools to long-term guerrilla warfare.

Employment Implications

These then are the major educational policy implications of teacher selection by urban school districts. But, as I have already mentioned, there is another side to the coin. There are obvious employment policy implications as well. Focusing on the *employment* aspects may actually lead to different perceptions about the nature of the process and about ways to reform it. Where educational and employment implications pull the reformer in opposite directions, as is sometimes the case, a decision has to be made about priorities. In my case, the priority has been stated—educational considerations will prevail.

School districts are major employers by any criteria. They account for almost two and one-half million teaching jobs alone. If most of these jobs have been effectively closed to the members of any racial or ethnic groups, for whatever reason, significant employment consequences follow. But that would be true of any comparable size employer. There are two things which distinguish the public schools and make their employment practices even more consequential.

School systems are *public* employers and their employment practices should serve as models for the private sector. If the state and its agencies don't extend equal employment opportunities to all citizens, who will? This is being increasingly recognized and has resulted in attacks across a broad front against alleged discrimination and invalidity in civil service selection and promotional procedures. Written tests have been singled out for special criticism. But teacher selection is just one part of the battle; challenges to procedures for employment of state police in Alabama, policemen in New York City, Newark and Boston, professors and administrators in the State University of New York, and federal government employees under the Federal Service Entrance Examination illustrate the scope of the attack. The battle is shaping up along traditional reformer versus supporter of the status quo lines. The reformers press their attack on the basis of the manifest racial imbalance among civil service employees and the questionable validity of many civil service selection processes to make meaningful distinctions in terms of job-related skills. The supporters, on the other hand, maintain that what is really at issue is whether selection will continue to be based on "merit" and "objectivity," however imperfectly realized in some cases, or whether there will be a return to the "pork barrel." Any significant change in the current system is, for them, a rejection of "civil service." This dispute may have to be resolved in the courts where many challenges to civil service procedures, including those relating to the selection of school professionals, are already pending. Chapter 6 discusses the legal issues in detail.

The second reason for the special importance of teacher selection to employment policy is that, nationally, teaching as a profession has always attracted disproportionately high numbers of minority group people. If they are being effectively excluded from positions in urban school districts, the ramifications would be especially destructive.

For these reasons, selecting teachers has broad employment consequences, and the primary goal sought by some reformers is an employment-oriented goal—more minority group teachers. Put in another way, the goal is an end to racial imbalance. How does one achieve that goal? By techniques such as affirmative employer action, compensatory hiring to redress past discrimination, or "benign quotas"? From an employment point of view these may be justifiable or even necessary steps to break historic patterns of discrimination and to open more jobs to minority groups. These are worthy goals but they cannot be considered in isolation. The educational consequences must be kept in mind; indeed, for me, the educational needs of children must prevail.

Scope and Structure of the Book

This book sets out to put the many questions raised by the selection of urban teachers into a meaningful context, and to suggest some answers. It is directed at the broad range of people who are vitally interested in public education and who can affect its future course. There are sufficient details concerning administrative, legislative, and judicial developments to make the book useful for school administrators, professional educators, academicians, and lawyers. Indeed, I have discussed many of the important new developments in those areas through December 31, 1972. At the same time, this book is written in a style and format which should make it readable and understandable to many parents and other persons interested in public education who have no formal background or training in the field, but whose stake in the system is monumental.

Except for the first chapter, the book is organized sequentially; Chapers 2 through 7 cover the various aspects of teacher selection, moving from the training of urban teachers through their recruitment, selection, and assignmeni to their accountability and promotion. Chapter 1 is designed to provide an overview of the urban teacher's world: what is the teacher like; what are the students like; what is the school and school district like; what important pressures bear down on the teacher; and how does he or she respond. For readers without substantial background in education, this chapter may be indispensable for a full appreciation of the remainder of the book. For other readers, Chapter 1 may provide both a useful refresher course and helpful citations to landmark and new authority in the field. Because of its nature and functions, Chapter 1 has more detailed footnotes than any other chapter and a different format is used. Numbers interspersed throughout the text refer to complete footnotes at the end of the chapter. The other chapters have bracketed short-form citations to the authority in the text and full references to the authority at the end of the chapter also.

CHAPTER 1

THE TEACHER, THE PUPIL, AND THE SCHOOL

School should be a place where potential is discovered and creativity encouraged; where teachers and students come together in mutual respect and affection to learn from one another and, in the process, to grow. But many argue that American public schools have never really functioned as if this were their primary goal. Developing discipline and the will to conform may be a more accurate statement of the actual goal, according to critics.

Whatever the goal, however, there is little dispute that public education in this country has never before been beset with problems of such magnitude and variety as now threaten it. Especially in the urban schools these problems threaten to destroy any remaining public confidence in the educational system. Without such confidence the system can not long survive in any meaningful form. For ultimately the public must be willing to support public education; by spending tax dollars for it and by entrusting their children's future to it.

The clear indicia of dwindling support for the present system are everywhere. Voters are increasingly rejecting school budgets and school bond issues.[1] At the same time, pressure is building for more substantial public accountability procedures. The New York City Board of Education has contracted with the Educational Testing Service for a school accountability design, and the movement toward full state funding of educational costs will certainly be accompanied by more extensive statewide evaluation.

Dissatisfaction is boiling up in other areas, too. Parents, especially those in urban school districts, have been pressing for decentralization and community control since at least the late 1960's. This movement grew in part out of a broader political self-awareness. But its deepest roots were imbedded in the frustration of seeing children's hopes and promise devastated by a public education system which seemed totally unable to reach the children or their parents. Those who see greater community control as a means to bridge the gap have won some battles but the war is far from over. Indeed, a much older war is still being waged with the likely victor uncertain. In 1954 the United States Supreme Court decided in *Brown v. Board of Education*[2] that racially separate schools were inherently unequal, at least when they resulted from state action. Since then, substantial progress has been made in most Southern states to end dual school systems. But most of the progress has come only in the past several years after more than 15 years of official foot dragging under the judicial sanction of "all deliberate speed." And even now, formidable efforts are under way to roll back the clock. A spate of proposed constitutional amendments and legislative bills attempts to prohibit busing of students to desegregate the public schools. Without busing, meaningful integration will be impossible in many school districts throughout the country. This is true of many large urban school districts in the North. Southerners point to this with irony. Only when Northern metropolises, such as Detroit, Denver, and San Francisco, were threatened with mandatory plans for achieving racial balance, they say, did serious efforts begin to prohibit the use of busing. And the Southerners have a point. Although most Northern school districts have not had legally required dual school systems, the schools in many large Northern cities are virtually segregated by race or ethnic background. The traditional defense that the segregation in the North is *de facto* rather than *de jure* has begun to be undercut as federal courts have either found a basis for *de jure* segregation in Northern cities or have ruled that the distinction should not be dispositive if the same harm flows to the children.

Yet another expression of dissatisfaction with the present public school system comes from those who should know best—the students. They have sought broader freedom of expression and action in the schools and a larger voice in determining how the schools should function. Some students, despairing of any real reform in the public schools, have even sought alternatives like the free schools.

In the middle of this maelstrom are the teachers. Who they are and how they got there is as important a part of the picture as what they face. This chapter will sketch a profile of the urban teacher and explore his or her relationship to the urban pupil and to the urban school environment in which they both try to function. To give a real sense of what the urban teacher faces requires that this chapter touch upon most of the problems which beset urban education. But the purpose is not to deal with them comprehensively. That would occupy many volumes. Rather, the overview provided should serve as a back-drop for this book's focus on the training, recruitment, selection and upgrading of teachers by urban school districts.

THE LEADING CHARACTERS

Who is the Teacher?

Most American public school teachers are white females from a middle to lower middle class economic background and with a relatively mediocre educational background. The median age of all public school teachers is 36 years; the median age for teachers in urban schools is somewhat higher.[3]

If recent trends continue, these characteristics will change, but not quickly. For example, in 1969—70, according to

National Education Association data, 32.4% of all public elementary and secondary school teachers were men.[4] In 1963—64 men comprised 29.9%. But in 1963—64 men constituted 36.2% of all teacher education graduates, as compared to only 31% in 1969—70.

There has also been an increase in the number and percent of minority teachers in the past decade. Blacks and other minorities accounted for 10% of all public school teachers in 1970, 3% more than in 1960.[5] In fact, historically, teaching has been the top professional attraction for black people in this country where, traditionally, more black college graduates have gone into teaching than any other profession or vocation.[6] The job market for black teachers has, however, been essentially a Southern phenomenon, where dual school systems provided jobs for black teachers, principals, and supervisors in all-black school districts. The reluctant demise of dual school systems in the South is now changing that picture. Particularly hard hit are black principals,[7] and because principals were often allowed to recruit their own staff, black teachers are also feeling the impact of desegregation. Thus, for many black teaching professionals, the present national oversupply of teachers carries a double threat.

The middle class, among both whites and blacks, was, for many years, the origin of many teachers and the aspiration of most other teachers. Historically, the profession has attracted a heavy proportion of women from the middle and upper-middle strata of society. However, with women in increasing numbers breaking into other professions which bring greater esteem and remuneration, this is beginning to change. Now, both men and women who enter the teaching profession come from lower-middle-class and blue-collar backgrounds. A 1961 United States Office of Education study of beginning teachers showed 51% of the women and 38% of the men claimed white-collar fathers, while 49% of the women and 62% of the men had fathers in blue-collar or farming

categories.[8] A 1965 Wisconsin study showed over 67% of the
men derived from the latter social classes.[9] Hence, more and
more, those who enter teaching see that profession as a step
up the social ladder.

This upwardly mobile group, for the most part, receive
their professional preparation in what professors rate, by salary
at least, as inferior institutions of higher education. A 1969
Education Professions Development Act report showed that
80% of all teachers are trained at "C" and "D" rated institutions on the American Association of University Professors'
scale of faculty salaries.[10] Nearly half were attending "D"
rated schools while less than 4% were attending "A" rated
schools in 1969. The faculty salary scale has traditionally
been one of the criteria by which the quality of an institution
has been measured.

When at these schools, studying what state departments
require them to study in the form that higher education serves
it to them, these future teachers, on the whole, seem not very
excited about learning. In fact, as compared with other professionals, teachers might be classified with those they typically prefer not to teach—underachievers. In 1952, 1964, and
1968, they ranked lowest of 16 professional categories on
Graduate Record Examinations; and a 1965 U.S. Office of
Education study of graduate students' undergraduate achievement showed that education majors did better only than business and commerce majors.[11]

Whether or not their underachievement in preparatory
studies indicates the intellectual caliber of individuals who
choose teaching as a career or indicates their reaction to
higher education's low investment in the courses they take,
one effect of it is inevitable. Teachers are not well prepared
to teach. Numerous studies in the late sixties showed teachers
poorly prepared to teach science, mathematics, civics, history,
world affairs, and English.[12]

The upward mobility of teachers is perhaps one important
reason for their political conservatism, their reluctance to

change the system in which they are progressing. It must be conceded, however, that restrictive legislation and prohibitive community norms for teacher behavior have made teachers leery of political involvement for change. Thus, the main thrust from the membership level of professional teacher organizations has not been toward needed change in the structure of the educational system, but rather toward greater security for the individual teacher and recognition of him or her as a professional.

For the most part, teacher security is embodied in teacher tenure (and the job security and due process guarantees it assures) and in a unitary salary schedule, with salary determined solely by level of education and years of experience, not by demonstrated ability to do a good job. So firmly and successfully have teachers in control of teacher organizations opposed moves to deviate from unitary salary schedules, that in 1970—71, not a single large school district — out of 80 districts with enrollments exceeding 50,000 children — had provisions for compensating teachers for superior service.[13] In his book, *What's Happened to Teacher,* Myron Brenton predicts that if teacher salaries continue to rise, such simultaneous eating and having of teachers' economic cake will be stopped by angry taxpayers.[14]

The fact that teachers' salaries have risen is due, in large part, to the strength of teacher organizations. The average teacher's salary rose 65% between 1957—58 and 1966—67.[15] The latest National Education Association figures on teachers' salaries show an increase of 31% from 1966—67 to 1970—71 in the minimum salary level of beginning teachers with bachelor's degrees.[16]

Thus, in school systems of 25,000 or more enrollment, the mean salary for a beginning teacher with a bachelor's degree was $5,258 in 1966—67 and $6,915 in 1970—71. The maximum salary for a teacher with a B.A. was $7,959 in 1966—67 and $10,284 in 1970—71. If the teacher had a master's degree, the

beginning salary was $5,717 in 1966—67 and $7,651 in 1970—
71; the maximum salary $8,890 and $11,789. Those teachers
with a Ph.D. or its equivalent (seven years of preparation)
started at $6,381 in 1966—67 and at $8,581 in 1970—71. The
maximums at this level averaged $10,046 in 1966—67 and
$13,400 in 1970—71.

All salary schedules varied, of course, from region to region
and state to state. There were also sharp differences in the same
state between average salaries in urban and suburban districts,
with teachers in high-income suburbs earning higher salaries.
Finally, there were appreciable differences between large and
small urban districts, with the larger districts paying higher
salaries. The 1970—71 mean maximum salary for B.A.'s was,
for example, $11,300 in districts of 100,000 or more enroll-
ment. In 50,000 to 99,999 enrollment districts, it was $10,030.[17]

This difference no doubt results from strong teacher organizations in large cities. It is probably also an indication of a
kind of "combat" pay demanded by teachers in urban areas,
and a genuine need for income required to live in urban
centers. Finally, it probably reflects the higher pay available
in wealthy suburbs with which urban districts must compete.
The NEA's data on selected wealthy suburban districts show
that their average maximum salary for a teacher with a B.A.
in 1970—71 was $11,672, with some such districts paying as
much as $15,530.[18]

Although teachers' salaries have risen dramatically in the
past two decades, they have, nevertheless, not overtaken the
rise in the cost of urban living. A comparison of the U.S. Department of Labor's estimate of required income for a city
worker in 1967 with the average city school teacher's salary
is revealing. In only one major urban center, San Francisco-
Oakland, did teachers earn enough to enjoy a *moderate*
standard of living.[19]

Teacher organizations, interested as they are in salary,
press even harder for the security of their members. Teacher

tenure, a hard won right which the organized profession is proud of, goes far toward making teaching the most secure of any profession. It has been called "the closest thing to an ironclad promise of job security with no strings attached."[20]

With the detailed safeguards built into union—school board contracts as well as state statutes, tenured teachers cannot be dismissed from their jobs except for certain specified causes, such as immorality, willful neglect of duty, or malfeasance. Dismissal for such causes is never summary. It is preceded by due process rights to a hearing, to have counsel or counsel substitute (sometimes a union representative), to subpoena witnesses, and to appeal the decision. Generally, the first decision is made by a specially constituted school board committee whose decision must be approved by a majority of the board. It can be appealed to the state education authorities and ultimately to the courts. (Some collective bargaining contracts also provide for resort to arbitration.) Although decisions of education authorities are not ordinarily reversed by the courts, court deference to school authorities is a minimal threat to the absolute security of tenure, for there are not many attempts to dismiss tenured teachers.

In their battles for contracts which assure job security, the *Riles Report* notes, as do most other serious commentaries on urban education, that "unions performed a vital function historically and continue to provide teachers with valuable protections."[21] The drive for teacher tenure originated as a result of wholesale and arbitrary dismissals of teachers, often for political reasons, through the 1930's. The treatment of black teachers in the South, where tenure statutes and union contracts are weak or nonexistent, illustrates the problem in a contemporary context. Such dismissals often follow desegregation orders. Nor, for that matter, have Northern school districts been reluctant to dismiss or refuse to rehire nontenured teachers who participate in civil rights or antiwar demonstrations.

The purpose of tenure, then, is to protect the teacher from arbitrary and capricious action, to allow him or her freedom of speech in the classroom. However, as many critics of public education point out, rather than producing bold, creative teachers, tenure has "sapped the incentive of many teachers to improve their competence or to bring to their jobs a strong, professional motivation."[22] Tenure, in combination with the unitary salary schedule, is seen as producing many teachers who are only timeservers.

It's not a question of tenure alone. It's a question of too many individuals with low job motivation — sheltered by a single salary schedule, shielded by tenure — doing work that, despite its apparent challenges, can easily become routinized — coasting along. . . . In almost every district one . . . finds teachers who can't control their classrooms, can't control their students, can't teach. Yet they remain as teachers. In almost every district one finds pure and simple timeservers and, worse, teachers who can't control themselves and who make school a cruel, unbearable experience for some or all of the children whose minds they're supposed to be enriching. Yet, they remain . . . remain as teachers.[23]

A stark illustration of incompetent teachers remaining in their jobs is found in the New York City school system, With more than 60,000 teachers on its payroll, only 12 teachers were formally discharged in a recent five-year period.[24] Since evidence of incompetence and even sadism in the classroom is not lacking, the obvious question is why teachers who victimize children are not dismissed. If they are tenured teachers, they are protected by elaborate dismissal procedures. Indeed, even if they are nontenured the present trend is for substantial safeguards to be afforded. And safeguards should be available. The answer to incompetent teachers is not rejection of due process. What has happened, however, is that procedures have become so time-consuming and costly, and supervisors so unwilling to rock the boat, that due process has become a straitjacket. For incompetent teachers are also protected by administrators who are reluctant to risk bad publicity and strained relations with their staff or with teachers' organizations. Finally, they are protected by their "professional" organizations which have not assumed responsibility for screening and policing their membership.

Moreover, individual teachers, who are most likely to know which of their colleagues really do not belong in a classroom, are ordinarily loathe to report or testify against those colleagues. Although there are some isolated instances of staffs demanding a voice in tenure decisions in order to rid their school of blatant incompetence, for the most part teachers are caught between professional responsibility and group loyalty. And group loyalty usually wins.

Thus teachers themselves, aiming upward on the social ladder, seem to have settled for moderate pay and high security. In this way, they avoid the risk-taking of most other professionals who produce or go hungry. Whether or not this type of "insurance" bodes well for children in their classrooms is questionable. That too many of those children are not learning is certainly clear. Furthermore, the pressure brought to bear by teachers to defeat merit pay and other forms of accountability does not bespeak a professional interest in genuinely improving education.

All of this is not to say, of course, that there are not many good teachers who are creative and who are dissatisfied with the public school system as it presently operates. Indeed, teacher self-criticism has helped focus national attention on teachers' failures and on the failure of the system which shields inadequate teachers.[25]

The sound that echoes through this self-criticism is the failure of the system to meet the educational needs of its largest clientele, urban children. As the *Riles Report* put it, "The system is failing the needs of its good teachers and its good teachers are realizing with increasing frustration that even they, while a part of the system, are failing the needs of the students."[26]

Who Is the Pupil?

Increasingly, the children whom the teacher deals with in large
urban school districts are different from her (or him). She is
usually white; they are black or brown or speak a different
language. She was reared by both parents; many of them are
fatherless. She may have known some physical deprivations,
but she didn't experience the ill-health and malnutrition her
children endure. Nor did she live in segregated, substandard,
overcrowded housing. Although she is not a top achiever, she
did fairly well in grade school and high school. Therefore, the
underachievement and dropout rate of her students is often
beyond her understanding. So, too, is their rebellion against a
system in which she has succeeded and which she grew up
revering. She does not understand their hostility toward her.
Nor does she understand the unique strengths and abilities
which they bring into her classroom. Instead, more often
than not, she is frightened by the unknown — the child she
faces — for she has not been taught how to teach him. If she
cannot escape to suburban schools — as have so many of her
white middle class peers — she remains to mark time until
seniority gives her the right to transfer out of the "worst
schools" and into the "better schools" of the city system.

In 1970, three out of every five blacks in the United States
lived in a major metropolitan area.[27] As of 1970–71, according to HEW's second national survey of racial and ethnic enrollment, 22 of the nation's 100 largest school districts had
enrollments of over 50% black and/or Spanish-surnamed
children.[28] Fifteen additional districts had minority enrollments of 40%–49%. Of the 26 U.S. school districts with enrollments of more than 100,000, 12 had over 50% minority
enrollments and three ranged between 40% and 49% minority.
Thus, 60% of the city school districts which serve more than
100,000 children and 37% of our 100 largest school districts
are either predominantly minority group enrollment or will
be soon.

Moreover, even in large cities whose minority school populations have not reached 40% or 50% proportions, most minority children — if they attend in large numbers — attend racially isolated schools. For example, Milwaukee serves a school population which is 26% black. But 76.2% of its 34,355 black students attend schools which are 80%–100% black. Similarly, Columbus, Ohio assigns 53% of its 29,440 black children (26.9% of the school enrollment) to 80%–100% black schools. And in Indianapolis, which has a 35.8% black student enrollment, 22,925 out of 38,044 black students (60.3%) attend 80%–100% black schools. For the most part, those districts with over 50% minority enrollments have an even greater degree of racial isolation in school assignment. Furthermore, the form in which HEW compiles its data (separate tables used in reporting isolation of each minority group) does not indicate schools which may be 100% black *and* Spanish-American, as opposed to schools which are either 100% black or 100% Puerto Rican.

Thus, even though composite enrollment figures indicate that black students comprise only 14.9% and Spanish-surnamed students only 5.1% of continental U.S. public school enrollment, the picture in America's largest urban centers is quite different. There the urban child will — for many teachers — be the black child or the Puerto Rican child. This is especially so for the beginning teacher, who usually serves his or her professional boot camp in a predominantly minority school.

It is appropriate, then, that in delineating urban school problems, the *Riles Report* devoted three chapters to examining the physical, educational, and social disadvantages of urban nonwhite students and their unique strengths and often unrecognized potential. Some of the *Riles Report* findings are worthy of summarizing here.[29]

Many impoverished black, Puerto Rican and Mexican-American children simply do not have enough food to eact, and they suffer severely from the effects of malnutrition. Almost 40% of the urban children examined in ten states for a 1969 National Nutritional Survey (those examined were 55% black and 25% Spanish-American) consumed less than half the iron they require. One-third of the children under age six were anemic. Similar proportions showed inadequate levels of Vitamin A and Vitamin C. Children between one and three years of age were considerably below the average height of children in the United States.

As a result of widespread malnutrition, children not only suffer many physical and neurological disabilities, they also suffer from a reduction in responsiveness resulting in various levels of apathy. This apathy is often confused with mental retardation by teachers. When such teachers lower their expectations for impoverished children, the self-fulfilling prophecy of "these children can't do better" begins.

The effects of malnutrition and resulting ill-health are also dramatically reflected in the short life expectancy of black males. Although life expectancy for all Americans is generally increasing, for the black man there has been no increase. As a result, more black women are widowed (20% as compared with under 7% of white women in 1960) and at an earlier age than white women. As the *Riles Report* notes, ". . . it is comparatively easy to infer the kinds of effects the lack of the male head of the household could have on a family's economic and emotional stability — and, particularly, on the family's children."[30]

An indication of the economic impact is seen in 1970 census data. The median income of black families headed by women (29% of all black families) was $3,340, while the median income of white families headed by women (9%) was $5,500.[31]

Although there were some encouraging changes in the employment and income level of black families between 1960 1970, 1970 census data show a downturn in the last year of the decade. Black unemployment figures had risen in 1970 to 8.2%, about the 1965 level, with minority teenage unemployment rising to 29.1%, close to the 1963 level.

While median minority family income as a percent of white family income increased between 1947 and 1969, the dollar gap had increased from about $2,500 in 1947 to about $3,600 in 1969. The median incomes in 1969 were $6,191 for minority families and $9,794 for white families.[32] In fact, since 1965 the only real gains in closing the income gap between black and white families were in the South.[33]

Outside the South, there was a rise in the ratio of black to white median income only for young husband-wife families in the North and West. Census analysts show that the increase occurred only where both husbands and wives worked. In these two areas, 7 out of 10 young black wives worked, as compared to 5 out of 10 young white wives.[34]

The need for multiplied earning power in black families is clear. In 1969 two earners in a black family brought in less (median: $7,782) than one earner in a white family (median: $8,450). Nor does this difference in earning power reflect a difference in completed education. For as of 1969, black male *high school* graduates 25 to 54 years old earned less (median: $6,192) than white *elementary school* graduates the same age (median: $7,018). So, too, black *college* graduates earned less ($8,669) than white *high school* graduates ($8,829).[35]

In examining similar data for 1967, the *Riles Report* comments on their implications, especially for the young black student being urged to accept the myth that "better" education means a "better" job:

> The immediate explanation that comes to mind — quite apart from the educational quality of the schooling received — is racial and ethnic discrimination on a grand scale. Moreover, it takes little effort for any member of any of the racial and ethnic groups to arrive at the same explanation. The typical admonishment to a high school student from the minority groups to stay in school now so he will have an opportunity for a better income later receives only partial support from the figures. ... He may have an opportunity for a better income in

comparison with those from the minority groups if he does stay
in school, but in all probability he won't have an equal opportunity
when compared with his counterpart from the white majority group.[36]

The facts of life for black students living in a central city
speak too loudly for them to docilely accept such a myth. For
they are surrounded by poverty which is so desperate that
they can't ignore it. They, themselves, may belong to one of
the 2,740,000 black families living in the central cities of
metropolitan areas which had below the low income level of
$3,743 for a family of four in 1969.[37]

The implications of such poverty are evident, as we have
seen, in malnutrition and ill-health. They are also evident in
overcrowded, substandard, segregated housing into which the
poor black family is forced.

In 1970, 65% of black families living in central cities lived
in renter-occupied housing, and 5% of those families lacked
some or all plumbing facilities.[38] The *Riles Report* held that
the findings of the Kerner Commission concerning housing
and living conditions were just as applicable in 1969 as in 1967.
Two of those findings were:

> Poverty is the foremost reason for the black to live in substandard
> housing.
>
> Discrimination in the housing market is the second major reason
> which forces nonwhites into ghetto housing.[39]

Moreover, the Riles Task Force examined for future implications a lack of federal commitment, in combination with
the higher birth rates and greater youth of the black population as well as the accelerating white flight to the suburbs.
They saw that by 1985, when approximately 70% of metropolitan area whites will be living in the suburbs and 75% of
metropolitan area blacks will be living in the central cities,
urban education systems will be facing gigantic problems.

> The problems created by the increasing numbers of children, by the
> inevitable deepening of the bitterness and frustration which racial

and ethnic isolation and discrimination have bred, and by the never ending cycle of poverty, are also increasing the magnitude of the problem confronting urban education. Specifically, the schools will face more children with more needs and parents with less tolerance for unsalable and invalid education and less acceptance of the schools' current brands of expertise.[40]

Not only do urban children bring to their schools handicaps resulting from discrimination and economic deprivation, but they also bring an environment and orientation reflective of the effects of oppression on the adults in their families and community. These are the "negatives" which the *Riles Report* describes as "the results of a pernicious and insidious combina- of economic poverty, discrimination, isolation, and sheer physical hardships," negatives which "are *not* to be considered as intrinsic to the impoverished urban family."[41]

With the nonwhite male divorce rate five times that of his white counterpart in the inner city, black children will have more immediate experience with problems resulting from divorce, as well as from separation or desertion. They also probably have some knowledge of the problems associated with drug addiction, prostitution, and theft within their neighborhoods — if not within their immediate families.

The adults in the urban child's family — which is likely to be an "extended" one, including as many as four generations within a household plus aunts and uncles — usually react promptly to the child in terms of physical discipline for stepping out of line. Within this family circle, he or she probably has been encouraged to develop a tough self-reliance and a spirit of cooperation. He or she has learned to endure a high degree of noise and has experienced considerable casualness in terms of daily routine.

Beyond that, the urban child has probably acquired concepts, language, and problem-solving techniques primarily geared to survival in the world of the neighborhood and the family. These are the techniques which are brought to his school, where, all too frequently, instead of being recognized as assets and built on, they are discredited and punished.

For instance, the impoverished urban student has learned early a pattern of generous cooperation for survival. But when friends turn quickly to help a youngster having trouble identifying words in the (all too often inappropriate) reader, they are reprimanded because "everybody is to do *his own learning by himself.*"[42]

Similarly, in the neighborhood, ability to fight is an important aspect of the male child's self-prowess and is a key to maintaining group leadership. But in school, even efficient fighting is not admired. Instead, it is viewed as the sign of a troublemaker or potential delinquent.

As a result, urban youngsters are forced early in life to work out sophisticated compromises between the values which they need to survive in their milieu and the values required of them by the schools. "And yet," comments the *Riles Report,* "the staff of a school will rarely register the conflict which this student experiences and resolves — let alone, capitalize upon his very real capability here."[43]

This is, perhaps, one important key to our urban school's failure with its inner city student, its failure to perceive and develop the strengths that that student brings to the school. As he or she continues through school, environmental obstacles persist. But daily the urban youngster is presented with an academic program unrelated to that environment, indeed indifferent to the toll that the environment exacts, and geared "neither to capitalize on his strengths nor respond to his needs."[44]

Therefore, too often, the ghetto student does what the teacher expects. He or she fails. Documentation of this failure abounds, and the data show almost identical patterns of students falling farther behind as they "progress" through the grades.

In 1969 the Center for Urban Education intensively analyzed over 200 studies of the academic progress of black and disadvantaged children. The analysis shows that these children score slightly below their more advantaged counterparts when first tested in grades one or two, and thereafter progress at steadily lower-than-normal rates. "The gap increases as the child proceeds through school until at the end of the ninth grade, he is generally two and a half years behind."[45]

Contrasting the urban black student with the white suburban counterpart, the *Coleman Report* found the average twelfth-grade black student in the Northeast 5.2 grade levels behind the white student in math, 2.0 grade levels behind in reading, and 3.3 grade levels behind in verbal ability. Figures were similar in the Midwest and worse in the Far West.[46]

But these figures do not give the full picture. They do not record the underachievement of black youths no longer in school who have rejected a system which has failed them. At practically every age level, the 1970 census shows that black youth's dropout rate is over twice that of white youths. In 1970, for example, 44% of all black male 19-year-olds were not enrolled in high school or had not graduated from high school, as compared to 12.9% of white males of the same age.[47] Among 18-year-old males, 29.8% blacks and 13.6% whites were dropouts. For those 16 years old in 1970, the percentages were 16% black and 7.6% white; and for 15-year-olds, 10.9% black and 5.0% white.

The *Riles Report* notes that dropout rates have grown steadily through the sixties, and, for individual cities, the rate increases with the size of the city.[48] In 1967, for example, approximately 65% of New York City black and Puerto Rican students left school before high school graduation.[49]

Also, for Mexican-Americans and other non-English-speaking children, the problem during the elementary grades is even more acute. "According to the Texas Education Agency, as many as 60% of the approximately 100,000 non-English-speaking first graders entering the system each year will have dropped out of school permanently before elementary school graduation."[50]

Moreover, dropouts, in increasing numbers, do not merely release their hostility toward the system by breaking their association with it. They overtly attack it with violence ranging from vandalism against property to assault and even murder of individuals associated with it.

The Urban Task Force on Education concluded that, generally, as school vandalism rates have increased, school officials have failed to heed the message of the vandalism. That message is clear when the targets are systematically analyzed. "The highest rates of school vandalism tend to occur in schools with obsolete facilities and equipment, low staff morale and high dissatisfaction and boredom among the pupils."[51]

Not only have big city school systems failed to heed the message of dissatisfaction, they have provoked more serious forms of violence by their often repressive response to vandalism.

> School administrators express their growing alarm at the rising tide of damage to school property by installing expensive electronic detection devices, changing building design, employing armed guards accompanied by dogs, training themselves in police methods, and even by flying helicopters at low altitudes with powerful searchlights each night — in short, doing those things which will further reduce pupil, parent, and teacher morale, and further destroy any feelings of mutual respect and openness so essential to good learning.[52]

There follows, logically, from students, the next step in violence, assaults and threats on people who represent the system. Such personal violence and reaction to it is increasingly alarming. In 1969, for example, three out of four East St. Louis teachers were reportedly carrying guns.

Although this is the extreme in teacher reaction, it is representative of a widespread fear on the part of teachers who, too often, instead of blaming the system that has failed the urban child, arm themselves — at least with stiff-necked superiority — to do battle with the system's product. And the war sounds erupt.

WHERE THEY MEET

Profile of the Urban School

The physical and psychological environment in which urban education takes place is hardly conducive to the kinds of drastic changes which are needed to remedy present deficiencies. There are whole school systems which have a difficult time attracting qualified teachers. There are also specific schools into which experienced teachers refuse to be transferred.

Although the present glut of teachers in the employment market may make it possible for urban school systems to attract a greater number of qualified teachers, the reluctance of teachers to take jobs in such systems will not necessarily change. Urban teachers continue to be faced with less desirable working conditions and more demanding jobs.

Beginning teachers assigned to a city school may find, if they accept the assignment, that they are expected to teach overcrowded classes in makeshift classrooms, housed in old, rundown buildings, and that they have insufficient books and supplies to use in teaching the children who attend in double sessions. The Kerner Commission found that conditions such as these are more likely to obtain if the school population is predominantly black.[53]

But for *all* city schools, the quality of facilities and the pupil-teacher ratio compare unfavorably with their surrounding suburbs. According to the *Coleman Report,* in the Northeast, 43% of the elementary schools in city districts are over 40 years old, while only 18% of suburban schools are 40 years old. In secondary schools, there are seven more students per classroom in the cities than in the suburbs.[54]

Largely because of the growing severity of the fiscal crisis in urban education, the causes of which will be examined below, pupil-teacher ratios in large urban centers have shown a steady rise in recent years. Between 1966 and 1968, for example, the pupil population in Washington, D.C., rose 1.9%

and the teacher population decreased 6.3%.[55] Of 12 large cities surveyed by the Center for Urban Education in 1968, 8 of them exceeded the national pupil-teacher ratio of 23:1 by as much as 5.1 pupils per teacher.

Besides having large numbers of children to teach in inadequate and often substandard facilities with insufficient equipment and supplies, beginning urban teachers are also likely to find themselves members of an inexperienced, perhaps incomplete staff, a staff including inadequately prepared teachers. What is more, they will discover, as the year wears on, that neither they nor their fellow teachers receive supervisory assistance to do the mammoth job expected of them.

For a long time, graduate schools of education, with few exceptions, have recommended their brighter students for placement in "good" suburban schools. Similarly, the most effective experienced teachers have generally selected suburban systems. Thus, the *Coleman Report* found in 1966 that the average black student is more likely than the suburban student to be taught by a teacher who: (1) scored lower on a verbal examination voluntarily taken for the report; and (2) attended a college which gives less than a regular teaching certificate.[56]

According to the *Riles Report,* recent studies show that in 15 major cities, 17% of the teachers have been in their ghetto school for one year and 63% in their present position for five years or less. Furthermore, the proportion of teachers remaining after five years drops off radically. Since the highest rate of turnover occurs among beginning teachers, it is not surprising that schools in deprived communities suffer a high rate of attrition among their teachers. The rate of exit from Chicago inner city schools, for example, is ten times that of less poverty stricken areas, and teachers' dropout rates are high nationally.[57]

A 1964 survey of all teacher turnover studies through the early 1960's revealed a stark picture of teacher dropouts.[58] Of 100 college graduates who had prepared to teach and who

satisfied state certification requirements, approximately 60 of
them took teaching assignments. An additional 7% dropped
out by the end of the first school year, and by the end of their
second year, 5 more had left. After 10 years, only 10 to 12 of
the initial 100 prospective teachers were teaching in elementary
and secondary school classrooms. Finally, those dropout studies
which compared teachers who had left with those who had
stayed concluded that generally the dropouts were rated better
as teachers and had superior college achievement records.

By examining schools within one urban school system, the
Kerner Commission showed the effect of teacher attrition on
ghetto schools in terms of both the lack of experience and
lack of qualification of teachers in those schools.

[A] 1963 study ranking Chicago's public high schools by the socioeconomic status of surrounding neighborhoods found that in the ten
lowest-ranking schools only 63.2 percent of all teachers were fully
certified and the median level of all the teaching experience was 3.9
years. In three of these schools the median level was one year. Four
of these lowest-ranking schools were 100 percent Negro enrollment
and three were over 90 percent Negro. By contrast, eight of the ten
highest-ranking schools had nearly total white enrollments, and the
other two were more than 75 percent white. In these schools, 99.3
percent of the teachers were fully certified and the median level of
teaching experience was 12.3 years.[59]

While many reasons can be and have been advanced for the
annual dearth of qualified and experienced teachers in schools
where they are most needed — and not the least of these is
urban school systems' lack of sufficient funds to pay competitive salaries — failure of school administrators to help their
beginning teachers must be considered a key.

For the most part, in large urban systems beginning teachers
are appointed by central administrations (although the school
principal may play some role). This process often turns out to
be bureaucratic body shuffling which results in indiscriminate
placement, without regard for an individual teacher's areas of

specialization or aptitudes. Misplacement, then, is the first administrative failure and, of course, it has serious repercussions for students.

A 1965 national misassignment study done by the National Education Association showed 677 cases of misassignment out of 1,035 survey questionnaires returned.[60] Of the cases reported, almost 60% involved lack of subject matter competence, and another common type involved assignment of teachers to grade levels they were not prepared to teach.

Thus, professional subject matter and methods training, whatever its quality, is of little help to many new teachers in urban schools. Although misassignment is not imposed only on new teachers, relatively junior teachers are more likely to have it imposed on them because they lack the seniority rights to help them get the assignments they want.

Secondly, the novice teacher gets little or no supervisory assistance once he or she starts trying to teach. This problem is dealt with in detail later in the book. Suffice it to say here that the complaints of beginning teachers made at a conference on the training of elementary school teachers at Harvard University in 1968 seem to reflect a widespread problem.[61] They said their principals, whom they had asked for help, weren't knowledgeable enough about the problems of teaching to help them or weren't around enough to try. They found supervisors dictatorial or superficial and resource people unavailable or nonexistent.

An added problem faced by beginning teachers within the small community of the school staff is racial polarization of teachers. Although this problem cannot be analyzed outside the larger societal context of American racism which has imposed segregation and discrimination on black people and other minority groups, there are peculiar causes within urban public school systems which have fostered hostilities between black and white teachers. These causes include discrimination in hiring and upgrading black teachers, racially segregated

placement of teachers, and failure of both professional educators and school administrators to prepare teachers to deal
adequately with urban children. More specifically, there has
been virtually no training of white teachers to understand
and work with black children.

As noted earlier in this chapter, although about 10% of this
country's teachers are black, until very recently black teachers
were largely concentrated in all-black school districts in the
Southern and border states. Until the World War II northern
migration of black people brought large numbers of black
children into Northern urban schools, there simply were no
black teachers hired by these schools. When the hiring of black
teachers began in the North, administrators uniformly placed
them in predominantly black schools. Data from the U.S. Commission on Civil Rights' 1967 study, *Racial Isolation in the
Public Schools,* which surveyed 75 school systems, showed
that in all Southern districts and in all but eight of the
Northern and border districts the majority of black elementary
school teachers were assigned to majority black schools.[62] In
most cases the percentage of black teachers so placed ranged
from 70% to 90%. Yet, despite that pattern and despite the
recognition by some school systems with large black pupil
populations of their need for more black teachers and administrators, school by school data on placement of teachers
still rarely show majority black staffs. This pattern holds even
for 90%—100% black schools. Thus, in all but the rarest
schools white teachers are in the majority.

Promotion to supervisory positions has come even more
slowly for blacks. Even those few schools with relatively high
percentages of black teachers usually have white principals.

During the last few years a few cities have initiated affirmative policies of recruiting, hiring, and upgrading black teachers.
But even in those cities, there are still relatively low percentages of black principals.[63] For example, in October 1969,
62.5% of Detroit's students were black, yet black teachers

represented 41% and black principals only 16.7%. So, too, in Chicago, with a 52.9% black and an 8.6% Spanish-surname population, 34% of the teachers and only 6.9% of the principals were black. None of the teachers or principals were Puerto Rican.

But in many urban school districts not even this level of affirmative action has taken place. New York City is typical of the long standing patterns of unrepresentative hiring and upgrading of minority professionals in cities where the majority of students are black and/or Puerto Rican. New York's pupil population was 31.7% black and 23.6% Puerto Rican. Minority principals were, of course, almost nonexistent. The ratios: 1.3% black and 0.1% Puerto Rican. And most of them were serving in an acting capacity.

Rationalizations for such figures and analyses of why they are so low, why they must be changed and how they can be changed are widely debated by education specialists, school administrators, teachers, students, and parents in public forums and in courts of law. These discussions and analyses constitute a large portion of this book. But one conclusion seems clear — in most urban school systems the effects of current personnel practices are deeply felt. Black teachers, themselves the victims of racial discrimination, identify much more easily with the demands of black students and their parents. At the same time, black teachers view teacher organizations with suspicion because they are usually controlled by whites and, in at least some urban school districts, are actively engaged in fighting growing black community demands for control of their own schools (as in New York's Ocean Hill-Brownsville controversy in 1968 and Newark's 1971 teachers' strike). Thus, teachers on the same staff are likely to have wide attitudinal differences toward the students they teach, with differences dividing along racial lines.

A study by David Gottlieb of Michigan State University pointed up such differences between black and white elementary school teachers in a low income Midwestern district. Almost twice as many white as black teachers considered black students "athletic"; by contrast, nearly twice as many black teachers perceived them as "ambitious." By considerable margins, black teachers saw the children as "cooperative" and "fun-loving." Conversely, white teachers in overwhelming numbers looked upon them as "high strung," "impetuous," "lazy," "moody," and "talkative." Similarly, much higher percentages of white than black teachers complained of parental disinterest and discipline problems.[64]

Complaints about discipline problems have, in fact, found their way to the teacher contract bargaining tables. Predominantly white teacher organizations in urban school districts in Wisconsin, for example, have demanded separate classes and even separate schools for disruptive students, with teachers at these schools receiving "battle pay."[65] One such school opened in Milwaukee in 1969—70 with an all-black enrollment.

If these attitudinal differences between white and black teachers are typical, the difficulty of attaining unity of purpose among school staffs serving minority children should be obvious. Even those beginning white teachers who prefer assignment to ghetto schools (and there are increasing numbers of such teachers) may consequently be faced with real problems in building rapport with their black peers. For racial polarization among teachers is now a fact in the teaching profession. It must be recognized and dealt with by the individual teacher.

Racial polarization has other faces, too. It may account for some of the students' hostility and for some of the parents' insistence that they be assured their children are learning, and that they will control and improve the schools in which non-learning is found.

An individual teacher's ability to perceive and deal with these forces may largely determine his or her ability to function in an urban school today. But the effort can not stop there. What many of the new breed of teachers seem not to realize is that their response to the sad plight of urban schools cannot stop with an honest effort to achieve results no matter what the built-in obstacles. Their greatest challenge is to work for change within the profession, within the schools of education, within the school bureaucracies and within the teacher organizations. For nothing short of fundamental structural change will save the public schools in urban districts, and the institutions which resist such structural change must be reformed.

PRESSURES ON TEACHERS

National Problems and Trends

The subsequent sections of this chapter move away from the problems of the individual teacher, the limitations he or she brings to the classroom, and the obstacles he or she faces in an urban school assignment. What follows is a brief analysis of the larger causes of unequal educational opportunity in urban public schools, as well as an analysis of pressures being brought to bear to equalize opportunity and to assure greater teacher responsibility for children's learning. These national trends are, of course, not divorced from the individual teacher's experience. But they can best be understood as pressures facing an entire profession. Indeed, reaction to them has come, not so much from individual teachers, but from large teacher organizations in major urban centers with their well-subsidized lobbying and public relations activities.

School Financing

Educational experts differ about the nature of the correlation between dollars and educational quality. But most of them would agree that a certain level of funding is necessary but not sufficient for quality education. Until adequate funding is available to urban schools, many of their other serious problems will not be solved. How the money should be used, who should control its expenditure and who should be paid for what kind of output are, for the most part, moot questions until there is adequate funding for urban schools. To expect students in an overcrowded, poorly equipped ghetto classroom taught by an inexperienced, unsupervised new teacher or a badly trained older teacher to learn as much as their suburban counterparts is, as teacher organizations are quick to point out, to ask the impossible. Similarly, to give control of schools to community boards (and make them accountable for results) and then to cut back on the funds they are given is to delegate built-in failure.

School financing is, therefore, a major problem for urban school systems. The problem has been escalating into a war, with angry taxpayers and militant teacher organizations the most visible protagonists. Caught between, facing growing public unwillingness to pay for rising local school costs substantially caused by heightened teacher organization demands for raises, are city school boards and state legislatures.

School financing legislation in most states makes school boards ultimately dependent upon the public's willingness to tax itself. Voter rejections of bond issues and tax measures are increasingly resulting in serious financial crises, which require program cutbacks.

A typical example from the *Riles Report* survey of nationwide fiscal crises in urban education is Houston, Texas. There, in the spring of 1969, voters rejected by a 2 to 1 margin a proposed $5 million tax measure and a $20 million bond issue. The result: no kindergarten or special education programs for 20,000 children in 1969–70.[66] More recently, the Detroit school system announced a 35% reduction in educational services because of financial problems.

In city after city this pattern obtains, with results ranging from increased class size and decreased curricula to school or systemwide shutdowns. Furthermore, with few exceptions, there is little relief forthcoming from state legislatures, which have responded to the taxpayer revolt with an economy drive approach to state aid programs. Most newly apportioned legislatures with increased representation from suburban districts refuse to consider revising state formulas to meet the financial crises in center city schools.

The roots of this widespread financial bind reach beyond current public disenchantment with education. Indeed, most writers agree that the American taxpayer — or his elected representative — has never been willing to put his money where his mouthed expectations of education are. The authors of *Private Wealth and Public Education,* for example, note that the share of gross national product spent on education has not changed since the nineteenth century.[67] But there is a real basis for today's rebellion of urban taxpayers. As a result of social and economic changes over the last two decades, the city dwellers are actually paying more and getting less.

The change in city populations, noted earlier in this chapter, has had a drastic economic effect in large cities. A 1971 analysis of federal aid to education prepared for the U.S. Senate's Equal Educational Opportunity Committee by Syracuse University summarized the process that has taken place.

> The shifts have not been random. A sorting out process has occurred — leaving the poor, undereducated, aged and non-white in the central cities and taking heavy manufacturing, many retail establishments and other kinds of business activities to the suburbs along with middle and upper income families. The result is that the tax base of cities has become insufficient to meet the resource needs of high cost city populations.[68]

This combination of the diminishing tax base and the higher cost of providing public services has placed an almost impossible burden on the urban taxpayer. Tax rates are at or fast approaching confiscatory levels in many cities even though the quality of the services leaves much to be desired.

Although under the U.S. Constitution, education is one of the functions reserved to the states and is generally recognized to be a state responsibility, all states (except Hawaii, which has a unitary state education system) legislatively delegate the bulk of school funding responsibilities to local or county school districts. Customarily, the local share of educational budgetary needs is met by local real property taxes.

Although the local percentage of total elementary and secondary education costs varies from state to state, it is invariably higher than combined state and federal expenditures. Nationally, in 1969, 52% of the fiscal responsibility was local. States provided 40.7% and the federal government 7.3% of funds expended.[69]

The burden on the urban taxpayer derives (1) from the state requirement that local real property be the major tax base for raising school funds, and (2) from state formulas for distribution of state education aid to local districts. Both operate to disadvantage most urban school districts: the former, because urban areas usually have a smaller tax base per pupil than the suburbs, and the latter, because state aid only inadequately equalizes the tax burden among districts of varying tax capacity.

(1.) Property Tax Inequities. As a result of the population shift described in the *Syracuse Study,* the city's real property base (traditionally quite high) has been threatened by a very slow rate of growth.[70] By contrast, suburban property growth rates have been steadily climbing. In the Northeast, suburban growth has tripled city growth, and in the Midwest, suburban property appreciation was more than six times that in core cities in the last few decades.

What makes the picture bleaker is that cities have the additional burdens of high cost populations and older physical plants, which result in greater demands for general government services. Demands for greater health, public safety, sanitation, public works, transportation, public welfare, public

housing, and recreational services require cities to devote 65%
of their budgets to noneducational services. Suburban budgets
generally devote only 45% of their funds to general governmental services. So, only a third of city funds can go for education, while neighboring suburbs spend more than half of
their public monies for schools. As a consequence, cities
raise about 30% less per capita for education, despite the fact
that when tax efforts are calculated as a percentage of income,
urban taxpayers are exerting a 40% greater effort than their
suburban counterparts.

In addition to paying higher taxes and having less money
to spend for education, city dwellers get less education for
their money. The reason: city education costs more per child
than education elsewhere. Not only does it cost more to provide the same educational programs but urban students have
special needs which require additional programs.

The higher urban cost differentials derive primarily from
higher teacher salaries due, in large part, to more attractive
salary schedules won by militant city teacher unions. Moreover, while city school districts have many new and inexperienced teachers, they also have many senior teachers who
cluster at the top of the salary schedule. Professor Charles
Benson in an unpublished study for the U.S. Civil Rights
Commission attributed this phenomenon to the slower growth
of central city school populations and to city districts'
tendency to promote from within. With teachers paid largely
on the basis of seniority (another right won by aggressive
city teachers' unions), cost per teacher runs higher in the
cities than in the suburbs.

Other more expensive budget items in cities include more
costly personnel expenses — for maintenance, secretarial, and
security services — which must meet higher urban standards
of living. Land for school buildings is generally more expensive in cities, with differences ranging, for example, from
$100,000 an acre for school land in Detroit in 1967 to $6,000
an acre in school districts surrounding the city.

But the most important cause of higher urban educational costs is the educational and socioeconomic characteristics of student populations. Special program requirements for the poor, the nonwhite, the immigrant, the handicapped — programs desperately needed to enable them to achieve normal grade level performance — are expensive. Examples of such programs are: education for the culturally disadvantaged, programs for non-English-speaking adults and children, programs for children to whom standard English is virtually a foreign language, general adult education, summer school, programs for the physically and emotionally handicapped (where per pupil expenditures are greater by a factor of four or five to one) and vocational schools which are generally 35% more costly than academic secondary schools.

But, as the *Riles Report* notes, the fiscal consideration must go beyond present cost levels. Clearly current educational approaches are not meeting the mark in most urban school districts, and needed improvements will cost still more. "More importantly, however, if improvement and change in curriculum, educational personnel, supplementary services, facilities, and attitudes are to take place to educate effectively the inner city population, it will cost more — more per . . . child."[71]

If reliance on local real property taxes continues, more funds can be provided for urban schools only by urban taxpayers agreeing to tax themselves at a still higher per capita rate. The prospects for that happening are not good.

(2.) State Aid Inequities. The disproportionately heavy property tax burden of city taxpayers is not alleviated by state aid. On the contrary, state aid formulas often actually add to urban disadvantages.

For example, state governments often assume the costs of teacher retirement systems. But in many states the large school districts are omitted from the state program. In some cases where they are not omitted entirely, the larger districts bear a heavier charge for retirement contributions than other districts.

Direct state aid to education may similarly discriminate against large school systems, for state aid in many cases is still operating on systems designed in the early 1900's to compensate for inequalities between what were then the rich cities and the poorer outlying and rural regions. Although the relative fiscal positions are now reversed, the formulas continue to give lesser proportions of aid to cities than to suburbs and to give more aid to rural than to metropolitan areas.

The *Syracuse Study,* which analyzed five industrialized states, found that metropolitan areas in New York, Texas and Michigan received from $17.00 to $58.00 less per pupil in state aid than nonmetropolitan areas. Within the metropolitan areas, the central cities in all states except Massachusetts were found to get less aid than their surrounding suburbs.

The whole concept of flat grants per pupil, regardless of school districts' wealth or proverty, works against meaningful equalization among districts. Although many states have moved from a simple flat grant system of aid to what Professor Coons, et al., call the "mythical foundation plan" — a system of equalizing state aid according to a district's per pupil property base — and have also added categorical aids for such expenses as busing, inequities in state aid remain. But the largest obstacle to equity is heavy state reliance on local property wealth as the determinant of educational spending. For even state equalizing grants, which do work to equalize, leave urban districts with higher tax rates and less money to spend.

It is precisely this wealth criterion which was found to be "invidious discrimination against the poor" and, therefore, in violation of the equal protection clause of the Fourteenth Amendment in the California Supreme Court decision, *Serrano v. Priest.*[72] In ruling that the lower court dismissal of a complaint by parents and their children must be reversed, the court found that public school education is "a fundamental interest which cannot be conditioned on wealth." [73]

Futhermore, the court found "no compelling state purpose necessitating the present method of financing." [74]

Noting the wide disparity in per pupil expenditure among cities and suburbs in California, with monies raised dependent not on tax rate but on property value, the court assessed present disparities visited upon urban education as economic starvation. It dismissed as without merit officials' arguments that expenditure differentials are partially determined by tax rates.

> [T]he richer district is favored when it can provide the same educational quality for its children with less tax effort. . . . [P]oorer districts are financially unable to raise their taxes high enough to match the educational offerings of wealthier districts. . . Thus affluent districts can have their cake and eat it too: they can provide a high quality education for their children while paying lower taxes. Poor districts, by contrast, have no cake at all. [75]

In assigning responsibility for this scheme of discrimination, the California Supreme Court Justices (with only one dissent) said that state action caused the wealth discrimination. First, the system arises from the constitution and laws of the state of California. Second, even though private action (residential and commercial patterns) are partially responsible for assessed valuation distribution, "such patterns are shaped and hardened by zoning ordinances and other governmental land use controls which promote economic exclusivity." [76] Third, the state drew school district boundary lines, "thus determining how much local wealth each district would contain." [77]

Serrano was the first real success by school finance litigants. Previous law suits, such as *McInnis v. Shapiro* and *Burruss v. Wilkerson,* [78] had failed because the courts found the "educational needs" test proposed by the plaintiffs as the basis of fund allocation a test without judicially manageable standards. The courts noted the inequities in current school finance schemes but concluded that remedies were the province of the legislative branch. The *Serrano* plaintiffs urged a different theory upon the California courts — "fiscal neutrality." The court need not determine how education funds should be distributed, whether according to educational need or otherwise. All the court was asked to do was to prohibit the state from using a system which differentiated between children and between taxpayers on the basis of local wealth. The California Supreme Court agreed that if wealth were used in any manner in determining school financing, it must be the wealth of the whole state.

Serrano was not a final determination. The case was returned to the trial court for consideration of the facts. But there is little doubt about the outcome there. Indeed, an increasing number of other courts have since struck down school finance statutes on grounds very much like *Serrano*.[79] The U.S. Supreme Court has agreed to decide an appeal from one of those decisions, *Rodriguez v. San Antonio Independent School District,* so the viability of "fiscal neutrality" as a constitutional argument may soon be determined.

Even if the Supreme Court affirms the *Rodriguez* decision, however, it is not entirely clear whether urban schools will be assured adequate funds. Professor Coons, one of the prime creators of the "fiscal neutrality" doctrine, characterized it as "half a loaf." For equal protection of the laws can be satisfied by giving all children the same treatment, even if that treatment is not very good. A state might therefore satisfy the doctrine by providing enough money for all children to receive a marginal education. Indeed, if the state made flat grants of the same amount per child to every school district and forbade local school districts to raise additional amounts locally, fiscal neutrality would probably be satisfied. But the plight of the urban school district would be only partially alleviated. As we have seen, it simply costs more to educate urban children.

Many critics of *Serrano* and its progeny fear that just such mediocratization of the public school system will occur. But

it is too early to do more than speculate. None of the successful school finance law challenges requires the legislature to
adopt a particular new approach. Of the broad spectrum of
possibilities previously available to the legislature, one type
has been eliminated — an approach dependent upon local
wealth. The challenge of devising an equitable and sufficient
plan for financing the public schools and of raising the
necessary funds remains where it should be — with the legislative branch. This is obviously an onerous and complex
task and the courts will retain jurisdiction to ensure that the
legislatures comply with constitutional requirements. But
pressure from informed citizens should play a role, too.

One of the school finance decisions, *Robinson v. Cahill*[80]
in New Jersey, goes beyond *Serrano* in a way which may
have great import for urban school districts and which may
respond to critics of *Serrano*'s lowest common denominator
effect. The plantiffs in *Robinson,* Jersey City and several
other municipalities, their mayors and councilmen, taxpayers
and school children, argued not only that they were entitled
to fiscal netrality but also that they had a state constitutional
right to a "thorough and efficient" education. The trial court
agreed, holding that New Jersey's school finance law was unconstitutional because of its wealth discrimination and its
failure at present funding levels to support a "thorough and
efficient" education. If, as the words themselves seem clearly
to require, such a standard connotes a high level of education
for all children, then there will be no mediocratization of the
public schools. Moreover, if the success of the state in meeting its constitutional obligation must be measured by educational *output (i.e.,* performance) criteria and must encompass
compensatory treatment for districts disadvantaged by the
existing school finance laws, then urban school districts should
fare quite well. These were the positions advanced forcefully
by *amici curiae,* the NAACP Education Committee, Newark
Chapter, and the ACLU of New Jersey, in *Robinson*. The trial

court agreed that a "thorough and efficient" education clearly meant something more than merely adequate or satisfactory, and that compensatory treatment might well be required. The court did not, however, deal with the matter of measurement criteria. Instead it underscored the duty of the State Commissioner of Education to evaluate the public schools.

The *Robinson* case is now before the New Jersey Supreme Court. (Because the trial court decision was based principally on *state* constitutional grounds, the New Jersey Supreme Court's determination will probably not be appealable to the U.S. Supreme Court.) A tax reform program sponsored by the governor, which included far-reaching school finance reforms thought by some to effectively moot the *Robinson* case, was defeated by the legislature. Further, legislative action is now likely to await the Supreme Court's decision in *Robinson*. Through one means or the other, New Jersey may wind up with a dramatically different approach to school finance, perhaps before any other state. The odds favor it being in the form of substantially full state funding, a format recommended by the governor's Tax Policy Committee in New Jersey, the Fleischmann Commission in New York, and the president's Commission on School Finance.

(3.) Federal Aid Inequities. Another recommendation of the president's Commission on School Finance was that the federal government initiate an Urban Educational Assistance Program to provide emergency financial aid on a matching basis over a period of at least five years to help large central city public schools develop experimental educational programs, replace or renovate antiquated and unsafe facilities, add needed special personnel, and provide instructional materials and services. This recommendation was made in recognition of:

> . . . the enormity of the problems of urban decay. . . . The big cities of the Nation are rapidly being left to the poor and the untrained. Whatever the causes of this concentration of human problems in

cities, the solutions are surely more than local or even State matters. We urge that the situation demands strenous effort now and a major part of that effort must be made through education. We urge that State governments assign a high priority to the critical problems of their major cities and especially to the schools of their cities. Education deficiencies are more concentrated within the cities and the educational opportunity gap between them and their suburban neighbors must be narrowed. The Federal Government must assist the States in this area. We must learn why past efforts have not worked, and more important, just what will work.[81]

As the president's commission conceded, federal efforts to deal with the problems of urban education have not worked. Although we cannot deal here in detail with the types of federal aid and their maldistribution, or with the scattered recordkeeping which makes federal, state, and local accountability almost impossible, it is necessary to point to some overall flaws in federal spending for education. The two basic flaws are an inadequate amount of federal funds and a failure of those funds to go consistently where they are needed most.

In 1968, 11 cents out of every federal dollar went for all social programs including education. During the same year, 43 cents went for national defense.[82] To make matters worse, since 1967–68, when federal expenditures for education rose to a high of 8% of total educational costs, they have declined steadily. In 1970–71, they represented only 6.9% of total educational revenues.[83]

To put this dollar input in hard cash terms, the *Syracuse Study* found that per pupil expenditure in the five states studied ranged from $475 to $1,000. Total federal aid in those states averaged only $22 to $50 per pupil, amounts totally inadequate in the face of education's massive financial problems.

Further, analysis of expenditures in the five states shows that even these small amounts of federal aid often do not go proportionately to the urban disadvantaged. Summary findings of the *Syracuse Study* which point to unequal distribution of federal aid in 1961 are: [84]

- Nonmetropolitan areas, largely rural and small town in character, tend to receive more federal aid per pupil than metropolitan areas.

- While overall central cities get more federal aid than suburbs, the amount received is too small to offset the suburbs' local and state revenue advantage.

- With the exception of programs under Title I of the Elementary and Secondary Education Act (ESEA), federal programs often provide more funds to suburban than to central city districts. Large cities seem to receive proportionately less money from ESEA Title II, ESEA Title III, NDEA Title III, and Vocational Education programs.

- Although districts with lower income tend generally to get somewhat more federal aid than higher income districts, there are many glaring exceptions. Federal aid shows no equalizing effect with regard to property valuation.

- Although somewhat more federal aid goes to districts with higher proportions of nonwhite students, these amounts are not proportionate to the added costs of educating the disadvantaged.

- Within these higher nonwhite enrollment districts, ESEA Title I money, designed to compensate disadvantaged students, has often been used improperly as general aid for system-wide purposes.

- During a four-year period (1965—68) amounts of aid received by local districts varied erratically, with almost half of the metropolitan areas reporting an actual decrease in the last year.

These were the major flaws found in a study of federal spending in five urbanized states. A broader look at all of the

states, with their wide variations in income and property
values, shows still another inequity in federal aid distribution.
Nationally, the poorest states spend the highest proportion
of their wealth on education and, at the same time, have the
least amount of money to put into education. The federal
government, following it seems the lead of state governments,
does not concern itself with equalizing this imbalance.

A serious examination of underexpenditure and careless expenditure at the national level, coupled with gross inequities
within states, bespeaks the need for a drastic change in national
priorities. This need has an urgency far beyond the press felt
by the overburdened and rebellious taxpayer. For it goes to the
social cost of inadequate and discriminatory funding, which
contributes to high dropout rates, low student performance
and difficulties in attracting and holding qualified teachers.
From these results flow the immense costs of higher welfare,
law enforcement, and job training expenses of the cities; of
the flight of the middle class to the suburbs; and of the human
tragedy and property destruction of urban unrest.

As the *Riles Report* urged:

> The crisis in urban education must be confronted. It is obvious that
> we cannot afford the financial and social burden that presently exists.
> We cannot afford the growing animosities and tension between blacks
> and whites in our cities and across the land. If it is agreed that the
> foremost socializing agency in the nation is the school system, then
> that is where an attack upon the problem must begin and the solution,
> at least in part, must reside.[85]

Integration

When the Riles Urban Task Force and the president's Commission on School Finance spoke as they did of the need for
the federal government to face and solve the crisis in education, they were speaking about the problem of funding inequities; but they were also speaking about the burden of segregation imposed on the urban child. Indeed, the two problems
have never been divorced in American public education in

spite of the myth "separate but equal." As a federal court found in *Hobson v. Hansen*,[86] one of the proofs of segregation is inequality of dollar input. Those who argue for integrated education contend that an expenditure differential is always an effect of racially segregated schools.

To speak of "the problem" of school integration is to talk about a hoary tradition of resistance to efforts aimed at ending "class tyranny" (the elder Justice Harlan's term for racial discrimination). Until recently, the tradition of active resistance to school integration has been confined largely to the South, perhaps because the thrust of early school desegregation litigation was aimed at Southern school districts. There, segregated schools and segregated faculties had been imposed by state law. And there, since *Brown v. Board of Education, supra,* the confrontations have come over implementation of court ordered plans to change dual education systems into unitary systems.

But with the 1971 school year, the confrontation has clearly moved North. The response to several recent court decisions indicates that the tradition of resistance knows no geographic bounds. Indeed, the 1971 bombing of school buses in Pontiac, Michigan, is a poignant reminder of the 1957 scene in Little Rock, Arkansas.

Although Pontiac citizens did not have the backing of their governor and the protection of state troopers in their resistance, they had the voice of a more powerful official, whose condemnation of busing was said by school officials and observers to have encouraged white parents in their opposition. The voice was that of the president of the United States.

On August 3, 1971, President Nixon made it clear, as he had during the 1968 presidential campaign, that he is "against busing as that term is commonly used in school desegregation cases." To further clarify, he added, "I have consistently opposed the busing of our nation's school children to achieve racial balance, and I am opposed to the busing of children simply for the sake of busing." [87] The president acted on his view eight days later when he ordered the Department of Justice and the Department of Health, Education and Welfare not to suggest to nonconforming school districts any more busing than that minimally required by law.

The policy statements and orders came in the wake of a U.S. Supreme Court decision in the case of *Swann v. Charlotte-Mecklenburg Board of Education,* handed down April 20, 1971, which found "no basis for holding that the local school authorities may not be required to employ bus transportation as one tool of school desegregation." [88] As the rationale for the *Swann* opinion and companion cases, Chief Justice Burger pointed out for a unanimous court that "bus transportation has been an integral part of the school system for years," and that the desegregation mandate for cases before the court could not be limited to walk-in schools.[89]

It was such reasoning which the U.S. Civil Rights Commission used on August 12, 1971, when it unanimously attacked the president's order limiting HEW's use of busing in Southern desegregation plans. The commission called student transportation "essential to eliminate segregation," and reminded Mr. Nixon that for purposes other than integration "busing has been a common feature of American education." [90]

There was a certain irony in the reaction to President Nixon's August statements. Many critics believed they had been addressed to the South as a part of the president's famous "Southern Strategy." Certainly, Southern school districts had been the subjects of virtually every desegregation suit brought before 1970, and it was there that the resistance to integration had been most obvious. Yet, the 1971–72 school year, which began a month after the president's statements, brought the prospect of widespread integration in the South, far more than the prior year's attendance of 39% black children in majority white schools. The opening of the schools there was relatively calm, in marked contrast to previous school year beginnings in the South and to some contemporaneous school openings in the North. Many Southern school officials, irked by the president's comments, told reporters that those comments had made their job harder and that whatever community recalcitrance they were experiencing cropped up only after the White House statements were made.[91]

Ironically, the presidential statements prompted much greater resistance and violence in Northern cities. Mrs. Gladys McNairy, acting president of the Pittsburgh Board of Education, gave her assessment of their impact in the North.

"He can only create chaos by his policies," she said. "When he says, in effect, don't bother about busing, you can imagine the effect on the people in the North who subtly support segregation. They've been waiting for something like this."[92]

Mrs. McNairy was right. Fist fights broke out at several San Francisco school board meetings called to discuss implementation of court-ordered integration. Students were injured in scuffles and 10 buses were bombed at night in Pontiac, Michigan, where a 1970 court order was going into effect. In Evansville, Indiana, the school board withdrew from a comprehensive integration plan agreed upon with HEW officials. After the president's August 3 statement, officials asked for new negotiations.

Northerners, of course, have not acquired the psychological conditioning to "the inevitable" which has eroded the recalcitrance of the South. For even though *Brown v. Board of Education*'s "all deliberate speed" seemed for many years after 1955 to mean "never if you're smart enough," the Supreme Court has ruled ever more clearly against state decreed school segregation. By contrast, the Court had never heard a Northern school case, although many — both wins and losses for integration litigants — had been appealed from circuit courts. Therefore, Northern resisters have perhaps been lulled into a feeling of imperviousness.

But lower courts, both federal and state, have been moving with greater vigor to order desegregation of intentionally segregated Northern schools. And the Supreme Court has finally agreed to hear a Northern school desegregation case, *Keyes v. School District No. 1,* arising in Denver.[93] So, too, some legislatures and state education departments have ordered efforts to achieve racial balance. But there has been resistance in the North. In some districts, such as Denver and Detroit, school board members voting for integration plans have been ousted by irate constituents. In Boston, where the State Board of Education cut off $21.3 million in state funds because of racial imbalance, the school board decided to sue rather than implement more than token integration.

In many Northern metropolitan areas, of course, white citizens have felt that they successfully avoided even the distant threat of court imposed desegregation by removing themselves from city districts to suburban districts. In at least three recent federal school decisions, however, even this escape has been threatened.[94] With these decisions, adverse public reaction has continued to mount, fed by prior and subsequent executive pronouncements and by election year one-upmanship.

Governor George C. Wallace used the specter of the yellow school bus to confuse the ranks of Democratic presidential hopefuls, and the Republican incumbent mused publicly about the possibility of permanently remedying this court-made evil by a constitutional amendment. The president rejected this route, however, at least partially on pragmatic grounds. It would take too long to get state approval and effective implementation. Instead President Nixon asked for congressional action which would (1) permanently prohibit increased busing for desegregation in the first six grades of school, (b) require the courts to use busing of older children only as a last resort, and (c) allow school officials presently under court orders to have those orders "reopened and modified."

The president's bills failed but an anti-busing rider was

successfully added to the Higher Education Act.[95] What the judicial response will be is widely debated. Certainly serious constitutional issues are involved.

Although teachers' organizations have not been vocal on the present busing issue, they have moved to the right from an earlier, liberal stand on school integration which saw them on the front lines, for example, backing with money and manpower a 1964 New York City school boycott for integrated, quality education. Teacher organizations still say they support integrated education. Their need to attract black teacher members dictates such a policy. But their unwillingness to actively back staff integration may belie a real commitment.

Part of the history of court remedies for state-imposed school segregation is a line of decisions holding that equal opportunity for both students and teachers requires integrated faculties.[96] These decisions, as well as HEW guidelines, have been required to meet school district efforts to avoid integrating teachers. The remedy customarily imposed by the courts has been to order school districts to change their policy (in Northern school districts, a pattern rather than an articulated policy) and practice of initially assigning teachers by race to schools where students of the same race predominate. Further, the courts have required reassignment of teachers formerly assigned on such a basis, with reassignments designed to achieve racially balanced faculties.

It is the latter requirement which has been actively opposed by teacher organizations. The basis of the opposition is contractual. Among the rights which many teacher organizations have won for their tenured members is the right not to be transferred involuntarily. (In some school systems, involuntary transfer of *any* teacher is prohibited by the contract.) Urban school systems, with large numbers of tenured teachers, therefore, may be effectively precluded from integrating their faculties unless they are prepared to violate the contract of a strike-prone teacher organization.

A 1971 report from Chicago demonstrates the dilemma.[97] A 1969 threat of court action by HEW against the Chicago Board of Education unless the board implemented faculty integration carried with it a suggestion that the faculty at no school be more than 65% of one race. In 1970 the Chicago board set its own goal of having no school with a teacher population more than 75% black or white. Measured in 1971 by board standards, only 46% of the Chicago schools had integrated faculties. By HEW guidelines, a mere 25% of the schools had integrated faculties.

Chicago administrators explained that new teachers and full-time substitutes had been assigned to achieve racial balance. However, because the teachers' union warned the board that the contract forbids involuntary transfers, there had been no move to transfer tenured teachers.

Another problem regarding faculty integration at all levels has been the paucity of black and Spanish supervisors. A part of the difficulty here, too, is traceable to union agreements. The 1968 agreement between the Newark Board of Education and the Teachers' Association required "merit appointment" to administrative positions and prescribed a promotional list procedure. The list had been in existence for some time and allowed only those teachers already in the system who had successfully passed examinations to be eligible for positions ranging from supervisory assistant through principal. As a result of this method of appointment, the percentage of black administrators was only about 10% in a school system with a 72.5% black student body. After negotiations with the Teachers' Association, the school board abolished the supervisor's selection method.

The board's action was challenged in state court as a breach of contract, and in federal court by white teachers as an equal protection violation. The Newark school board action was upheld by the state courts, by both the federal district and circuit courts, and by the State Commissioner of Education.[98]

The Third Circuit reasoned that "boards of education have a very definite affirmative duty to integrate school faculties and to permit a great imbalance of faculties . . . would be in negation of the Fourteenth Amendment to the Constitution and the line of cases which have followed *Brown v. Board of Education.*" [99]

As illustrated by the Chicago situation, however, not many school boards seem willing to take such affirmative action even in the interest of faculty integration. For this reason, many parents have pressed for local control in still another effort to win the long promised equal educational opportunities for their children.

Accountability to the Community

Many people, both inside and outside the education profession, have reacted negatively to the drive for accountability to the community, or to community control, in Northern urban school districts. However, parental control of their children's education is not a new or revolutionary phenomenon in this country. As Dr. Kenneth B. Clark, a noted psychologist and Regent of the State of New York, pointed out in the introduction to *Community Control and the Urban School,* only the present advocates are new in pressing for community control, and they took it up in desperate response to the failure of American education to reach their children.

> Community control of schools is a given in many of the towns, smaller cities, and suburbs of the nation. If an epidemic of low academic achievement swept over these schools, drastic measures would be imposed. Administrators and school boards would topple, and teachers would be trained or dismissed. If students were regularly demeaned and dehumanized in these schools, cries of outrage in the PTA's would be heard — and listened to — and action to remove the offending personnel would be taken immediately. Accountability is so implicit a given that the term "community control" never is used by those who have it. "Community control" . . . is to be understood rather as a demand for school accountability by parents to

whom the schools have never accounted, particularly those parents
of low status groups in Northern cities. It is a demand that their
children be respected as human beings with the potential all normal
children have and that they be taught by those hired for the purpose
of teaching. It is a demand that schools cease finding scapegoats and
stop making excuses for their failure by claiming that these children
are uneducable or too "disruptive" or too "culturally deprived" to
respond. It is a desperate response to the subtle and flagrant racism
that afflicts so many of the institutions of American education.[100]

Even organized teachers, who adamantly resist the notion
of individual teacher accountability, admit that "there is justification for the cry from the ghetto."[101]   Delineating the
stand of the Association of Classroom Teachers, Joseph
Stocker conceded that:

Children of the poor, and especially the minorities, *are* leaving school
unable to read, write, or add. Who is responsible? It matters not in
the least. What matters is that a democratic society cannot endure
with the problem of widespread poverty unsolved — with a large
portion of our population deprived, alienated, and hostile. The only
route out of poverty is education.[102]

The pressure for community control in many Northern
center cities grew out of the massive frustration among ghetto
parents as they watched integration efforts fail. As Dr. Clark
noted, most of the individuals in minority communities now
fighting for community control have been consistent fighters
for integration. He calls the present fight "a strategy of
despair, a strategy determined by the broken promises of
the white community."[103]
   Dr. Clark also warned in 1970 that the concept of accountability to the community could achieve new educational purpose and effectiveness for *all* children only if that concept
were not corrupted. In light of his 1972 statement that community control has not worked in New York City to improve
education for minority children, one wonders whether or not
it was ever given a chance. These are the potentials for misuse
and the requirements for success which he foresaw in 1970:

One cannot assume that the strategy of community control will be successful. It may be used and exploited by those who are concerned only with personal profit and power. It may be manipulated by established institutions of power in the larger communities for their own ends. It may further isolate the poor and the minority groups from the majority society and bring the customary consequences of racial and class isolation — eroded facilities, inadequate teaching and administrative staffs, and minimum resources. Isolation does not bequeath power to the powerless; as the South learned over generations, there is no such thing as "separate and equal" when the separation is a function and a manifestation of inferior status. As most of the community action projects of the antipoverty program demonstrated, unfamiliarity with power and status, lack of experience with organization skills, and apathy, disunity, and cynicism associated with long repression often characterize the communities of the poor, weakening their capacity to compete effectively with reinforced power and rendering the community vulnerable to those who would exploit it for their own ends.

Community control, therefore, requires a commitment of the city as a whole, genuine delegation of power, and continued efforts to relate the community to the larger society. Perhaps, paradoxically, the lower-status community will never have genuine power until its isolation is ended.[104]

It was, in fact, the very isolation of minority communities from school decision-making bodies which gave political impetus to the call for accountability to the community. Statistics showed, and community groups pressing for institutional change discovered, that school boards, whether elected or appointed, were usually not representative of (and did not consider themselves answerable to) large segments of the population.

According to a 1962 U.S. Office of Education national survey of boards of education, business and professional people constitute more than three-fifths of the membership.[105] Housewives constitute 7.2% and skilled and unskilled workers 9.4%. Larger school systems contain the highest proportion of business and professional membership, 74.2%.

As the authors of *Community Control and the Urban School* noted, the result of this pattern has been unresponsiveness to those unrepresented. Paradoxically, those whose children are most tragically failing have been largely unable to have their voices heard in the councils of power. This state of affairs has proven increasingly intolerable.

> In another day, wide social and economic disparities between governing bodies and the electorate were not so suspect. But such benevolence does not prevail in a climate of educational failure and suspicion by low income, minority communities of the effectiveness, and even the motives, of school authorities, especially when a large system's power is concentrated at the center.[106]

Thus, community control, in attempting to make educational systems more responsive to the community, has focused on restructuring and redistributing this centralized power. Accountability to the community, then, can perhaps best be seen as a function of decentralization and of community involvement in school governance.

The *Riles Report* described four variations on decentralizing the responsibility and authority of a central, duly constituted legal school board.[107]   They are:

1. Decentralizing certain administrative matters (e.g., personnel placement and selection of materials and equipment) to a geographical subdivision of the school district with all major policy-making and decision-making power still residing in the central board and administration.

2. Shifting authority for certain administrative matters within the educational system from the school board and superintendent to area superintendents who, acting under the authority of a city board and superintendent, have considerable decision-making power in their geographical subdivisions.

3. Informally granting some decision-making authority and responsibility to a community advisory board or plan-

ning council for a school or subsystem administered by an area superintendent, with the grant of power ranging from program planning, budgetary decisions, and hiring practices, on the one hand, to merely airing complaints. Within such *de facto* decentralization, final formal authority is retained by the central board and administration although considerable actual policy-making may shift to the local board or council.

4. Full, contractual delegation of authority and responsibility by the state authority or central board to a duly constituted legal entity, such as a nonprofit corporation or a local school board operating within a geographical subdivision of a school district. Such a contract would specifically grant authority for a particular period of time or until rescinded.

There are also a number of basic patterns for community involvement, which generally means more participation by neighborhood residents in the operation of a school or subsystem. They are:

1. *Participation,* with a possible combination of advisory and policy-making functions. The meaningfulness of community input will depend, of course, upon the genuine cooperation of the area administrator. This form of involvement has had an uneven pattern of success in ESEA Title I, Head Start and Follow Through programs, in which parental advice has often been ignored. For this reason, the Riles Task Force saw community participation as unlikely to effect the major institutional change required by the magnitude of urban educational problems.

2. *Partnership,* implemented either formally or informally. This is a dvision of authority, a sharing of decision-making. Technical assistance, as well as the financial and material resources of the larger system, remain available to the partnership unit. The critical element to success in

community partnership is the actual authority provided. If the role of the community is that of a junior partner, this form of community involvement cannot effect adequate institutional change either.

3. *Control* involves full authority in fiscal, programmatic, and hiring matters. "Control" connotes legal replacement of the central school board by representatives of the community. Most advocates of community involvement press for this pattern as affording the greatest opportunity for rapid institutional change. The *Riles Report* lists four critical success factors: (a) maintaining sufficient funding; (b) training community members to operate the educational unit; (c) securing appropriate personnel; and (d) utilizing appropriate technical assistance.

Clearly, these factors for successful community control are interdependent. Clearly, also, the commitment of the entire community is indispensable. A reading of the transcript of the hearings which gave rise to this book seems to indicate that New York City, the cradle of community control, has fallen short of the requisite degree of commitment.

Despite the problems community control has encountered, however, the underlying call for accountability of the schools has gained momentum. It is the demand for accountability that has inspired judicial and legislative challenges to teacher and supervisor selection, retention, and promotion methods; proposals for performance criteria to replace these methods; repeal or reduction of tenure statutes in a number of states; district school boards' challenges to central board mandates concerning hiring and firing of teachers and administrators; federally proposed voucher plans which allow parents to shop for the school which *will* produce results for their children; incentive pay proposals for teachers with compensation based on the performance of their pupils; performance contracting with private firms whose level of payment depends upon achievement results. Moreover, if school finance laws are reformed to provide full state funding, or if state courts impose serious qualitative requirements on the public schools, then statewide evaluation will inevitably become more significant.

All this movement toward accountability has drawn resistance from those in whom big city educational power has for so long been vested. Where the movement for bona fide accountability to the community has gained momentum, in fact, the real power centers have revealed themselves. Central school boards have been shown to be far weaker than their broadly stated legislative powers would suggest. Their power has been offset, not only by accrediting agencies, universities, and national teacher associations, but by local power groups as well. For example, the multileveled, vertical hierarchies of supervisors, specialists, department chairmen, principals, and district superintendents have often worked together formally and informally to preserve the system which spawned them.

In some instances, these organized professionals have attempted to use court challenges to stop the actions of community school boards. In others, their spokesmen have publicly berated city administrators who have not clamped down on what was perceived as errant community school boards. They lobby untiringly against legislation which provides educational alternatives to centrally controlled public school systems. And always they raise the issue of violence in the schools and danger to teachers to demand strong-armed central control. Indeed, because they are so serious about retaining their power, they have also manipulated to their own advantage the very strategies that community accountability efforts have produced.

A recent instance of such manipulation has been considered by Dr. Clark. He has vehemently criticized an accountability contract signed by the New York City Board of Education and the United Federation of Teachers with Educational Testing Service of Princeton.[108]

This contract is unlike performance contracts or turn-key contracts which several cities have entered into with educational firms. These agreements are oriented toward specific achievement results in all students, and, in the case of performance contracting, the responsible educational company is not compensated for its services unless an agreed upon percentage of students reaches an agreed upon performance level in basic skills within a specified time.

The New York plan, designed by Henry S. Dyer, then vice-president of Educational Testing Service, differs in several ways from such result-oriented plans. First, although the New York plan would allow parents to have some say about plan objectives, the objectives do not focus on basic skills alone, but also include other measurable aims, such as growth in pupil self-regard, social behavior, vocational development, and health. Dr. Dyer's objection to concentrating all effort on basic skills is that "it encourages the notion that, as far as the school is concerned, training in basic skills is all that matters in a society where so many other human characteristics also matter." He also feels that such narrow concentration "neglect[s] the fact that if a school gives exclusive attention to this one area of pupil development, it may purchase success in this area at the expense of failure in other areas — social behavior, for instance. . . ."[109]

Dr. Clark sees in this approach "a substitute of fuzzy concerns that may be valuable in themselves but are less so than the schools' main job — the training in those basic skills, such as reading, which alone can serve as the foundation for future learning." He points out that since failure in basic skills "has long served as the basis for rejection of the children of the poor and especially of minority groups . . . [s]uch failure must not be reinforced."[110]

But Dr. Clark's strongest objections to the New York contract go to Dr. Dyer's fundamental approach to accountability which (1) sets different output goals for each school according to past pupil achievement and socioeconomic background, and (2) requires that the entire school staff have joint responsibility (rather than each child's teacher having individual responsibility), with the staff accountable collectively for keeping itself informed about pupils' needs and for doing the best it can to meet those needs. [111]

It is the last measure of accountability which Dr. Clark calls "a sham of accountability," for it clearly requires no results. Rather, in the proposed "pupil-change model" it requires that teachers acquaint themselves and try to work with the index of their school population which administrators must provide them (through the Educational Testing Service). This index predicts what the performance level of each grade should be. It is limited by the "input" of each child, *i.e.*, his past performance, health, self-image, as well as the "hard to change" surrounding conditions of the school community, for example, the socioeconomic level of pupils' parents.[112] It is this school by school variation in expectations which Dr. Clark sees as an elaborate rationalization for mandating continued failure of minority children.

> The Dyer approach would formalize and give sanction to negative expectations for poor and minority-group children. It would run counter to the consistent finding of educational psychology that the schools' expectations for the child are a significant, perhaps the most significant, school-related factor in his achievement. In this, it is more insidious than previous, less "scientific" foundations. It would give official sanction to multiple and relative standards of student performance, and would institutionalize and reinforce the present educational discrepancy. The Board would, in effect, by relying on the Dyer perspective concretize class stratifications and, of course, racial distinctions; thus it would become an agent in contributing to the continuing deprivation of the poor and of black and Puerto Rican children. . . . Such an approach to accountability would make inevitable separate and unequal education in the city schools.[113]

But it is this and only this kind of approach to accountability which Albert Shanker sees teachers accepting. In speaking at a 1971 national conference on accountability, he made

clear that teachers oppose any notion of accountability which
treats them as "hired hands," which dictates "what the
teacher should be doing, or what practices are good and
which are bad, without considering those . . . outside influ-
ences that limit the performance of even the best of
teachers." [114]

As Shanker assesses teacher reaction, "it will be easier for
teachers to believe that a system of professional accountability
does not, necessarily, imply an individual threat," once they
understand the Dyer principle of joint accountability.
Shanker explained that principle:

> The individual student, his family, his socioeconomic background,
> and the school system itself, must all be held accountable in degrees
> apt to be determined for everyone involved. [115]

Dr. Clark calls the principle "blam[ing] the victim for being
victimized." [116]

But Shanker, in his acceptance of this approach to accountability, demonstrated his ability to successfully manipu-
late the strategy of control to the advantage of teachers. For
once people started talking about accountability, organized
teachers knew who the "victims" would be. At least on the
New York scene, they were successful in finding professional
allies to save them from their fate of being treated like
"hired hands."

New Approaches to Teaching

Teacher response to new educational approaches has, by and
large, been as negative as the response to individual accountability. Indeed, the roots of the response may be similar.
Teachers may well see proposed innovations as implied criticisms of the jobs they are doing. Or they may simply be fear-
ful of the new and unknown. In any event, there has
commonly been teacher reluctance and consequent failure
really to try to make new techniques work. This has certainly

contributed to the less than impressive results traceable to these innovations during the past two decades. Whether they would have been successful with enthusiastic teacher response unfortunately may never be known.

Language laboratories are one of many examples of a technological aid that has failed to produce the kinds of results expected. In 1968, Fred T. Wilhelm of NEA's Association for Supervision and Curriculum Development said that most language laboratories have met one of two fates:

(1)   Too many classes share a single lab, diminishing student-use time to the point where it does little good;

(2)   Foreign language teachers have little faith in the labs or don't know how to use them, and they remain idle.[117]

Team teaching is another innovation, which theroretically provides teachers with greater flexibility and an opportunity both to observe and measure one another's work. But too often it degenerates into "turn teaching" — "I'll teach today and it's your turn tomorrow." [118] The failure even to give the program a chance to prove itself is regrettably typical. It probably stems in part at least from the teacher's reluctance to share his or her classroom, as well as the aversion to a free-wheeling analysis of each other's methods.[119]

When education innovations require radical restructuring of the school program — as do, for example, nongraded organization, differentiated staffing and the open or free school — resistance from supervisors is often added to teacher resistance. For both tend to be oriented toward autonomy and fixed routines, and these innovations certainly require more effort than traditional teaching to make them work. Their combined resistance is usually sufficient to end the program altogether or to effectively retain the old approach but rename it.

The threat teachers seem to perceive as most serious, however, comes in proposals that neighborhood paraprofessionals assist them in the classroom. Although teachers have justifiably complained for years about the paperwork and other non-teaching duities they must shoulder, they have tended to be less than completely hospitable to paraprofessionals hired to assist them with these and other responsibilities.

Perhaps it is because in some situations paraprofessionals have performed so well with the difficult, "disruptive" child. If the teacher were willing to learn from and work with the paraprofessional, their relationship could be a boon to all involved in urban education. If, however, the teacher instead reacts with concern because the paraprofessional is "too good," the opportunity is lost. All too frequently this is the pattern as teachers fear living proof that some kinds of teaching may not require a college degree or teaching license.

This threat to the professional standing of teachers, and the threat that paraprofessional presence in the classroom is a step toward community control of the schools, have colored the situation. Organized teachers have not formally opposed paraprofessional help but they have sought to control it carefully. Thus, largely through contract stipulations, teacher organizations have been working to limit the classroom activities of aides, and especially preventing them from assuming real teaching duties. While positive steps have been taken on paper to fashion a career ladder by which paraprofessionals can ultimately become teachers, in practice the requirements are so onerous that almost none are likely to reach the promised land.

The Teacher's Response to Pressures: *Organize and Then Organize Some More*

An individual teacher may be for or against innovation, community control, equal funding, merit pay and accountability, or integration. But that teacher is likely to have few avenues within a large urban school system for even expressing his or her views let alone having an impact on the way the system functions. The teacher can, of course, give up in disgust and leave public school teaching or seek a job in the suburbs. And many teachers do exactly that. But if the teacher opts to stay in the same school system (and that will be increasingly common if the personnel surplus develops as projected), the only way in which he or she can reasonably hope to influence trends in education is by active membership in a teacher organization.

Teacher organizations came into being in response to genuine needs of the American teacher who began in this country as an indentured servant and who continued into the twentieth century still bound in social, political, and economic servitude to the school system. Without teacher organizations the right to decent wages and some semblance of personal freedom would still be a vague hope for most teachers. But teacher organizations did come and are by now assuming enormous proportions on the American educational scene. For they have become major political forces to be reckoned with on local, state, and national levels.

The two largest teacher organizations began with dramatically different orientations but have come more and more to resemble one another. The National Education Association, still by far the larger, does not have labor union affiliations, nor did it begin with an organized labor orientation toward direct action and social reform. It was, and to some extent still is, a "professional association" designed to work quietly, sedately, and cooperatively for better education. The NEA represents more than 70% of all public school employees across the country with its membership including both teachers and supervisors. The American Federation of Teachers is a much smaller, but much noisier, organization. Representing approximately 20% of the nation's public school teachers, it is an affiliate of the AFL–CIO.

The NEA's preference for teacher professionalism influenced the character of its activities from its earliest days. Over the years it has played an important role in raising standards and status in the teaching field and in upgrading education preparation generally. But the NEA has, for the most part, avoided controversy, perhaps because until recently it was dominated by school supervisors and administrators. Unlike the AFT, for example, it was not in the forefront in calling for school integration in Northern cities. In many cities, in fact, local association officers publicly defended school boards and administrators accused of racially discriminatory policies. Similarly, until the mid-1960's, the NEA did not advocate school personnel strikes. As the rivalry of the two organizations grew, however, the AFT's militancy, particularly in its effective use of the strike, forced the NEA to change its position toward direct action. And with this concerted move into the center of the public forum, organized teachers have effected both a new self-image and a new image in the eyes of the public.

> The growing pugnacity of the teachers' organizations — the National Education Association (NEA) and its affiliates, the American Federation of Teachers (AFT) and its locals — is forcing a change both in the teacher's image of himself and in the way the community perceives him. "Front page pictures of teachers striking and marching, breaking open schools and going off to jail have just about finished off our lingering image of the mythical American educator as a long-suffering pedagogue, sustained more by dedication than hard cash, willing to accept second-class status in his efforts to educate our children," noted Harold Howe in his final [1969] report as U.S. Commissioner of Education. Since the 1960—61 school year, 189 teacher strikes involving 263,200 staff members have been called by the rival teachers' groups. They involved an estimated 1,593,638 man days lost.[120]

The growth in the number of strikes per year effectively indicates the increasing insistence of teachers on salary increases and fringe benefits. There were 5 teacher strikes in 1963—64;

12 the following year; then 34; and in 1967–68, 114.[121] *The Education Daily* reported on September 13, 1969 that some 75,000 teachers in at least 13 states were involved in serious disputes with their school systems.[122]

This pattern of increasing teacher strikes has come in the face of clear prohibitions against public employee strikes in virtually all states, and the repeated jailing of union leaders and regular members for contempt of court orders enjoining illegal strikes. Yet, the teacher organizations have hardly been deterred. They are moving with heightened vigor to openly challenge school boards, the courts, and ultimately, the legislatures. The UFT in New York City has been one of the leaders in this effort. A perfect example of its strategy is found in the comments of Albert Shanker, the union's president, when he discussed prospects for the impending bargaining with the New York City Board of Education over the 1972 contract. Said Mr. Shanker, "[The] complex structure of the negotiations this time [community school board representatives were to participate in the bargaining for the first time] makes a strike more likely. I would say, that there is better than a 50–50 chance there will be a strike in the fall." [123]

In addition to this obvious sabre-rattling, the teacher organizations have also been actively trying to eliminate or reduce the strike prohibition. Several states, including Pennsylvania, have recently enacted limited strike laws for public employees and their impact will be watched closely. The principal argument advanced by the teacher organizations and their supporters is, in the words of lawyer and labor mediator Theodore Kheel, "the right to strike and the right of an employer to take a strike is indigenous to the process of collective bargaining."[124] Put simply, collective bargaining can't work unless public employees, like private sector employees, have the ultimate right to strike. The only exception recognized at a conference called by the Workers' Defense League to protest the jailing of public employee labor leaders is if

"government employees render an essential service." [125] Since
it was Albert Shanker who stated this sole exception, and since
he obviously believes teachers should have the right to strike,
his definition of "essential service" must be a rather
restrictive one.

Certainly recent public sector experience does suggest that
the existing legal framework is not effective. But will legitimiz-
ing public employee strikes actually reduce their frequency,
as Mr. Kheel has maintained? Will it protect the public interest
better in the long run? Some labor law experts think not.
Writing in *The New York Times,* Professor Harry H. Wellington
and Professor Ralph K. Winter, Jr., of Yale Law School,
argued that a public employer is fundamentally different than
a private corporation and what has worked to promote labor-
management relations in the private sector will not necessarily
work in the public. They distinguish the two situations on a
number of grounds. The most obvious is that "disruption of
public services is more apt to endanger the health and safety
of a municipality's citizenry." [126] But there are less obvious,
although perhaps equally important differences. "Unions of
public employees are less restrained by the fear of unemployment among their members. . . . The demand for most
municipal services does not quickly decline when cost increases." Yet another significant difference is that public
officials "are highly vulnerable to the disruption of public
services by strikes. . . . All public employee strikes worth
staging inconvenience voters who will press for a quick settle-
ment often without sufficient attention to its cost." Finally,
according to Professor Wellington and Professor Winter, if
strikes were made legal for public employees they would presumably be more, rather than less, frequent and would further
increase the power of public employee unions.

> What is at stake is not simply economic efficiency but the distribution
> of urban political power. When public employees strike for higher
> wages, they are exerting political force not only on the voters they

inconvenience but also on other groups making political claims on the municipal budget. Nor do public employees use their power only to affect the allocation of government funds. Increasingly, their attention is turning to matters such as police civilian review boards and the governance of schools, matters which, while they affect the employment relationship, ought to be resolved through a political process in which all competing groups of interested citizens have a meaningful say.

Professor Wellington and Professor Winter recognize the difficulty of enforcing the strike prohibition, but they attribute part of the problem to those, such as Theodore Kheel, who in their judgment have "done much to destroy the moral imperative of laws against strikes." Their answer is to take steps to reduce the political vulnerability of public employers to strikes. "Principally, this can be achieved," they say, "through making the costs of settlements more visible and imposing them directly on the voters involved."

There is no evidence that this controversy will be quickly or easily resolved. Indeed, there are signs that teacher organizations may be preparing for a long and desperate struggle over this and related issues. One sign of this preparation may be the substantial movement toward the merger of the NEA and the AFT into a single teacher power bloc. After years of being at one another's throats, the signs of *rapprochement* are everywhere. And this has become almost inevitable. For, just as the NEA began to gear its own tactics to the more militant AFT actions, the AFT has found its philosophy and aims moving closer to the conservatism of the NEA. A pattern for actual merger is evolving. A number of NEA and AFT affiliates have already merged at the local level, and the United Teachers of New York, the statewide AFT unit, and the New York State Teachers Association, NEA's counterpart, have agreed to merge into the New York Congress of Teachers. According to David Selden, AFT president, this will provide the impetus for similar merger efforts in other states. But Albert Shanker sees an even more grandiose pattern emerging. Mr. Shanker has said that a nationwide joining of the two organizations could take place within five years. His prediction was strengthened in December, 1972 when a large block of classroom teachers from urban areas, members of both NEA and the AFT, formed the National Coalition for Teacher Unity. This coalition, claiming affiliates in 150 cities in 34 states and the support of one-third of NEA's members and all of AFT'S members, has a stated purpose of bringing about a merger within two or three years.[127]

If the changes predicted as a result of the New York State merger can be extrapolated to the national level, the whole face of public education will be dramatically changed by a merger of the two parent organizations. For, in New York State, Albert Shanker and Thomas Hobart, president of the New York State Teachers Association are confidently predicting that the new congress will provide them with vastly increased muscle. With more than 200,000 teachers, two-thirds of all the teachers in the state, under unified leadership, the new organization is expected to push hard on the statewide legislative level for such things as repeal of the "punitive" provisions of the state's Taylor Law which bars strikes by public employees and enactment of laws to strengthen teacher tenure (the trend has recently been moving in the opposite direction with the probationary period for teachers increased to five years from three and with tenure eliminated entirely for supervisors). There will be other changes as well, often having to do with economic matters; for the teacher organizations see many recent unfavorable developments resulting from the money squeeze. Thus, changes in the tenure law are attributed to pressure from school boards to permit economizing by replacement of more experienced and expensive teachers with less experienced ones. Performance contracts, the increasing demand for "productivity," voucher programs, the freeze on sabbatical leaves — all are seen as consequences of the dollar pinch. An answer, according to Albert Shanker, is merger and redirected energies.

The merged group will be the largest state teacher organization in the nation. Instead of spending hundreds of thousands of dollars in costly jurisdictional disputes, as they did in the last few years, the organizations will be able to concentrate on massive statewide political action to improve education and on a large-scale program of legal, public relations and negotiations assitance to teachers throughout the state.[128]

Writing in Mr. Shanker's weekly column/advertisement about a month later, Thomas Hobart made ever clearer the impact expected of the merged teacher organization:

In the State Legislature, the voice of teachers will be heard with undiluted clarity. They will have in abundance what is needed for effectiveness in politics — votes, lobbying, dedication. Statewide public relations programs will give the people of New York a better idea of what their schools and teachers do — and what they need in order to do their jobs better. . . . The impact of education's lobbyists on Congress and the Department of Health, Education and Welfare will be strengthened — not only by teacher unity in New York State, but also by the NEA-AFT cooperation that NYCT will encourage. . . . It is this prospect of unprecedented teacher strength that commands the attention of editorial writers and broadcasters. They see very clearly the advantages which merger will bring to teachers. They see less clearly — or do not see it at all — that merger will also benefit children, schools, and society itself. . . . The typical teacher contract is . . . as much concerned with improved education for children as it is with better terms and conditions of employment for teachers. . . . Teachers have worked to win a voice in curriculum. . . . NYCT will strengthen the voice of teachers in educational decision-making. . . .[129]

It is precisely the prospect of "unprecedented teacher strength" which deeply worries some educational commentators. For teacher organizations seem to be moving with new fervor into two areas of controversy — the political arena and educational decision-making.

As Mr. Hobart suggested, teacher organizations will increasingly involve themselves in lobbying and delivering votes in abundance. The effort is already under way according to Dr. Benjamin Fine. The NEA and AFT, even before serious merger talk, had indicated an intention "to make teachers' voices heard, as never before, in the 1972 campaign."[130] The AFT decided to endorse candidates for president and vice-president for the first time in its history and a campaign chest of $1 million was to be devoted to the aid of "pro-education" candidates. Voter registration was also to be a focus of a number of AFT locals. The NEA's efforts were to focus on congressional candidates but the possibility of endorsing a presidential candidate was left open.

The endorsement of a presidential candidate by either of the organizations raised interesting issues. For, while President Nixon has been castigated as "anti-education," the majority of American teachers are now considered politically conservative. A study by the NEA's research division found that 60% of the teachers label themselves conservative.[131]

The expanded involvement of teacher organizations in educational decision-making is greeted by critics with even greater concern than the unions' political involvement. As Professor Wellington and Professor Winter pointed out, certain basic decisions are better made "through a political process in which all competing groups of interested citizens have a meaningful say."[132] Traditional collective bargaining is not that forum. Indeed, Mr. Shanker predicted a 50—50 chance of a teachers' strike in New York City because the involvement of three community board representatives made the structure of negotiations too complex. Despite the essentially closed nature of the bargaining process, however, if teacher organizations have their way, broad educational issues will be decided there. The issues may be decided, right or wrong, but the process will be intentionally shielded from public scrutiny. For it is a well-known rule of collective bargaining that the positions into which the parties are settling during the course of negotiations should be kept confidential. Absent some kind of public referendum to approve the contract before it becomes effective, anything the public can do smacks very much of locking the barn door too late. That has been the exact plaint of members of the black and Puerto Rican communities in New York City and Newark, among other places, in recent years.

The scope of the demands put forward by the UFT in March and April 1972 may suggest the shape of things to come. There were of course the financial demands — a basic salary scale of $12,500 to $25,000 (as compared to the current range of $9,400 to $13,950), increased pensions, and an increased welfare fund. But there were many other substantial benefits such as increased sick leave and personal days and expanded sabbatical program. And that was just the beginning.

According to a Public Education Association report on June 12, 1972, "the issue in this negotiation is not as it once was, fair teacher salaries and working conditions. The issue is whether the old rigid bureaucracy that so paralyzed the education of our children in the past is to be replaced by a new rigid bureaucracy imposed by contract." [133] For among the UFT proposals were the demand that no teacher be laid off or reduced in rank for budgetary reasons or because of a staffing decrease or total elimination of a class of positions. The only acceptable method of decreasing staff, according to the UFT, is by natural attrition. Also, the union demanded the continuation of existing experimental education programs and the expansion of each program to 10 additional schools during each year of the contract. John Lotz, a former New York City Board of Education member, used to say that all experimental programs in the city school district were "doomed to success," and the UFT demand seems very much in that tradition. Other contract demands similarly raised the issue of who sets educational policy for the public schools. The approximately 700 demands included: expansion of the Early Childhood Pre-School Center program; a Junior Guidance program in every elementary school; a full-time corrective reading teacher in every elementary school with more added

as the number of educationally retarded children rises; at least
one full-time mathematics, health education, science, music,
art, and library teacher in every elementary school; a $2 million
annual contribution to an Education Development Fund
under the auspices of the UFT; relief of teachers from most
"non-teaching" duties, such as patrol duties, escorting children
to and from the classroom, and all clerical duties; limiting
evaluation of teachers' performance to one per year after
tenure and requiring that only the teacher's supervisor can conduct the evaluation; permitting teachers to transfer to a new
school after three years of service (as compared to the present
five years); and requiring acting supervisory positions to be
filled by qualified applicants within the school solely on the
basis of seniority.

Reasonable people can differ about the merits of each of
the proposals. Indeed, one could favor the policies or programs
advanced by each and still be sorely troubled about using the
collective bargaining process as the forum for making educational policy. Albert Shanker, in his weekly *New York Times*
column/advertisement, asked, "Shall Teachers Have a Role in
Educational Policy?" [134] He leaves little doubt about his
answer. After an excursion into whether the teachers' demands really intrude into educational policy-making,
Shanker says:

> But even if these proposals go beyond working conditions in the
> traditional sense, it is significant that in teacher-board bargaining, not
> only in New York City but elsewhere across the country, teachers
> are pressing for a voice in changing the schools while school boards
> are unsure of the role they want teachers to play. . . . The question
> of a teacher voice, through the collective bargaining process, in the
> formulation of educational policy still remains. [135]

The verdict is still out on this crucial question, but the
teacher organizations, especially the American Federation of
Teachers, have left little doubt that they will press forcefully
for increased teacher involvement in educational policy-making

throughout the country. Strong resistance from boards of education, community groups, and many parents can be expected. So, an important battle is predictable.

Ironically, the teachers' pressure for a larger voice in educational policy-making, in the name of reform, puts them into conflict with parents and others (in New York City, elected community boards) who believe they should be the ones with a greater say. All too often this seems to be the result of teacher organization positions. For example, teachers' pressure for higher salaries brings them into conflict with taxpayers resisting increased school taxes. Teachers' efforts to improve working conditions and the safety and security of school buildings often bring them into conflict with students who object to disciplinary rules they regard as overly strict and dehumanizing.

This puts great pressure on individual teachers and ultimately on their organizations. If there is any chance to solve the problems of urban education, it must come through vigorous cooperation among all those whose lives and livelihoods are involved in the system. Yet on numerous issues, including many where the teachers are taking forward-looking positions, the teachers find themselves in opposition to those who must become their allies. Solving this dilemma is one of the highest priorities in public education. The willingness to put aside high blown rhetoric and reach rational compromises is an essential starting point. Perhaps the current New York City negotiations provide a basis for hope. Despite the enormously costly and far-reaching union proposals and the constant talk of impending strike, agreement was reached in a spirit of cooperation. Albert Shanker described it well:

> Meanwhile, New York has done more than avoid what would have been a disastrous strike. The ability of the union, the community boards and the central board to work together in this set of negotiations and the atmosphere of good faith and cooperation which prevailed give hope that in the three years under this new agreement

a new relationship can be developed — one in which each party will be sensitive to the needs and interests of the others and will turn from political and economic conflict toward finding answers to the educational problems before us.[136]

This is a far cry from the Albert Shanker who has been quoted as likening community boards to "vigilantes fighting over the goodies." [137] Let us hope the real Albert Shanker has stepped forward and that teachers and their organizations, standing as they do at the center of educational ferment, will again be able to work in tandem with the other major actors in this contemporary drama. If they can not, the direst predictions about urban education may come true.

Notes and References

1. *See, e.g.,* U.S. Dept. of Health, Education and Welfare, *Bond Sales for Public School Purposes, 1970–71* (Government Printing Office, Washington, D.C., 1972), pp. 2–3.

2. 347 U.S. 483 (1954).

3. Myron Brenton, *What's Happened to Teacher* (Avon Books, New York, 1970), p. 28 (hereinafter *"What's Happened to Teacher"*).

4. National Education Association, Research Division, *Teacher Supply and Demand in Public Schools, 1970,* p. 15, table 3.

5. U.S. Bureau of Census & Bureau of Labor Statistics, *The Social and Economic Status of Negroes in the United States,* 1970, p. 61, table 49 (hereinafter *"1970 Census"*).

6. In 1970, black and other minority group members constituted 7% of professional and technical personnel in the United States with the two highest professions being teachers (10%), and medical and other health personnel (8%).

7. J. C. James, "The Black Principal, Another Vanishing American," *The New Republic* (Sept. 16, 1970), pp. 17–20.

8. U.S. Office of Education, "Beginning Teachers, Status and Career Orientations," *Final Report on the Survey of New Teachers in the Public Schools, 1956–57* (Government Printing Office, Washington, D.C., 1961)

9. Ronald M. Pavalko, "Aspirants to Teaching: Some Differences Between High School Senior Boys and Girls Planning on a Career in Teaching," *Sociology and Social Research* (Oct. 1965).

10. John Chafee, Jr., "First Manpower Assessment," *American Education* (Feb. 1969).

11. Philip R. Harvey, et al., *Graduate Record Examination Special Report* (Educational Testing Service, Princeton, 1965), pp. 1–29; J. Scott Hunter, *The Academic and Financial Status of Graduate Students—Spring 1965* (Government Printing Office, Washington, D.C., 1967), p. 15

12. .*What's Happened to Teacher*, pp. 46–52, with references in notes 3–19.

13. National Education Association, *Salary Schedules for Teachers, 1970–71* (Research Report 1970–R12), p. 24, table 19 (hereinafter *"Salary Schedules"*).

14. *What's Happened to Teacher*, p. 221.

15. *Id.* at 82.

16. *Salary Schedules*, p. 14, table 7.

17. *Id.* at 7, table 4.

18. *Id.* at 16, table 9.

19. *What's Happened to Teacher*, p. 85.

20. *Id.* at 224.

21. "Task Force on Urban Education to the Department of Health, Education and Welfare," *The Urban Education Task Force Report* (Praeger, New York, 1970), p. 265 (hereinafter the *"Riles Report"* after the Task Force's chairman Wilson C. Riles). This report systematically documents both the problems of urban schools and a federal plan for dealing with those problems. Commissioned by the secretary of HEW, Robert Finch, it was effectively buried in the Office of Education until Congressman Jeffrey Cohelan of California included it in the *Congressional Record.*

22. *What's Happened to Teacher*, p. 225.

23. *Id.* at 225–26.

24. *Id.* at 227.

25. *See, e.g.*, Nat Hentoff, *Our Children Are Dying* (New Viking Press, New York, 1966); James Herndon, *The Way It Spozed to Be* (Simon & Schuster, New York, 1968); John Holt, *How Children Fail* (Pitman, New York, 1964); Nathaniel Hickerson, *Education for Alienation* (Prentice-Hall, Inc., Englewood Cliffs, New Jersey, 1966); Herbert Kohl, *36 Children* (New American Library, New York, 1967); Jonathan Kozol, *Death at an Early Age: The Destruction of the Hearts and Minds of Negro Children in the Boston Public Schools* (Houghton Mifflin, Boston, 1967).

26. *Riles Report* p. 183.

27. *1970 Census*, p. 1

28. Department of Health, Education and Welfare, *Report A66* (June 18, 1971), table 3—A ("Negroes in 100 Largest (1970) School Districts, Ranked by Size") and table 3—B ("Spanish Surnamed Americans in Selected Large School Districts, Ranked by Size in 1970").

29. *Riles Report*, Chs. 3, 4, & 5 (pp. 82—201).

30. *Id.* at 94.

31. *1970 Census*, p. 2

32. *Id.* at 26, table 17.

33. *Id.* at 27, table 18.

34. *Id.* at 31, table 22.

35. *Id.* at 27.

36. *Riles Report*, p. 108.

37. *1970 Census*, pp. 37—38, table 29.

38. *Id.* at 88, table 72, and p. 91, table 75.

39. *Riles Report*, p. 123.

40. *Id.* at 129.

41. *Id.* at 130.

42. *Id.* at 199.

43. *Id.* at 191.

44. *Id.* at 166.

45. *Id.* at 166. Results of the CUE analysis cited at pp. 166—69.

46. James Coleman, et al., *Equality of Educational Opportunity* (National Center for Educational Statistics, U.S. Office of Education, Government Printing Office, Washington, D.C., 1966), pp. 274—75 (hereinafter *"Coleman Report"*).

47. *1970 Census*, p. 77, table 63.

48. *Riles Report*, p. 170.

49. *Carnegie Quarterly* (Fall 1968), p. 1.

50. *Riles Report*, p. 172.

51. Stanley M. Cohen, "Politics of Vandalism," *The Nation*, (Nov. 11, 1968), pp. 497—500.

52. *Riles Report*, p. 178.

53. *Report of the National Advisory Commission on Civil Disorders* (1968), p. 432 (hereinafter *"Kerner Report"*).

54. *Coleman Report*, pp. 68—69, 71.

55. *Riles Report*, pp. 154—55.

56. *Coleman Report*, pp. 134, 137, 140.

57. *Riles Report*, pp. 157—58.

58. W. Wolf and W. C. Wolf, Jr., "Teacher Dropouts Still a Dilemma," *School and Society* (Apr. 18, 1964).

59. *Kerner Report*, p. 428.

60. National Commission on Teacher Education and Professional Standards, *The Assignment and Misassignment of Teachers* (National Education Association, Washington, D.C., 1965), pp. 1—68.

61. Institute for Development of Educational Activities, *A Symposium on the Training of Teachers for Elementary Schools* (Melbourne, Florida, 1969).

62. U.S. Commission on Civil Rights, *Racial Isolation in the Public Schools* (Appendixes 1967), pp. 8—11, table A—2.

63. Data obtained from a survey by the Office of Civil Rights, Department of Health, Education and Welfare and from individual school districts, as published in "Discriminatory Merit Systems: A Case Study of the Supervisory Examinations Administered by the New York Board of Examiners," 6 *Columbia Journal of Law and Social Problems* 374, 394, 395, table V (Sept. 1970)

64. P. J. Graff, "Culturally Depreived Children: Opinions of Teachers on the Views of Riessman," *Exceptional Children,* Vol. 31, No. 2 (October, 1964).

65. Robert B. Moberly, "Causes of Impasse in School Board-Teacher Negotiations," 21 *Labor Law Journal* 668, 676 (Oct. 1970).

66. *Riles Report,* pp. 61—62.

67. John E. Coons, William H. Clune III, and Stephen D. Sugarman, *Private Wealth and Public Education* (Cambridge, Mass., 1970), p. 272· (hereinafter *"Private Wealth and Public Education"*).

68. Joel S. Berke, Stephen K. Bailey, Alan K. Campbell, Seymour Sacks, *Federal Aid to Public Education: Who Benefits?* (U.S. Senate Select Committee on Equal Educational Opportunity, Committee print, Government Printing Office, Washington, D.C., April 1971), p. 14 (hereinafter the *"Syracuse Study"*).

69. *Riles Report,* p. 55.

70. *Syracuse Study,* pp. 16—23, is the source of this and subsequent data in this section unless otherwise noted.

71. *Riles Report,* p. 54.

72. 5 Cal.3d 584, 487 P. 2d 1241 (1971).

73. 5 Cal. 3d at 589.

74. *Id.*

75. *Id.* at 599—600.

76. *Id.* at 603.

77. *Id.*

78. McInnis v. Shapiro, 293 F. Supp. 327 (N.D. Ill. 1968), *aff'd mem. sub nom.,* McInnis v. Ogilvie, 394 U.S. 322 (1969); Burruss v.

Wilkerson, 310 F. Supp. 572 (W.D. Va. 1969), *aff'd mem.*, 397 U.S. 74 (1970).

79. Rodriguez v. San Antonio Independent School Dist., 337 F. Supp. 280 (W.D. Tex. 1971), *prob. jur. noted,* 406 U.S. 966 (1972); Van Dusartz v. Hatfield, 334 F. Supp. 870 (D. Minn. 1971); Robinson v. Cahill, 118 N.J. Super, 223, 287 A. 2d 187 (1972); Hollins v. Shoftstall, Civ. No. C-253652 (Super. Ct., Maricopa County, Arizona, January 13, 1972).

80. 118 N.J. Super. 223, 287 A. 2d 187 (1972).

81. President's Commission on School Finance, *Schools, People and Money: The Need for Educational Reform* (Final Report, 1972), p. xiv.

82. *What's Happened to Teacher,* p. 80.

83. *Syracuse Study,* p. 32.

84. *Id.* at 31–32.

85. *Riles Report,* p. 224.

86. 327 F. Supp. 844 (D.D.C. 1971). *See also* 269 F. Supp. 401 (D.D.C. 1967), *aff'd sub nom.,* Smuck v. Hansen, 408 F. 2d (D.C. Cir. 1969).

87. *The New York Times,* Aug. 24, 1971, p. 19, col. 1.

88. 402 U.S. 1, 30 (1971).

89. *Id.* at 29. *Cf.* North Carolina State Board of Education v. Swann, 402 U.S. 43 (1971); McDaniel v. Barresi, 402 U.S. 39 (1971).

90. *The New York Times,* Aug. 13, 1971, p. 1, col. 4.

91. *The New York Times,* Sept. 7, 1971, p. 20, col. 1.

92. *The New York Times,* Aug. 31, 1971, p. 1, col. 4.

93. 445 F. 2d 990 (10th Cir. 1971), *cert. granted,* 404 U.S. 1036 (1972).

94. Bradley v. School Board, 338 F. Supp. 67 (E.D. Va. 1972), *order stayed,* 456 F. 2d 6 (1972) [Richmond, Virginia] ; United States v. Board of School Commissioners, 332 F. Supp. 655 (S.D. Ind. 1971) [Indianapolis] ; Bradley v. Milliken, 433 F. 2d 897, *remand for trial on merits,* 438 F. 2d 945 (6th Cir. 1971), *order denying motion to join suburban school districts,* 338 F. Supp. 582 (E.D. Mich. 1971) [Detroit].

95. Public Law 92–318 Supp. 719 (assignment to non-neighborhood schools not required). Note the stronger language and more thorough treatment of busing in the bill passed on Aug. 18, 1972, by the House (H.R. 13915), which prohibits any U.S. court, department or agency from ordering busing beyond the second closest school to a child's residence. Busing is prohibited if a desegregated school becomes segregated as a result of shifting residential patterns. The bill also authorizes reopening of court orders on desegregation plans already in effect, and

termination of court orders requiring busing if the court finds that the school system is no longer being operated in a racially segregated manner, regardless of past discrimination.

96. *See, e.g.,* Lee v. Macon County Board of Education, 453 F. 2d 1104 (5th Cir. 1971); U.S. v. Plaquemines Parish School Board, 336 F. Supp. 992 (E.D. La. 1971); Baker v. Columbus Municipal Separate School District, 329 F. Supp. 706 (N.D. Miss. 1971); U.S. v. State of Texas, 330 F. Supp. 235 (E.D. Tex. 1971), *modified and aff'd,* 447 F. 2d 441 (5th Cir. 1971); and Davis v. School District of City of Pontiac, 309 F. Supp. 734 (E.D. Mich. 1970), *aff'd,* 443 F. 2d 573 (6th Cir. 1971).

97. Seth S. King, "Chicago Reports Segregation Is Up," *The New York Times,* Nov. 28, 1971, part 1, p. 69, col. 1.

98. Porcelli v. Titus, 108 N.J. Super. 301, 261 A. 2d 364 (1969); Porcelli v. Titus, 302 F. Supp. 726 (D.N.J. 1969), *aff'd,* 431 F. 2d 1254 (3rd Cir. 1970), *cert. denied,* 402 U.S. 944 (1971); Porcelli v. Titus, N.J. School Law Decisions 218 (1968) [Commissioner decision], *aff'd,* N.J. School Law Decisions 188 (1969) [State Board decision].

99. 431 F. 2d at 1257—58.

100. Kenneth B. Clark, "Introduction," *Community Control and the Urban School,* Mario Fantini, Marilyn Gittell, Richard Magat (Praeger, New York, 1970), pp. ix—x (hereinafter *"Community Control"*).

101. Joseph Stocker and Donald F. Wilson, "Accountability and the Classroom Teacher," *Today's Education,* Vol. 60, No. 3, Mar. 1971.

102. *Id.*

103. *Community Control,* p. x.

104. *Id.* at x—xi.

105. *Id.* at 66.

106. *Id.* at 67.

107. *Riles Report,* pp. 268—72.

108. Metropolitan Applied Research Center, Inc. (MARC), *MARC Memo,* released March 18, 1971 (hereinafter *"MARC Memo"*).

109. Henry S. Dyer, "Toward Objective Criteria of Professional Accountability in the Schools of New York City," *Phi Delta Kappan,* Vol. 52, No. 4, Dec. 1970, p. 211 (hereinafter *"Dyer"*).

110. *MARC Memo,* p. 2.

111. *Dyer,* p. 206.

112. *Id.* at 207—09.

113. *MARC Memo,* pp. 2—3.

114. "Possible Effects on Instruction Programs," *Proceedings of the Conference on Educational Accountability* (sponsored by Educational Testing Service, March 1971) F—5, 6.

115. *Id.* at F—6.

116. MARC, *Accountability as a Rationalization for School Failure*, released March 18, 1971, p. 11.

117. National School Public Relations Association, *Education U.S.A.* (Sept. 23, 1968, weekly report).

118. *Id.*

119. *Id.*

120. *What's Happened to Teacher*, p. 18.

121. *Id.* at 106.

122. *The Education Daily*, Vol. 2, No. 165, Sept. 13, 1969.

123. *The New York Times*, March 22, 1972, p. 36, col. 1.

124. *The New York Times*, March 12, 1972, p. 32, col. 4.

125. *Id.*

126. *The New York Times*, June 12, 1972, p. 35, col. 1, is the source of this and subsequent quotes from Professor Wellington and Professor Winter. *See also* Harry H. Wellington and Ralph K. Winter, Jr., *The Unions and the Cities* (The Brookings Institution, Washington, D.C., 1971).

127. *The New York Times*, Dec. 24, 1972, p. E—5, vol. 1.

128. *The New York Times*, April 9, 1972, p. E—13, col. 5.

129. *The New York Times*, May 7, 1972, p. E—9, col. 5.

130. *Newark Star-Ledger*, March 26, 1972, p. 48, col. 7.

131. *Newark Star-Ledger*, March 12, 1972, p. 43, col. 1.

132. *The New York Times*, June 12, 1972, p. 35, col. 1.

133. Public Education Association, *Education Information Service Report*, Vol. II, No. 9, June 12, 1972, p. 1.

134. *The New York Times*, Sept. 17, 1972, p. E—5, col. 5.

135. *Id.*

136. *Id.*

137. Nat Hentoff, "School Hearings: 'F' for the Times," *Village Voice*, February 4, 1971, p. 12, col. 2.

CHAPTER 2

TRAINING THE URBAN TEACHER

The process through which urban (and other) school districts obtain their teachers customarily begins in the teacher training programs. Most of those programs are offered in institutions of higher education which have existed mainly to prepare teachers. Indeed, many of them grew out of the old normal schools which qualified high school graduates to enter teaching after a one- or two-year program.

It is in these teaching training programs where prospective teachers develop, solidify, or lose their interest in teaching in urban schools. It is also where they should be developing the skills and insights to become effective teachers of urban children. What actually happens in teacher training programs is, therefore, critically important to all urban school districts. And the urban school districts should have some power to affect what goes on in the colleges. After all, the colleges exist to prepare their students to gain teaching positions. A teacher training program is judged in part at least by its ability to place graduates in school districts they prefer. The urban school district, as a large employer, can establish eligibility criteria which should influence the character of the teacher training program.

This seems obvious and straightforward. But in practice it is far more complicated. Most school districts have not been noted for their aggressiveness in advising teacher training institutions of their requirements. Indeed, communications of any kind are often sparse. Moreover, most school districts leave personnel matters, including liaison with the sources of teachers, largely with the district's professionals who are themselves usually products of traditional teacher training programs. This is not an approach likely to yield dramatic departures from prevailing practice.

Many urban school districts, because they are often rated "less desirable" by prospective teachers, seem to have less influence than their suburban counterparts.

Other factors work to diminish the real power of all school district employers. The teacher training institutions themselves have great influence in educational circles. "Circles" is a particularly appropriate word here. For cyclical movement of people and theories has long characterized the education establishment. Some graduates of teacher training programs go into the "field" to teach. If they are ambitious, they aspire to supervisory positions which often require graduate credits and degrees in education which usually means back to the school of education. It also means back into contact with other graduates of teacher training institutions who stayed on as faculty members.

Still other education professionals (sometimes the same ones at different stages of their careers) find their way to additional bases of power which influence teacher training and which tend to reduce the role of the school district. State education departments typically establish teacher certification standards that constitute a statewide floor. Individual school districts may add their own special requirements. If each of the almost 800 school districts in New York State actually developed significantly different knowledge and skill requirements, the teacher training institutions would be hard pressed to reflect those demands in their curriculums. Most districts, however, have not established their own special demands. Consequently, the colleges have been free to direct their attention to assuring that their graduates meet state certification standards. If, as is commonly true, those standards have little or nothing to do with the special educational needs of urban schools and their children, state certification may offer the urban district little assurance that candidates have the necessary knowledge, skills, and personal characteristics.

Indeed, the kind of teacher training programs that most state certification standards inspire may deter people who would be effective urban teachers from ever entering the field. For state certification still puts a premium on traditional education courses in most states. It may in fact be based on little more than a determination that the applicant has taken sufficient credit hours of "straight" education courses (that is, courses with little subject matter content, or, as some observers would say, little content of any kind). A substantial number of state education departments don't even make this determination. They use "program" certification. Once a particular teacher training program is approved, any graduates of that program certified by the institution are given state certification. The evaluation which leads to program approval may be carried out by state education department personnel or the state may rely on an accrediting agency. When the state does the latter, it has effectively delegated its certification function to private agencies and the state has ceased to be a meaningful force in the area of teacher training.

The accrediting agency is yet another stomping ground of education professionals. The National Council for the Accreditation of Teacher Education (NCATE, affectionately known as N-kate) has for the past 20 years been the principal accrediting body in teacher education. It was created as a "super" agency by various professional education organizations, most notably by an accrediting arm of the venerable National Education Association. It is no coincidence that NCATE's governing body is dominated by appointees of the various departments of the NEA. Virtually all the members represent traditional bastions of professional education.

NCATE has reached a position of great power in teacher education. Whether or it not it can rise about its relatively parochial origins to lead the reform of teacher training is unclear. For its power is at once a great opportunity and a great danger. About ten years ago, James Koerner's *Miseducation of American Teachers* raised six serious questions about NCATE:

1. ... [T]he efficacy of accreditation itself, as an instrument for improving the education of teachers, is not self-evident, whether done by NCATE or any other group. The question of whether some kinds of accrediting do more harm than good in higher education ... is a question, say many academics, that should have been explored at length by all the principal interests concerned before the creation of any national agency to accredit programs or institutions in this field. [Koerner, 1963, p. 230]

2. ... [A]ssuming that accreditation *is* a good way of improving the training of teachers, who should make policy about how to do it? ... To the academic eye, this concentration of Education specialists [in NCATE] has, to say the least, an insular look. [*Id.*]

3. NCATE attempts to accredit only the professional part of a teacher's education, and relies on the six regional associations to insure adequate quality in the liberal arts work and in everything else about the institution. While it is obvious that NCATE in its present form is incompetent to accredit the academic program of future teachers, it seems equally clear that the use of the regional associations for that purpose is ill-conceived. [*Id.* at 231]

4. NCATE has developed a set of seven standards that constitutes the instrument with which it measures and judges institutions. ...These standards appear to many an academician decidedly like a way of replacing the old rigidity of state certification requirements with

a new and equally invalid, but more dangerous, rigidity of their own. They are based on two extremely controversial assumptions: that the way to get good teachers in public schools is to look chiefly at what goes *into* the training programs and not at what comes out; and that the things which should go into these programs are well known, agreed upon, verified, and that they can be measured. [*Id.* at 231—32]

5. NCATE is naturally committed to the idea that there is one and only one permissible preparation for teaching — exposure to an orthodox program of courses in pedagogy in a college or university, preferably one accredited by NCATE. This commitment makes it impossible for institutions to experiment with other ways of training teachers, such as internships and apprenticeships involving little or no course work in Education. [*Id.* at 232]

6. . . . [T]he most serious charge against NCATE is that it threatens to become a vast academic cartel that will ultimately prevent the employment of any person for any job at any level in any public school . . . who has not been through an NCATE-accredited program. . . . State teachers, organizations as well as national associations like those within the NEA talk frankly about the time when NCATE will furnish the only acceptable entree to the public schools. [*ID.* at 232—33]

Dr. Koerner perceived these dangers through his concededly "academic" bias, but they are issues to be reckoned with. Although there has been recent evidence of increased flexibility by NCATE and although Dr. Koerner's direst predictions have not yet been borne out, NCATE has not proven an especially progressive force in reforming teacher training either. It has certainly not used its enormous power agressively enough to cause teacher training programs to be refashioned in the interests of desperate urban school districts.

Nor, incidentally, have the NEA and other important professional associations played a consistently constructive role. They too have enormous potential power to initiate, or at least support, efforts to find the key to training teachers so that they can reach urban youngsters. They have made some useful efforts but not nearly enough.

Ideally, the pressures on teacher training institutions from these various sources, and from within, should be forcing teacher training in the same general direction — better preparation for meeting the diverse needs of today's schools. This should be especially true now. For many years teachers were in short supply, and school districts had to be content with the best candidates avilable, whether or not they seemed well-trained or particularly suited to the district's needs. During the past several years, however, there has been a marked turnabout. Current predictions indicate we are heading toward a period of large teacher surpluses. According to U.S. Office of Education figures, in September 1971 there were already 19,000 more elementary and secondary school teachers than positions available. By 1978, the U.S. Office of Education predicts, the number of surplus teachers will rise to 93,000. Illinois State University's Bureau of Appointments has made a far more alarming prediction. By 1975, it says, there will be 600,000 unemployed teachers. The NEA goes still further; it projects a surplus of 730,000 beginning teachers within five years.

The reasons for the teacher surplus appear to be a declining birth rate, the reduction of local funds for educational expansion, and the entry into teaching of unemployed professionals from other fields and of young men who receive a draft deferment. Whatever the reasons, Geoffrey H. Moore of the U.S. Department of Labor warns that:

> We must either cut down the number of teachers educated or increase funding to hire new teachers, thereby reducing class size

and improving education, or we will soon have a vast army of unemployed teachers. [*Parade Magazine,* July 11, 1971, p. 18, col. 2]

Whether or not the number of teachers educated will be cut
down is not yet clear. Several major universities, such as
Michigan State, Ohio State, Penn State, the University of
Illinois and the University of Iowa, have begun to limit ad-
missions into their schools of education. In some states, state
college systems, which have traditionally produced high percentages of teachers, are being retooled. New Jersey's Chancellor of Higher Education, Ralph A. Dungan, has said that he
hopes to see "a drastic reduction" in the size of education
departments at the state colleges and in the number of education majors. But elsewhere, most institutions of higher education still take the position that they have no right to tell
prospective teachers that they cannot enter the field. Advisers
and faculty members are increasing their efforts to make students aware of the poor employment prospects for teachers.
But such counseling has not made much of an impact, partly
because of failure on the part of both high school and college
guidance counselors to make women students aware of the
variety of professions open to them. Instead of semi-auto-
matically funneling women into teaching, now obviously an
oversupplied field, counselors themselves must be retrained.
to present a full spectrum of opportunities to young women.
Many teacher training programs, such as the one at the State
University of New York College at Brockport, continue to
increase their enrollments and the number of their graduates,
a "dubious distinction" according to the college's Dean of
Certification.

There is little likelihood of greatly increased funding to
hire new teachers, at least based on *voluntary* action. Given
the taxpayer revolt described in Chapter I, the prospects for
greater overall funding of public education turn largely on
the possibility of increased federal funding. The U.S. Commissioner of Education, Sidney Marland, has talked about a

federal government contribution of as much as 30% of the total costs. If that happened, more teachers might be hired. If it does not, which is more likely in view of the present 7% level of federal aid, unemployed teachers may have to look to other fields. For the only other real prospect for greater educational funding lies with the effort to overturn existing school finance laws in the courts. The theory is that these laws discriminate against children and taxpayers in "poor" districts. The relief sought is a statutory pattern which equalizes the wealth available to every district. This can be accomplished without changing the overall level of educational funding in a state by leveling up poor districts to an average expenditure. But this is not politically or educationally feasible. The more likely result is that wealthy districts will continue at a relatively high expenditure level while poor districts will be brought up substantially. This will mean some new money for education but not necessarily for additional new teachers. The choice will probably rest with the currently poor districts. Should they spend their increased funds on more teachers so that class sizes can be decreased? Or should they improve physical facilities? Or should they increase their salary schedule so they can compete more successfully for the better teachers? The options go on indefinitely. Only one thing is clear — teacher training programs will have to meet the test of the market place in trying to sell their products to school districts. And, ironically, it is likely to be the poor urban districts which will have relatively greater buying power.

Thus, the projected oversupply of teachers carries with it the potential for great improvement in this country's educational system, especially in the urban centers. School districts, which until recently were unable to find even a live, fully licensed teacher for each class, will be able to pick and choose among many candidates. Dr. Glenn Gamble, director of counseling and placement at Rutgers University, described it well:

> Administrators have had to settle for so many years for the question-
> ably qualified teachers because of a shortage, but now they have the
> opportunity to be very selective. It might even be a good time for
> them to suggest to obviously unqualified teachers that another voca-
> tion would be a good idea. [*Newark Star-Ledger,* June 6, 1971,
> p. 1–10, col. 1]

This opportunity to be selective will make teacher training
far more important; but, as we shall see in later chapters, it
also means personnel selection by school districts will become
more difficult and more important. Selection will involve
choosing the most qualified by the standards of the particular district from among an abundance of applicants instead of
merely screening out incompetents as has been the case in a
number of larger school districts including New York City.

If funds permit, districts may be able to experiment with
team teaching, individualized instruction, and other teaching
techniques which rely on professional staff members trained
in nontraditional ways. Fortunately, some teacher training
programs are already moving in this direction, albeit for
reasons of self-preservation. A number of colleges and universities are altering their programs to stress practical experience over educational theory. Others are encouraging
teacher candidates to enter special areas, for example, education of the mentally, physically, and emotionally handicapped,
whose needs have not yet been fully met. An article in *The
New York Times* began with the following revealing paragraph:

> Last year, when many would-be teachers were forced to drive taxi-
> cabs or take jobs in department stores, all of the graduates who had
> studied special education at Jersey City State College were placed in
> attractive positions. [*The New York Times,* Mar. 5, 1972, p. 76, col. 3]

Hopefully, teacher training institutions will even begin to
fashion specialties in such esoterica as teaching urban children
to read. Perhaps the marketplace will compel them to. In
just this manner a few colleges are beginning to develop

approaches to training teachers for "open classrooms." Indeed, as Roland Barth and Charles Rathbone pointed out in *The Center Forum* in July 1969, even then:

> A few teacher training institutions are beginning to reorient themselves towards open education and are now struggling with the problem of preparing teachers for this kind of setting. . . . Open education . . . faces serious perils as well as opportunities: with its emphasis on student choice and initiative, open education can easily become a cover for those who don't know how to relate to children and who are unsure of what is best for children. Like a similar groundswell in the '30s, open education when employed by those who little understand it, can easily degenerate into sloppy permissiveness and wistful romanticism. For open education if anything demands of teachers the deepest thinking through of what learning is, what knowledge is, and what their craft is. [*The Center Forum,* Vol. 3, No. 7, July 1969, p. 1]

This challenge is before the teacher training institutions today as they struggle to find a productive role in the roiled world of public education. In the words of Dr. Ewald Nyquist, New York State Commissioner of Education, "one of the most important aspects of making this kind of change [to the open classroom] is, of course, teacher training. It will mean a different kind of a job on the part of our teacher training institutions, and a lot of retraining of present teachers." [Nyquist, 1971, p. 13]

It would be a mistake, however, to believe that all the challenges regarding teacher education confront colleges and universities. As Commissioner Nyquist implied, not all teacher training takes place there. Many school districts sponsor programs of in-service training for their pedagogical staffs. The concept has great potential. For one of the chief educational problems, especially in urban school districts, is that many of the senior teachers have lost touch with the children and with the new learning techniques. The problem is aggravated in urban centers which are experiencing a rapid ethnic or socioeconomic turnover. School districts with 90% white, middle class, "achievement-oriented" children may become populated with 90% black or Spanish-speaking, lower income children within a decade or less. An in-service training program which really helped teachers and their supervisors adjust to the new demands is obviously a high priority. That it almost never exists is a tragedy. There is little evidence that the programs attempted have had more than marginal effect in changing attitudes, extending awareness or even imparting significant knowledge or skills.

Every school district, but particularly the urban district, must begin trying to understand and deal with the problems of teacher training in all their dimensions. Blame for shortcomings can't blithely be placed on the colleges and universities, or on state education departments, or on accrediting agencies, or on professional organizations (although none of them are blameless). If teacher training is to be molded to the needs of urban schools, it can only come through the active involvement of the districts themselves and of all those who care about the education of children.

An effective way to begin appreciating the problems of teacher training is to look at the experience of the New York City school district through the prism of the Commission on Human Rights hearings. It offers a valuable case study. The criticisms of the current approach there and suggestions for reform open areas of inquiry for other school districts.

The New York City Experience

Over 90% of the teachers in the New York City public school system receive their training in a New York City college; 65% of them, at the City University of New York. The most common kind of education that candidates for New York City teaching licenses present is a baccalaureate degree which includes 24 semester hours in the professional study of education and a college supervised student teaching experience. In the last few years, an "Alternative B" examination has been offered to candidates who have baccalaureate degrees with only 12 semester hours in education (the remaining 12 hours to be completed within five years).

The Board of Education, at a time where there was a teacher shortage, set up several programs in conjunction with City University for candidates who wanted to take this alternative route to licensure. One was the Intensive Teacher Training Program (ITTP) which allowed liberal arts graduates to take the required 12 hours of education credits in an intensive summer program. Another, Training Experience for New Elementary Teachers (TENET), was a one-year program for liberal arts graduates who needed education credits or the student teaching experience. A third, Teacher Education Masters Program for Urban Schools (TEMPUS), is the master's degree component of TENET.

Candidates who want to take the examination for New York City licenses are also eligible if they have been permanently certified by New York State in the appropriate field. Educational requirements for state certification are in some cases somewhat higher than for licensing by the city.

The school system is directly involved only in limited ways in the training of teachers. According to Dr. Jay E. Greene, who was a member of the Board of Examiners, the Board of Examiners keeps in touch with schools of education through an Advisory Council of Colleges in Teacher Education.

The most direct links between the school system and the training of teachers are in the areas of student teaching and post-licensing training. Students who major in education typically practice-teach in their senior year, if possible in the school district where they hope to be employed.

The school system does provide new teachers with a training program during their first year. In fact, such in-service training has been mandated by the Board of Education's agreement with the United Federation of Teachers. The contract requires: 1) the principal to direct the new teacher to "devote a reasonable number of his preparation periods, not to exceed twenty, to observing classes conducted by more experienced teachers, or to consulting others familiar with classroom problems"; and 2) the superintendent to direct "that teacher to participate in an after-school training program of not more than two hours per week and extending over a period of not more than fourteen weeks in each of the two terms of the school year, designed to heighten the capabilities of inexperienced teachers."

Two other programs of the Board of Education have training aspects. One is the paraprofessional career development program, which provides paraprofessionals with an opportunity to acquire sufficient college credits to qualify eventually to take examinations for teaching licenses while developing classroom skills in their work as paraprofessionals. The other is the Program for Oral and Written English Reinforcement (POWER), a series of courses for applicants who fail the oral or written parts of the teaching examination and need remedial work, and for applicants for whom English is a second language.

Aside from these direct connections with the training of teachers, the school system, by virtue of the fact that it establishes eligibility requirements for teaching candidates, should have an important indirect connection. For, clearly, any teacher training institution which sends a substantial number of its graduates to the New York City public schools should be influenced by the character of these requirements and should gear its curriculum to them.

Criticisms of the Current Approach to Teacher Training

The main criticisms of the relationship between teacher training and the New York City school system, and of teacher training generally, are of two kinds — that teacher training programs and the people involved in them are of a poor quality. and that these programs are often characterized by a lack of communication with and commitment to large urban school districts and their special problems.

According to many witnesses at the Human Rights Commission hearings and many other education commentators, teacher education suffers from serious deficiencies in almost every area. Dr. James Koerner put it in these terms:

> ... [T]he education of American teachers is trapped in a series of circular problems that makes reforms extremely difficult. A weak faculty operates a weak program that attracts weak students. Strong students are deterred by these weaknesses from entering the field and forcing improvements. Graduate programs in Education put large numbers of incompetent persons through a variety of incompetent degrees, and these persons then become school administrators who hire teachers, or they become professors of Education who train teachers and who run other graduate programs to train other administrators and professors of Education. [Koerner, 1963, p. 242]

This is strong stuff, vaguely reminiscent of the old saw that "those who can, do; those who can't, teach; those who can't teach, teach teachers." But to an alarming degree it seems borne out by the data. In Chapter 1, we saw evidence that teachers as a group rank very low on most standard indicators of intellectual ability and academic preparedness. Koerner and others apply these conclusions to most teacher training programs staffs as well.

The results of this "weak faculty" operating a "weak program" for "weak students" is, according to many critics, exactly what one would expect—weak teaching candidates. Thus, a number of witnesses at the Human Rights Commission hearings testified that successful completion of a teacher training program, even in the most prestigious institutions, does not guarantee that the graduate possesses minimum competency in his subject matter field or even in spoken or written English. In supporting this criticism, Dr. Jay Greene of the New York City Board of Examiners cited a "chamber of horrors" culled from examination answers. He reported that:

> You would be amazed to see some of the deficiencies that applicants
> who have degrees and . . . master's degrees [have] in their own sub-
> ject, written English, and literacy. Unless you are familiar with the
> results that cross your desk it is almost difficult to believe that this
> is so. There are applicants . . . who don't possess the knowledge of
> mathematics of an average 13-year old youngster in our junior high
> schools. . . . In written English there are some amazing examples of
> illiteracy. [*Selection of Teachers,* 1972, p. 141]

Further in his testimony Dr. Greene said:

> I think City University is in the forefront of teacher education. But
> that doesn't mean that all their young people, with their host of
> faculty, host of problems, that they can give the sort of guarantee,
> the sort of impartiality and selection for public employment that
> we need. [*Id.* at 161]

This criticism was echoed by Albert Shanker, president of
the United Federation of Teachers, when he said:

> . . . a good many teachers on a national basis barely manage to get
> out of [teachers'] college after they were pushed out of every other
> institution. It is precisely because of the low standards maintained by
> the colleges and institutions that it is so important for the Govern-
> ment to maintain a standard of entry. [*Id.* at 353]

These sorts of criticism did not go unanswered, however.
John Fischer, president of Columbia Teachers College, generally rejected them out of hand:

> I believe that if we assume that the possession of a bachelor's degree,
> or an advanced degree, is sufficient indication that the holder of the
> degree has met certain minimum requirements, . . . we are making an
> entirely safe assumption. [*Id.* at 512]

Dr. Fischer agreed that "our universities and colleges, being
. . . humanly managed institutions, fall somewhat this side of
heavenly perfection." But, in his opinion, reliance on a personnel system like the Board of Examiners, which he characterized as "quite objective but of highly questionable validity,"
was "much the greater and more serious error." [*Id.* at 513]

The choice need not, however, be between the lesser of two evils, despite what representatives of the interest groups say. Teacher training *and* selection techniques can and must be improved. To focus on one or the other as the villain of the piece is neither accurate nor helpful. Certainly the teacher training institutions should not be let off the hook because they may be doing relatively better than the boards of examiners. Dr. Ewald Nyquist, Commissioner of Education of New York State, should be seeing the bigger picture and he has refused to absolve the colleges and universities. In his presentation to the Public Education Association, Commissioner Nyquist said:

> Teachers need more adequate preparation in the technical aspects of the teaching of reading. The Beginning Teacher Survey, conducted by the State Education Department in the spring of 1968, showed that in the elementary schools, 50 per cent of first-year teachers with the bachelor's degree had no specific preparation for teaching reading beyond a general elementary methods or language arts methods course. Often lacking in the teacher's preparation is sufficient attention to the specific aspects of the reading task, training in the design of instructional systems, and training in the assessment of individual progress toward instructional goals. These are the technical skills which would allow teachers to design, select and/or modify a program as a continuous activity so that children and adults may learn to read more efficiently and effectively.
> [Nyquist, 1971, p. 8]

Commissioner Nyquist's criticism of teacher education did not stop with technical or basic knowledge and skills deficiencies. In common with other critics, he found that teacher training institutions are too narrow and traditional in their approaches. Criticism of this kind has come from within the teacher education establishment as well. This is an encouraging sign; more "Young Turks" are participating in the system and working to change it. Dr. James Shields of the City College's Education Department had this to say:

If you want to become a teacher you must present a Bachelor's degree and some evidence of having taken courses. Now, in teacher
education . . . no one really expects that what goes on in that institution that provides for credentialing . . . has anything to do with
performance on the job.

. . . [W] hat happens now is a student takes, for instance, in most of
the city universities, 12 hours of courses in the sociology of education, psychology of learning, child development, and adolescent development. And only after that experience are they allowed to have
an experience in a school of any significance. But what they have
been doing recently is providing two hours here and there hap-
hazardly and calling it field work. And this is ridiculous. [*Selection
of Teachers*, 1972, p. 538, 540]

Traditional courses taught in traditional ways seem all too
often to epitomize teacher education. One of the leaders in
the field, Dr. Fischer, agreed that more was necessary.

. . . [A] cademic training, though essential, is not sufficient. Understanding of the people with whom one works, understanding of the
situations from which those people come, is at least equal in importance to possession of the traditional types of academic and
systematized professional preparation. [*Id.* at 512]

Whether teacher training institutions or the employing
school district should be responsible for developing these non-
academic skills was a matter on which witnesses differed.
Some, like Dr. Fischer, Dr. John Theobald, a former New York
City Superintendent of Schools, and Dr. Robert Dentler,
Director of the Center for Urban Education, believe this development should come principally during a greatly improved
probationary period. During probation, the new teacher or
supervisor should be carefully observed and assisted by his
superiors to insure a meaningful on-the-job learning experience. At the same time, of course, his potential should be
evaluated. At the conclusion of this two-way street, whether
one calls it probation, provisional licensure, or internship, an
informed decision can be made about more permanent status.

Unfortunately, however, current school district efforts at both in-service training and support, and evaluation provide little basis for optimism. Dr. Shields, who has been evaluating in-service teacher training programs for the New York State Education Department, stated that the kind of programs New York City provides was not effective.

> The union mandates a two hour-a-week workshop on Monday afternoons or so for beginning teachers. And this has been a total failure. It seems to have nothing to do with anything. I have spoken to new teachers around the city about it, and mostly they try not to go. As a matter of fact, many of them just stop going. [*Id.* at 542]

The second major problem area identified by critics of teacher education is related to the narrowness of scope. The colleges and universities tend to view their role in teacher training as technical, or if you will "professional," training. The human element which is so central to education gets only short shrift. This problem is intertwined with the lack of meaningful communication between teacher training institution and school district, and the consequent failure of most teacher education programs to reflect the real needs of many school districts, especially large urban districts.

Here too, Commissioner Nyquist was on target. He said in his PEA presentation:

> Of equal importance [to the technical skills] are the humane aspects of the reading task. Present teacher education programs are not designed to produce teachers who must cope with the individual characteristics and diverse backgrounds of each learner. Too often they experience a culture shock in coming to classrooms of poor children from minority groups. The problem is compounded by the fact that today's student population includes an increasing proportion of the functionally illiterate, the non-English speaking, and the economically disadvantaged of all ethnic groups. Teachers need to understand these problems and must become increasingly sensitive to the uniqueness of the individual and the personal experiences which he brings to the reading process. It would help immensely if teachers had sincere unflagging expectations that every child can learn. In order that equal emphasis be given to the technical and

humane aspects . . . teacher training programs must be changed —
what we have has been characterized as the Great Training Robbery.
Our colleges and universities must share the responsibility for our
present deficiencies. [Nyquist, 1971, p. 8]

An obvious way to help teaching candidates develop some
understanding and appreciation of ghetto children is through
the effective use of student teacher programs. But these have
often failed, due in large part to a lack of communication. As
a result, they are held in low estate by school administrators
and teacher trainers alike. Dr. John Theobald made this
comment at the commission hearings:

I don't believe there has been nearly adequate cooperation between
the system and the colleges. This works both ways. The system, for
the most part, has been negative on college students coming in for
student teaching. When I say negative, they have a system . . . where
it is the principal's judgment whether or not he wanted student
teachers. Colleges in general tried to put their youngsters into the
"better schools," and the net result was, we didn't have anybody
who knew how to work in a ghetto school. [*Selection of Teachers,*
1972, pp. 43–44]

Another alumnus of the New York City school system,
Dr. Mortimer Kreuter, who is now director of teacher preparation at the State University of New York at Stony Brook,
agreed about the lack of effective interaction. He too saw it
most vividly demonstrated by student teaching efforts. "It is
self-evident," said Dr. Kreuter, "that any teacher training
institution should have close and fruitful ties with its local
system. But an analysis of existing relationships between
teachers colleges and the New York City schools reveals a
number of areas of interaction that need improvement."
The main point of contact is student teaching. "There," said
Dr. Kreuter, "the relationships are random in character and
lack a structured approach by both teacher educators and
personnel in the school system." [Kreuter, 1969, pp. 30–31]
But the problem may stem from more than just lack of
structure. Many of those who criticize teacher education

point to a total lack of involvement by the training institutions in the life and problems of urban and rural areas. Chancellor Ralph A. Dungan of New Jersey, for example, has sharply criticized colleges and universities for failing to act "in the face of continuing deterioration of urban and rural public schools." He finds as the source of the problem that:

> Most teachers coming out of most colleges are unequipped to teach in the poorer urban and rural areas, for a number of reasons. In the first place, the people who are teaching them have no experience with the environment of an urban or rural school. And the institutions themselves are not addressing the problems of those areas in a broad framework which includes considerations of housing, family life, health and nutrition. Universities and colleges genuinely have got to decide they are part of society. They've got to let the critics from the outside in and stop pretending they have some kind of monastic hold on the truth. [*Newark Star-Ledger,* May 17, 1972, p. 1, col. 5]

Dungan's approach has itself been criticized as an effort by the political system to squeeze more "productivity" out of education to make up for the political system's own failures. But whether teacher training institutions can do it all should not be the question. The question is whether they can do more and better than they have been doing. About that there is unanimity. The ultimate issues are what the more should be and how the better should be accomplished.

ALTERNATIVES TO THE PRESENT TEACHER TRAINING SYSTEM AND SUGGESTIONS FOR REFORM

The changes proposed for teacher education range from relatively minor, almost cosmetic ones, through total revamping of teacher training institutions, as we now know them, to elimination of any formal teacher education programs. Each proposal has its adherents and each has some merit. But the extremes at both ends seem unlikely to gain substantial support. There is increasing agreement that basic reform of teacher training is essential; there is also agreement that teachers must be helped to develop the necessary attitudes, techniques and skills through well-formulated educational programs.

This discussion of reform, therefore, is best organized around two main foci — proposed adjustments in the existing teacher training programs; and proposed alternatives to the existing programs in the form of dramatically different institutions, but teacher training institutions nonetheless.

Adjustments in Teacher Training Programs

Suggestions for reform of existing programs cover the waterfront. They extend from curricular modifications of all kinds to new techniques for evaluating the end products. A number of proposals have, however, emerged as serious possibilities and it is these that warrant discussion now.

The most general adjustment recommended is that teacher training become more "relevant." Relevancy has many faces. One is, of course, giving more emphasis to the problems teachers will face on the job. Dr. Harvey B. Scribner, then Chancellor of the New York City school system, made a number of specific proposals in that regard:

> . . . I believe in training and re-training of teachers in the natural setting of the actual classroom. To train teachers in isolated laboratory schools with select groups of youngsters is unrealistic. Worst of all, it provides a built-in excuse for the teacher-in-training, whereby he reverts to established ways on return to his own classroom because "my kids are different" and "my classroom is not a laboratory classroom."

> . . . I believe in involving colleges and universities in programs of school reform which include the training of student teachers and in-service teachers. But only if the . . . college agrees to assign at least some of its student-teachers as interns in the schools it seeks to help reshape; . . . only if the college will involve . . . in more than token fashion — its own faculty in on-site work beside regular classroom teachers and supervisors. . . . [*Special Supplement to New York City Board of Education Staff Bulletin,* Feb. 22, 1971, pp. iii–iv]

The *Riles Report* illuminated another aspect of relevancy — helping teachers to develop sound attitudes toward their children. One way to do that is through a reconnection between teacher training institutions and the communities from which the children come. As the *Riles Report* put it:

> If a comprehensive education plan directed to the needs of the disadvantaged child is to be effective, teacher-training programs must concentrate on changing the attitudes of teachers and preparing them to effectively employ new ideas and educational materials quite different from those methods and materials which might be employed in a typical suburban school. ... The program ... would have to be based on a reconnection between the teacher-training institutions and the communities which the teachers will serve. The institutions will need to ask the urban communities what their goals are in terms of the kinds of teachers they feel are needed in their schools. And they will need to design special student teaching experiences approved by the community and which take place in the city. In addition, university professors must come to understand, experientially, the actual problems that school teachers face daily in the classroom in order to help them arrive at better approaches to teaching. [Riles, 1970, pp. 242–43]

In advocating routes to more relevant teacher education both Chancellor Scribner and the *Riles Report* touched upon student teaching. And there are good reasons for that. In most school districts the student teaching program is the most direct and substantial connection between the teacher training institution and the school district. Careful use of this opportunity is important on a number of levels. From the student's point of view, it can provide a unique learning experience, a crucible in which the student's interest and ability in teaching urban children can be tested. From the college or university's point of view, careful evaluation of the student teacher's performance and impact can assist in counseling that student and in the continuous process of monitoring and reshaping the entire teacher training program. Finally, from the point of view of the school district, an effective student teaching effort affords the best opportunity to screen prospective permanent teachers.

Another point of substantial contact between the teacher training institution and the school district may be in the area of retraining or "staff development." Often school districts undertake programs of in-service training on their own, but nothing in the natural order of things requires this. Indeed, it may reflect the failure of the colleges to capture the confidence of the school systems. Many critics have bemoaned the weaknesses of in-service training efforts regardless of who conducts them. One of the main problems has been the lack of focus and the haphazard nature of the programs. This suggests a two-pronged approach to reforming them — decentralization of the program to the individual school and involvement of the entire school staff, but the introduction of a creative role for the teacher training institution to insure that the big picture is kept in mind and that the latest educational developments are considered.

The *Riles Report* saw great promise in such an approach which harnessed the cooperative energies of principal, supervisors, teachers, paraprofessionals, university specialists, parents and other community resources. The inclusion of the principal is something of a departure from traditional conceptions of in-service training. Virtually all the attention has been directed to teachers. Certainly effective teachers are crucial to a functioning educational system, but many educators would agree that it is the principal who sets the tone of the school. And this tone may encourage good, creative teaching or it may stifle creativity. Dr. Benjamin Fine expanded on the importance of retraining principals:

> Unless educational leaders, such as principals or school administrators, are offered help in improving their know-how, the nation's schools will not achieve the high goals expected of them. . . . School administrators have been ignored as an important vehicle for attaining educational reform. . . . But . . . the principal is easily identifiable

as the key determiner of the climate at the school. It is the principal who can make something work or frustrate it. . . . Yet no major national program has ever focused on the development of this leadership group. The United States Office of Education, for example, is directing only .08 percent of its annual budget to leadership training. Moreover, none of this is directed toward the school principal. Upgrading the teacher continues to be a major focus of school personnel development. But the task of upgrading the nation's two million teachers is infinitely more complex and costly than the development of the 88,000 school principals who are in charge of the schools, making the major decisions that affect the schools, and who are crucial to the implementation of change within the classrooms. [*Newark Star-Ledger,* May 28, 1972, p. 50, col. 6]

Expanding efforts to retrain principals is all the more important in light of the findings of the first detailed study of school leaders, The survey, conducted by Dr. Donald P. Mitchell for the Academy of Educational Development, found that school leaders are characterized by "localism" at a time when the issues facing them are often national in scope. School administrators, more than any other professionals, remain in the geographic area where they were born and raised. Typically, they rise to their positions through a single school system, often under the watchful eye of a patron in the central office. The result of these trends is that the school principal is likely to be a "right thinker" who may take more pride in the neatness and promptness of his reports than in the quality of education in his school. To alter these characteristics through meaningful retraining should be a high priority.

Efforts to revise the teacher training institution's curriculum constitute another major area of proposed reform. These efforts, as we have already seen, consist partially of pressure to have courses dealing with new techniques and skills added to the curriculum. As Commissioner Nyquist pointed out, there are new approaches to reading which teachers ought to know about. The *Riles Report* listed, as necessary elements of any teacher education program, "courses such as urban sociology, cultural anthropology, and the psychology of the disadvantaged; experience in working with highly aggressive students; and a working knowledge of behavior therapy in preparation for conflict situations likely to arise between the values of staff personnel and students from urban areas." [Riles, 1970, p. 243] Also, the movement toward the open classroom and individualized instruction requires new skills of teachers. Finally, areas of special education are, in many school districts, still not fully staffed with qualified teachers. The teacher training institutions should be expanding their offerings in those areas and channeling students into them.

Perhaps these curriculum changes could be effected within a rather traditional teacher education structure. Most critics, however, believe they must be accompanied by a redesign and refocus of the entire curriculum approach. More experimentation and field work, and less formality and methods courses, are undoubtedly the directions of the future. Professor Shields testified about an experimental program he is supervising which may influence teacher education in fundamental ways. This four-year program virtually does away with traditional course work. Instead, students spend most of their time in the field working with children. As Dr. Shields put it, ". . . instead of taking a course in child development, they work with children and watch their development. . . ." [*Selection of Teachers*, 1972, p. 541]

This approach may also attract more minority group students to teacher training institutions. Murry Bergtraum, former president of the New York City Board of Education, expressed the view that "many minority college students, seeing the formalistic system of those courses [in schools of education] , are turned off and do not go into teaching, because they feel immediately that the total curricular structure . . . doesn't relate to what they are and to where they came from and to what they want to do." [*Id.* at 10] If Mr. Bergtraum is right, and many people agree with him, the implications of a broad change in curriculum should go

beyond more minority group students in teacher education.
It should result in other types of education students who depart from the traditional mold. And this is essential if teacher
training is really to be made equal to the challenges besetting
it. For at the outset of this chapter the cyclical dilemma of
teacher training was exposed — weak students trained in weak
programs by weak faculty. Stronger, more relevant programs
will tend to attract stronger, more relevant students. This
trend must be encouraged and nurtured by all available means
until is is certain that the patient has been permanently re-
juvenated. As a minimum, teacher training institutions must
supplement new curricular approaches by adding to their
faculties people who can make them come alive. This means
actively recruiting faculty members who have had first-hand
experience in urban schools; who are open to new ideas; and
who are deeply committed to the principle that urban children
can and must learn.

This brings us to the final reform in the existing teacher
education system, a reform which is central to many aspects
of this book. The success of the training of teachers must be
measured at every stage by the performance of the teachers
in the classroom, not by some indirect standard. Many
witnesses at the Human Rights Commission hearings agreed
about this. Commissioner Nyquist suggested "a very tough
look at the validity of typical course work, student teaching
experiences and examinations for licensing and certification
purposes. Perhaps a better way to license teachers is to base
certification on performance." [Nyquist, 1971, p. 14]
Chancellor Scribner said the colleges and universities should
be involved in basic educational reform "only if the college
agrees to judge the professional competence of student and
in-service teachers seeking academic credit by some kind of
performance criteria (which the college might help to construct); . . . and only if the college will agree to grant credit
on the recommendation of advisors in position to judge the

performance of teachers-in-training. . . ." [*Special Supplement to Staff Bulletin, supra,* p. iv] Dr. Kreuter, a teacher educator with broad experience in urban schools, contributed his own important perspective:

> . . . [T]he whole teacher evaluation procedure must be changed. From his training period on, the new teacher will have to learn that tests are not a religion and that children can learn with and without tests and he himself can be judged on various professional criteria other than tests; namely by the way he performs in classrooms. The new teacher must be able to (1) make instructionally sensible and accountable decisions by using analytical methods; (2) manage the educational inputs of a widening cast of players in the open school scene — paraprofessionals, community persons, mental health workers, consultants, specialists, parents; (3) guide children to teach themselves and their peers; (4) fit into a team of teachers when that approach is needed; (5) foster throughout the entire school experience the non-punitive attitudes conducive to children's development. This kind of new teacher training will require the re-training also of the current teacher staff. Nothing less will do than a drastic reshaping of pre- and in-service teacher training. . . . In my judgement, the on-the-job evaluation of teachers to work in this context will be a necessary component of the teacher training changes which must come about in this decade. The almost total reliance of teacher evaluators on test scores will inevitably give way in this movement to the more difficult to determine but much more powerful techniques of performance evaluation. Nobody cares what his doctor scored on his boards but whether he is able to doctor well. [*Selection of Teachers,* 1972, pp. 732–33]

An impressive array of more recent study reports also discuss and, in most cases, strongly recommend a performance-based approach to teacher training. They include: The New York State *Regents State-wide Plan for the Development of Post Secondary Education;* the Fleischmann Commission Report; *The Power of Competency-Based Teacher Education,* a report of the U.S. Office of Education's Task Force 1972 Committee on National Program Priorities in Teacher Education; and *Realities and Revolution in Teacher Education,* a November 1972 report of the Commission on Public School

Personnel Policies in Ohio. The Ohio report had this to say about performance-based teacher education:

> Competency- or performance-based teacher education is a growing movement within the teacher education community which essentially focuses on what the teacher can do to help children learn, not simply on what the teacher knows. Competency-based programs are designed on the premise that the program should prepare teachers to accomplish observable goals. Competency-based teacher education is predicated on the following assumptions:
>
> 1. There are specific skills, strategies, and dispositions which the beginning teacher should possess to be effective with children.
>
> 2. Certain of these skills, strategies, and dispositions should be chosen and made the core of the program of training.
>
> 3. The behaviors which constitute successful performance of each skill should be clearly stated and these should be the criteria of successful completion of the teacher education program.
>
> 4. Since teacher education students differ one from the other, they should be able to move through the program at their own rate, depending on their ability to demonstrate mastery of the skills. [pp. 71–72]

The Ohio and other reports have characterized a performance-based approach to teacher education as one of the most hopeful developments in teacher education in recent decades, and a growing number of state legislatures and state education departments have already moved toward mandating performance-based teacher education programs (and certification procedures). But there is a danger in the too hasty and uncritical acceptance of this promising concept. The historical landscape of educational innovation is strewn with the bleached bones of "promising concepts." Often the demise has been occasioned by the traditional education community's tendency to grasp at promising innovations as instant solutions. The Ohio report and the U.S. Office of Education study reflect special awareness of this problem in relation to performance-based teacher education. There are difficult questions to be answered before a sound program can be fully implemented. Among the most significant problems are the determination of the particular competencies required of the teacher and how they can be validly measured. Despite the complexity of the problems, virtually all agree they are not insoluble. What is essential is an immediate and whole-hearted start in the development of sound approaches and instruments.

This movement away from test scores and toward other measures of ability to perform is not taking place only with respect to evaluation of teacher training. In licensing and selection of teachers and supervisors and in measuring the performance of pupils, parallel movements are occurring. Hopefully all will reach the common point where how well life tasks are performed will be more important than the ranking on formal written tests.

Whether or not the kinds of changes in teacher training that many of the witnesses urged can be accomplished within existing institutions was an issue on which people differed. Some, most notably Dr. Kreuter, argued that totally different institutions are necessary.

New Teacher Training Institutions

There is extensive discussion of what kind of institution should conduct teacher training for the changing schools of the future. According to Dr. Kreuter, "Some contend that teacher training should be moved totally to the public school sector; others that only in a university atmosphere where knowledge is being created can teachers be trained to transmit the subject matter of a discipline." But Dr. Kreuter finds the "either-or" approach lacking. "Neither institution is primarily disposed to train teachers and where they do take up the training role, too often the result is . . . second-rate treatment of it. Moreover, the community and other interested agencies rarely can affect either the university or the public school training effort even though they have vital stakes in the outcome." [*Selection of Teachers,* 1972, p. 733]

The problem is that teacher training lies somewhere between the two institutions — the universities and the public schools. The solution advocated by Dr. Kreuter and others, including the *Riles Report* and Albert Shanker, is to create an "interface structure" which pools the resources and talents of all facets of the education community. Said Dr. Kreuter, "This priority is important to all school systems, but to the city schools in particular because if educators fail in New York and other urban centers, the surrounding suburban areas will immediately suffer as the failure of the system radiates outward." [*Id.*]

The theory of the interface structure is that teaching "is learnable as a set of conscious and purposeful behavior rather than a mystical talent born only to some." [*Id.*]   In Dr. Kreuter's judgment:

> In order for this view to become actualized, the university level teacher training would have to move beyond the usual academic course practice teaching stage. The public schools would have to offer teachers an opportunity to gain continued training in a non-authoritarian setting separated from the supervisory reports and ratings which get in the way of their training programs. The community and other agencies would have to help to guide as well as to monitor an interface type of training organization. Critical to this entire concept is the building of confidence among teachers that they will gain skills which are useful to them in the classroom practice of the open, non-competitive school. [*Id.*]

A number of concrete models have been proposed. Dr. Kreuter's testimony before the Commission on Human Rights described in detail the "teacher training complexes" advocated by the report for the American Association of Colleges of Teacher Education, *Teachers for the Real World.* In short, these compexes would be neutral settings which combined the talents of universities, schools, communities, and other agencies. Operating on the assumption that enough research exists about teacher training, they would set out to engineer the research and evaluation findings into a training system.

The training orientation would be decidedly performance
based, with emphasis on performance of the professional skills
necessary to meet the complex technical and human relations
dimensions of teaching in urban schools. The objective of
the program would be to train students to develop a set of defined skills found necessary for successful performance. These
skills would include diagnosing pupil needs and learning difficulties; communicating and empathizing with pupils, parents,
and others; reinforcing learning efforts of pupils from diverse
backgrounds; and evaluating student achievement. Although
fiscal support for the teacher training complex is not yet assured, some promising beginnings have been made. The U.S.
Office of Education's Bureau of Educational Personnel
Development has funded four simulation projects in different
parts of the country to gain the experience necessary to install
the concepts of the teacher training complex on a full-scale
basis. One of the projects is at Stony Brook where Dr. Kreuter
is Director of Teacher Preparation.

Two variations on the teacher training complex model have
already been proposed in New York City. One was a specialized
College of Urban Teacher Education to be located in Harlem;
the other a teacher training cooperative for each borough
of New York City.

As Assistant Director for Educational Personnel at the
Center for Urban Education, Dr. Kreuter directed the feasi-
bility study for a special teacher education college in Harlem.
(The master plan for the college is available from the center,
and Dr. Kreuter also published an article summarizing the results of the inquiry in *The Urban Review.*)

The central conception of the college was that a new teacher
training institution located in Harlem could "become a powerful voice for upgrading the ghetto and the students who attend its schools" by producing teachers "with substantial
backgrounds in . . . urban affairs and [with] teaching ability."
[Kreuter, 1969, p. 28] New methods for teaching urban

children would be a high priority. To accomplish this, an effective working relationship would have to be established with the community. Indeed, the college might serve the community by operating some schools and by researching the educational needs of the entire community from pre-school through adult education, as well as by training effective educational personnel. This active involvement of teacher educators in the day-to-day problems of urban schools should eliminate the communications gap between teacher educators and classroom teachers, which has been cited as one of the major failures of teacher training.

The second variation on the theme of teacher training complexes was put forward by Albert Shanker. Mr. Shanker's conception of a teacher-operated training center grew out of the same failure of present teacher training. According to him, the most common complaint of teachers is that professors of education tend to be "too far removed from the day-to-day problems of the classroom to be of much help." [*The New York Times,* Dec. 26, 1971, p. E—7, col. 5] Add to that the inability or unwillingness of school supervisors to help the teacher and you have an unsavory brew. The result, says Mr. Shanker, is that "the quality of teacher classroom performance is largely determined by how successful each teacher is in discovering his own teaching skills and in developing his own techniques," *[Id.]* The conclusions which Mr. Shanker draws from this are that the teacher is the key to educational reform and that teacher centers are the means to accomplish such reform. Actually, teacher centers, like open classrooms, come from England. Professor Stephen K. Bailey, Chairman of the Policy Institute of the Syracuse University Research Corporation, described the origin and concept of teacher centers in an article in the November 1971 issue of *Phi Delta Kappan,* entitled, "Teacher Centers: A British First." The primary function of teacher centers is to make possible a review of existing curricula and other educational practices by groups of teachers and to encourage teacher attempts to bring about changes. During the past five years, English educational authorities have funded over 500 local teacher centers where teachers have been able to share with colleagues information about successful techniques. Rediscovering the wheel may be good for one's character but it is neither efficient nor good for teachers' morale. Professor Bailey believes other attempts to improve teacher performance have failed. In his words, "What the teachers' center idea does is to put the monkey of educational reform on the teacher's own back." Perhaps this will succeed where outside criticism, supervision and prodding have failed. Mr. Shanker, who ought to know, believes it may and is pushing the idea in New York City. It should be noted, of course, that this variation differs from the urban teachers college in that it is principally directed at the in-service training of classroom teachers. If the idea works, however, it can easily be extended to training prospective teachers, perhaps by applying it to the student teaching experience.

The final proposal for a new teacher training institution comes from the *Riles Report*. It has aspects of all the other ideas. It is like the teacher training complex or the urban teachers college in the sense that it deals with the education of prospective teachers in the local community. But it is like the teacher centers in that it would replace professors of education with other kinds of personnel. The *Riles Report* itself described the proposal succinctly:

> . . .[There should be] funds for experimental approaches in the area of teacher preparation apart from colleges and universities. These approaches could take the form of new training centers either publicly operated by a school system, or privately operated by a profit or nonprofit organization. The centers would be located in the ghetto as autonomous units and should be accredited by the State. Such experimental approaches should be operated on two basic premises: (1) that training should take place in the local community rather than on college campuses; and (2) that the community (including community service agencies and other local groups) should have a major

part in the planning and implementation of the training programs and in the policy decisions. [*Riles Report,* 1970, p. 243]

Whatever shape and direction reform of teacher training ultimately takes, it should be obvious that thorough reform is one of the cornerstones of any program to improve the quality of education in our schools. Certainly, it is an essential part of restructuring the process by which teachers wind up in those schools. Who those teachers are and what skills and attitudes they bring with them will in turn go far toward determining the quality of the educational program.

References

James E. Koerner, *Miseducation of American Teachers* (Houghton Mifflin, Boston, 1963).

Mortimer Kreuter, "A New College for an Old Ghetto," *The Urban Review,* Vol. 4, No. 1, Sept. 1969.

Ewald Nyquist, *New Directions for Education in New York City* (Presentation to Public Education Association, Feb. 23, 1971).

Task Force on Urban Education to the Department of Health, Education and Welfare, *The Urban Education Task Force Report* (Praeger, New York, 1970) (the "Riles Report" after its chairman, Wilson C. Riles).

Paul Tractenberg, ed., *Selection of Teachers and Supervisors in Urban School Systems* (Agathon Publication Services, New York, 1972).

CHAPTER 3

RECRUITING THE URBAN TEACHER

Organized recruiting programs have become increasingly common among school districts, especially large urban districts. Efforts to reach out for qualified professionals began in earnest during the period of dramatic teacher shortages in the 1950's and 1960's. But active recruiting will no doubt continue during the current period of general oversupply. This can be explained in part by bureaucratic reasons. At least in larger school districts, special recruiting offices have been established and they will not easily allow themselves to be eliminated.

But there are other, more important reasons. School districts have finally begun to recognize that there is a positive virtue in seeking out personnel of diverse backgrounds even when enough applicants who meet the minimum qualifications are otherwise available. All pupils — white, black, Spanish-speaking, Chinese, wealthy, poor, urban, suburban or rural — can benefit from having teachers with varied origins and life experiences. Homogeneity may be comfortable but it tends to be stultifying.

Urban school districts have other compelling reasons for reaching out. One is the obvious need to attract more representative numbers of minority group professionals to school systems populated with a preponderance of minority group children. Vigorous recruiting programs are essential to this end. Although in New York City and some other larger urban school districts the selection procedures — written tests, oral interviews, review of records — have been singled out as the main reason for the low percentages of minority group teachers and supervisors, ineffective recruiting has been a significant contributor. (Of course, the presence of a selection process which is believed to discriminate against minority group applicants is a substantial deterrent to effective recruiting.) The close nexus between recruiting efforts and equal employment opportunity is evidenced by the heavy reliance on expanded and redirected recruiting in affirmative action programs undertaken by employers, private and public, whose employment practices had been found unsatisfactory.

There is a second important reason why urban school districts should continue vigorous recruiting programs. Even during periods of general oversupply of teachers, there are desperate shortages in some license areas. This is especially true for urban districts which tend to have a higher percentage of educationally disadvantaged and otherwise handicapped children than other school districts. Remedial reading specialists, teachers of the emotionally disturbed and physically handicapped, teachers with sociological and behavioral backgrounds, all these and many others are in demand. But perhaps the most pressing need in many urban school districts is bilingual teachers. In New York City alone there is a need for thousands. The problem is not limited to Spanish-speaking students, for in many urban areas, immigrants from around the world populate the public schools in increasing numbers. But the problem of reaching Spanish-speaking youngsters, because of the numbers involved, must receive special attention.

Studies conducted by the Puerto Rican Forum and by the Puerto Rican Educators' Association, among others, make all too clear the enormous dimensions of the problem. Almost 300,000 pupils in the New York City public schools are Puerto Rican or of other Spanish-speaking origin. This represents nearly 25% of the entire student population. Yet, only .08% of the city's public school teachers and only five of the principals (out of more than 900) are Puerto Rican. Of the Spanish-speaking students, almost half, 130,000, speak principally Spanish. But only 4,000 of them are in comprehensive bilingual programs; only 10,000 receive one period of instruction per day in English as a second language. Indeed, of the almost 300,000 Spanish-speaking pupils in the school system, 75% receive absolutely no help for their special language problem. [Puerto Rican Educators' Association, 1971].

The effect of this dreadful failure of the school system should be obvious. In the words of Luis Fuentes,* one of the five Puerto Rican principals, as he testified before the United States Senate Select Committee on Equal Educational Opportunity:

> The suffering of the Puerto Rican student in the foreign, cold and alien classroom environment is an experience few of you have shared with me or some of the other people in this room.
>
> a. This child doesn't understand what's going on. This child can't share his own experiences or share in the experiences of other children or in the relationships the others are developing.
>
> b. But equally sad — no one understands the child and consequently, cannot know his needs, his wants, his ideas, his fears, his customs, his traditions.
>
> c. This youngster eventually winds up in the corner of a room with a picture book, with orders to learn English — sometimes emphasized by a well-insulated perpetuator of Anglo culture who thinks the child can learn English best if the teacher yells louder and louder in English.
>
> d. Finally, this youngster finds himself isolated in a crowd of 20 to 30 other youngsters. And the breeding grounds for boredom and frustration are laid out for him, in many instances going

*Mr. Fuentes has become an especially controversial figure after his appointment as Community Superintendent of District 1. A number of organizations, predominantly Jewish-based, have charged he is unsuited for the position because he has allegedly made anti-Semitic remarks.

beyond failing the child educationally and developing significantly into the first symptoms of HATE. [Fuentes, 1970, p. 11]

An inevitable consequence of this process of alienation
and retardation is that the lowest reading levels in New York
City are found in schools with high concentrations of Puerto
Rican students. It is estimated that they fall two to three
years behind in reading because of their language problems.
Further consequences flow from this. Less than half of the
Puerto Rican students entering the tenth grade complete high
school, according to the Puerto Rican Educators' Association
study. About 59% drop out between the tenth and twelfth
grades. Moreover, although 46% of Puerto Rican students entering high school go to academic schools, most of them are
placed in the general program "and are not given the required
academic subjects to qualify them for college." [*The Manhattan Tribune,* Dec. 15, 1971, p. 3, col. 2]

Some responses to this staggering problem have little to do
with recruiting of teachers. A selection process which screens
out disproportionately high numbers of Spanish-speaking applicants, inadequate funding, poorly conceived programs,
inefficient use of personnel, all require corrective action. The
selection process will be discussed in subsequent chapters of
this book; the other facets of the problem are beyond the
scope of the book. But inadequate recruitment, the subject
of this chapter, is central to the problems of non-English-
speaking children in urban school districts. For the thresh-
hold cause of those problems is the overwhelming shortage of
bilingual teachers.

According to a February 3, 1971 staff memorandum for
Senator Jacob Javits entitled "Non-English Speaking Pupils
in the New York City Public School System," the Board of
Education then employed about 195 teachers of English as
a second language and about 188 bilingual teachers. The latter
figure may be misleading, however. There are several categories
of bilingual teachers, including Bilingual Teachers of School

and Community Relations, whose principal function is to assist pupils in guidance matters and to establish liaison between the schools and parents and community people. The Javits memorandum states that:

> It would appear from incomplete data that the true bilingual instructors are actually a very small number. . . . Experts from the Puerto Rican Forum estimate that there may be *seven to ten* such teachers. [p. 18]

Whatever the precise current number of classroom teachers able to assist non-English-speaking students, it is dramatically below the needs. That this is the case has been demonstrated by community district budget requests. Almost two-thirds of the 31 districts have listed bilingual teachers and teachers of English as a second language as top priorities. According to the Puerto Rican Forum, to achieve the recommended ratio of one teacher of English as a second language for every 100 non-English-speaking children, would require more than 1,200 such teachers. That is an increase of more than 1,000 over the current level. Similarly, hundreds of additional bilingual teachers are needed.

Assuming funds can be found to hire the necessary bilingual personnel (and the Javits memorandum recommends increased federal and state financing), the problem of finding and recruiting qualified persons remains. But Luis Fuentes and others believe this should not be a problem. With one million Puerto Ricans and one million other Spanish-speaking people residing in New York City, he has maintained that there are certainly several thousand qualified to help New York's school children. Indeed, Mr. Fuentes went further to say:

> There are at least 5,000 qualified bilingual educators in the city working outside of their profession, many of them with years of teaching experience and possessing state certificates. [Fuentes, 1970, p. 2]

The reason their skills have not been utilized by the school system, according to Mr. Fuentes, is because of the district's selection process. In subsequent chapters we will explore this charge, but for purposes of this chapter the point to focus on is the availability of substantial numbers of prospective bilingual professionals. The Puerto Rican Forum agrees that sufficient numbers of competent prospects are readily available. It believes, however, that the school district's recruiting efforts should be expanded to three other groups: (1) Puerto Ricans who have graduated from high school; (2) Puerto Ricans now in college; and (3) Puerto Rican paraprofessionals. If necessary, college expenses and stipends should be offered those who train to be teachers.

Current Recruiting Procedures

During the past several years the New York City school system has tried to develop an effective recruiting program, especially to reach black and Spanish-speaking candidates. The steps taken and the reasons for their conceded failure to attract more minority group teachers should be illuminating for other school districts.

The Division of Recruitment, Training and Development of the Board of Education's Office of Personnel has primary responsibility for identifying and recruiting sufficient numbers of qualified candidates. Overall, the recruiting effort has increasingly been able to fill all vacancies with regularly licensed personnel. Less than a decade ago, one-third of all teaching positions were filled by persons with substitute licenses. That figure has declined to 12%–15% and the Board of Education has announced it will not license any more permanent substitutes (although it will have a category called per diem substitutes). But consistently the vast bulk of recruits have come from the New York metropolitan area.

In recent years recruitment efforts outside the New York metropolitan area and those aimed specifically at black and Spanish-speaking candidates have increased dramatically. For example, about 75% of the total recruiting budget has been spent on out-of-town recruiting. Moreover, almost $500,000 has been allocated to the Board of Education/UFT Joint Recruitment Program which has consisted largely of out-of-town recruitment. Trips are made regularly to Puerto Rico and to predominantly black southern colleges. In 1970–71, 81% of the division's public relations and advertising budget was spent on media directed toward black and Spanish-speaking audiences.

CRITICISMS OF THE CURRENT RECRUITING PROCEDURES AND SUGGESTIONS FOR REFORM

Despite increased emphasis on out-of-town recruitment and its focus on black and Spanish-speaking candidates, most New York City teachers still come from the Greater New York Metropolitan area, with about 65% from the City University of New York alone. And there have been only negligible increases in black and Spanish-speaking professionals in the school system. The recruitment of adequate numbers of minority group teachers and supervisors has today surpassed getting enough qualified candidates to fill all regular teaching positions as the major recruiting problem. According to Dr. Theodore H. Lang, Deputy Superintendent of Schools in charge of personnel for most of the period during which there was intensified minority group recruiting:

> . . . results have been very disappointing to those of us who have exerted so much effort to advance this objective. . . . Insofar as blacks are concerned, the percentage of blacks [teaching] in the system increased from˙ 8.2% in 1963 to 8.8% in 1966 to 9.1% in 1969. This is disappointing indeed. . . . We made an ethnic count of the supervisory staff only in the years 1966 and 1969. Lumping together appointed supervisors and acting supervisors, we still have a very disappointing figure of approximately 4% black supervisors in 1966 and only approximately 8% in 1969. . . . I caution you that in these figures the blacks are more heavily represented in the acting posts percentage-wise than they are in the appointed posts. [*Selection of Teachers,* 1972, pp. 69–70]

As we have seen, the statistics regarding Puerto Rican and other Spanish-speaking teachers and supervisors are even more discouraging. Puerto Ricans hold less than one percent of the professional positions — teachers, guidance counselors, Bureau of Child Guidance, assistant principals and department chairmen. Meanwhile, the number of Puerto Rican and other Spanish-speaking students in the New York City public schools is fast approaching 300,000 or 25% of the total pupil population, with the consequent problems discussed earlier in this chapter.

Dr. Phyllis Wallace, Vice-President of the Metropolitan Applied Research Center, put the New York City minority group figures into a national perspective. She testified that:

> When the recruitment and promotion of minority group teachers and supervisory staff in the top five cities in the United States are compared, it becomes apparent that New York City's record is, over-all, the poorest. ... [I]n Chicago, Detroit and Philadelphia, the percentage of minority group teachers is at least three and one-half times as great as New York City. Los Angeles, next lowest to New York City, has almost twice the percentage of black and Spanish-speaking teachers as New York City. [*Id.* at 529]

Because substantial numbers of full-time substitutes were included in the New York City statistics, the discrepancy is, of course, even greater for regularly licensed teachers. According to Dr. Wallace, New York City also has the poorest record among the largest cities in terms of the percentage of minority group personnel in supervisory positions, and the ratio of minority group teachers and principals to minority group students.

How much of the problem rests with recruiting as opposed to selection or other factors? The answer is still not clear. Until recently no pertinent statistics were available. The Board of Education's Office of Personnel and the Board of Examiners, for the first time, compiled data about the pass-fail performance of black and Spanish-speaking candidates on their examinations, as compared to white applicants. Unfortunately, this inquiry was not voluntarily undertaken by the school system. The compilation was required by the federal district court for the southern district of New York in connection with a suit brought by the NAACP Legal Defense and Educational Fund, Inc., challenging the legality of the school system's supervisory examinations. This suit, *Chance v. Board of Examiners* [330 F. Supp. 203 (S.D.N.Y. 1971), *aff'd*, 458 F. 2d 1167 (2d Cir. 1972)], is discussed in considerable detail in the selection chapters for it has great importance there. But it is also revealing in its insights about the relationship between selection and recruitment. The data produced by the school system showed that white applicants passed the Board of Examiners' tests at a 44% rate. Black and Puerto Rican applicants, on the other hand, passed at significantly lower rates, 31% and 27%, respectively. Yet, the difference in the pass rates would not seem sufficiently great to account for the entire disproportion among professional personnel. Recruiting too must play a role. And this is borne out by the reactions of those who have had first-hand contact with school system recruiting efforts.

Dr. Lang, in considering reasons for the small percentages of blacks and Puerto Ricans in the system, said, "We do not know the impact of our selection system in New York City as compared with the systems in other sections of the country." [*Selection of Teachers,* 1972, p. 70] He testified that in his view the factors which affect the recruiting effort are small percentages of black and Puerto Rican college graduates and intense competition for them from private and public employers. Indeed, scarcity of qualified black and Puerto Rican applicants was the principal defense of the system's recruiting efforts offered at the hearings. And, it was said, the problem is in the process of curing itself.

Programs like City University's open enrollment program, it was predicted, will significantly increase the percentages of

black and Puerto Rican graduates from the local colleges.
This was emphasized not only by Dr. Lang but by others, such
as Albert Shanker and Walter Degnan, who basically defended
the current system.

Is it then just a matter of time and patience? Will the system
really cure itself? Mr. Shanker suggested it would:

> We know that we live in a society in which the number of years which
> one has been in the country, the amount of wealth or poverty that a
> particular group has, that these are factors in terms of what particular
> jobs in this society a group gets. And we know . . . that, as various
> groups move into the cities, the first thing they start doing in their
> move towards upward mobility is to buy small businesses, become
> candy store owners, etc.; and that their children, who are the first to
> go to college, then go into professions like teaching and then the
> teachers go into other professions. Therefore, it has almost always
> been that the teachers in urban school systems represented pre-
> dominantly the immigrants of the previous generation who were
> teaching the children of the newer immigrants. [*Id.* at 341–42]

But even if there is sufficient time and patience (Dr. Lang
suggested the various positive forces should be allowed "to
mature over the next five years without pressing for immediate results in a one or two year period of time" [*Id.* at
71]), many witnesses predicted that the system will not
cure itself.

Daisy Hicks, Director of the Board of Education's out-of-
town recruitment program, said that out-of-town recruiting
has not succeeded. In her words, "If you do not get what
you are going after, it certainly reflects on [out-of-town re-
cruitment] . . ." [*Id.* at 111] Ms. Hicks attributed her
difficulties to several factors: (1) a cumbersome, confusing
selection process; (2) uncertainty about New York City's
commitment to minority group professionals; and (3)
the lack of guidelines with respect to professional staff integration. Concerning the last point, Ms. Hicks said:

> I am very happy to see that these hearings are being held because I
> hope out of this will come some guidelines for most of us who are

involved in recruiting to follow. Although the New York City school system has been a leader in the field of education . . . I do not feel that this same leadership will be shown in the area of integration, regardless of the procedures now in use by the Board of Examiners or the NTE, unless guidelines are spelled out for New York. . . . The federal government is fully aware that very few businesses or institutions have adopted fair employment policies in hiring and firing, unless a watchful eye was focused on the situation. In the case of the New York City Board of Education, assistance must be given. . . . [U]nless we get some guidelines, I just don't feel we are going to meet with the success that we are trying to achieve. [*Id.* at 104]

Ms. Hicks did not attribute the inadequacies of minority group recruiting to malicious motives or lack of awareness or concern. She pointed instead to systemic or institutional problems. This viewpoint was confirmed by James Watkins, a teacher in the New York City school system and an expert in teacher recruitment. Mr. Watkins based his observations on his personal participation in Board of Education out-of-town recruiting efforts.

The response of Dr. Phyllis Wallace to a question at the commission hearings also points to the importance of a clear-cut and systemwide commitment.

Mr. Tractenberg: Does that suggest that recruitment is one of the main areas in which this school system has fallen down in relation to the others that you have mentioned in your study?

Dr. Wallace: I think that it's clear. All of the cities that we have examined pointed out that they had deliberately introduced vigorous recruitment procedures. And, in fact, they would laugh when the question would come up about the difficulties of New York City in finding qualified black and Puerto Rican graduates. [*Id.* at 535–36]

So, the suggestions for reform focus on three interrelated aspects: (1) the elimination of any unnecessarily complicated and burdensome requirements and procedures; (2) the adoption of specific guidelines or goals for the employment of minority group teachers and supervisors; and (3) the development and publication of a vigorous commitment to succeed in these recruiting efforts.

The Detroit school system's recruiting approach may be worth emulating. Aubrey McCutcheon, Deputy Superintendent in charge of staff relations, testified at the commission hearings that:

> . . . [If] there is some sincere desire to increase the number of minority administrators [and teachers] . . . then I submit to you it is a very simple task. I think we have shown that in the City of Detroit. . . . [W]hat you have to do first, I believe, in any school system is to make up your minds that you do want to increase the number of minority group administrators [and teachers] in your system. You have to declare that publicly, you have to be willing to take the criticism that is so often blurted out about reverse discrimination, and things of this sort and yet go about doing the job. Then you have to hire somebody to do that job and give them the power to do that job. . . . The story is always told — we have been looking but nobody applied — so maybe when the applications are in and you find out you do not have a large number of blacks or others who have applied and you are looking for a particular group to be represented on an eligibility list, maybe you have to decide you have to do some greater advertising or you will extend the time for people to apply for a particular job — and these are all things personnel administrators have done for many, many years for a number of reasons and I see no better reason for exercising this kind of flexibility than to achieve a greater minority group membership. . . . [*Id.* at 644; 647; 649]

This type of attitude, coupled with flexible recruiting and hiring practices (Detroit recruiters can offer jobs on the spot to applicants in the upper half of their class who make a favorable impression during the interview; New York City requires applicants to take a written examination, sometimes in New York City, and await placement on an eligible list before a commitment can be made), has enabled Detroit to increase its percentages of minority group teachers and supervisors to more than 40% in each category. Whether the Detroit approach may amount to reverse discrimination or to a racial

quota and the legal issues involved in that possibility, will be
discussed in Chapters 6 and 7.

Undoubtedly, shortcutting the selection procedure is important. The best of the prospective teachers will be in demand
even with a teacher surplus. This is especially true of minority group candidates. If a candidate is sought by two school
districts, one offering him a job on the spot and the other saying he must take an examination and wait at least several
months for a decision, the problem is obvious. But even if a
school district wishes to retain some form of examination,
there are ways to expedite the process. New York City has
used a so-called unassembled examination, which consists of
a review of record without written test, for certain limited
purposes. Also, it has used one-day "walk-in" examinations
with short form written tests. Both of these approaches permit the determination of eligibility to be made within a few
days and an offer of a position to be quickly extended. Alternatively, the National Teacher Examination, which many
prospective teachers take as a matter of course, could be used
in lieu of any local written test.

Other modifications in the examination and licensing procedures may also have important positive impacts on recruiting. The New York City Board of Education has been trying
to find a format which will attract more bilingual teachers.
In 1970, according to Luis Fuentes, the first test for bilingual
classroom teachers was administered. In May 1971, the *Staff
Bulletin* reported that four bilingual teaching licenses, which
had covered service in elementary schools only, had been combined into a single license for service on all levels. The change,
said the article, "was based on improved achievement by
pupils in elementary grades and a request by parents and
others for bilingualism in secondary school instruction. ..."
[New York City Board of Education, *Staff Bulletin,* May 3,
1971, p. 1, col. 3]. In 1972, according to Albert Shanker's
weekly column, "Where We Stand," the board established

separate bilingual licenses in almost all subject areas. [*The New York Times,* June 18, 1972, p. E—9, col. 5] Thus, there would be bilingual elementary teachers as well as regular ones, bilingual junior high school social studies teachers as well as regular ones, and so forth.

In theory each of these efforts has constructive underpinning. In practice they have been criticized for different reasons and from different directions. The bilingual teacher examination, for example, has been denounced by many Puerto Rican educators as inappropriate for Spanish-speaking candidates. Luis Fuentes said in his testimony to the Senate Select Committee:

> Some of us really believed that one of our problems was on the way to solution; but most of us really knew better and the contention of the majority was confirmed when the exam turned out to be 75% in English (with only two questions dealing with Puerto Rican history or culture). An exam supposedly intended to bring in more native Spanish-speaking teachers turned out to be another frustrating exercise in futility and another way of keeping us out of the system. [Fuentes, 1970, p. 2].

If Mr. Fuentes' reaction is in fact shared by a majority of the Puerto Rican community, the structure of the examination would certainly be a deterrent to recruiting able bilingual teachers. Interestingly, during the Spring of 1972 the board began giving examinations wholly or principally in Spanish.

Separate bilingual licenses, as an effort to spur recruitment of bilingual teachers, have also come in for their share of criticism. Leading the negative reaction has been Albert Shanker and the UFT. They charge that these licenses may become second-class licenses "in which competence in another language will be a substitute for competence in mathematics, social studies, science or any other subject." [*The New York Times,* June 17, 1972, p. E—9, col. 5] That might happen, but surely it need not. And the "danger" certainly does not justify maintenance of a system which fails to reach out for adequate numbers of qualified bilingual educators. The UFT has also argued that the separate licenses "will create job insecurity for both [regular and bilingual teachers] and will result in vastly increased ethnic conflict." *[Id.]* No justification for or explanation of this inflammatory statement is even offered by Mr. Shanker. Finally, he has asserted that "separate 'bilingual' licenses will mean permanent ethnic segregation of both teachers and students." *[Id.]* This is the weightiest of the criticisms. For there is tied to the notion of separate bilingual licenses separate schools for non-English-speaking students. The Puerto Rican Forum has advocated such schools, as have individual Puerto Rican educators. There are already two totally bilingual schools in New York City and there is pressure for more. While they may hold the promise of improved education for children who enter the school system unable to speak English, they also hold the threat of a sub-system of Puerto Rican schools to which only Puerto Rican teachers will be assigned. Indeed, Mr. Shanker has said another aspect of the separate licenses and separate schools troubles him — that Puerto Rican teachers, in effect, would be licensed to teach only Puerto Rican pupils. As he put it:

> This would deprive the students, Puerto Rican and others, of the integrated experiences they should have; it would restrict Puerto Rican teachers to *el barrio* and deny them job opportunities throughout our school system. Puerto Rican teachers of mathematics should be able to teach anywhere in the system. *[Id.]*

This fear is shared by Alfredo Mathew, New York's first Puerto Rican community superintendent. In a speech before the Second Annual Conference on Bilingual Education, he warned against "cultural isolation and inbreeding that would result if bilingual education became a disguise for a new form of segregation or resegregation." *[Id.]*

A balance must certainly be arrived at. Bilingual education must be expanded through the recruitment of qualified teachers. But it must remain an open system, open to all ideas and to all people.

Several other specific recommendations for improving recruiting were made at the Human Rights Commission hearings. One is to actively recruit candidates for supervisory positions from outside the system. Thus far, little effort has been made in this direction in New York City or in many other school districts. This contributes to a school district's reputation as a closed system, especially for minority groups. But more than that, it leads to a kind of in-breeding which is unhealthy for any school district, large or small, urban, suburban or rural.

Another, far-reaching recommendation is that much greater use should be made of the paraprofessional program for recruiting teachers. Most large school districts use paraprofessionals as teacher- and school-aides. By and large, they do not have the academic background to meet current licensing standards for regular teaching positions. Yet, many of them have a deep commitment to education and to ghetto children. They constitute a large and untapped reservoir of potential urban teachers. In New York City there are about 15,000 paraprofessionals employed in the school system in a variety of job titles, mostly educational assistants. The head of the Board of Education's Auxiliary Education Career Unit estimates that 48% of the paraprofessionals are black and 16% are Puerto Rican. *[Selection of Teachers, 1972, p. 125]* Although many have been working in the schools for three years of more, less than one-third are enrolled in career development programs in local colleges. The career ladder designed for paraprofessionals predicates progress on college course credits. Under current released time provisions, it will take, on the average, eight years of combined work and study to acquire a bachelor's degree. At the time of the commission's hearings, none, except five who had prior college credits, had achieved the associate arts degree, a level on the

ladder providing a small pay increment, but no clear enlarge-
ment of function. No provision has been made to evaluate or
accredit the years of teaching experience and the skill acquired
in in-school work, except in certain college programs which
accord teaching experience some weight in counting total
credits.

Witnesses, both paraprofessionals themselves and those who
plan and conduct training for them, testified to the hardships
endured, especially by the many who are mothers of young
children. There are the long years of working and studying;
the lack of job security, of transferability of experience;
there is the uneven and often unsupervised quality of work
experience, an insufficient in-service training, and the seeming
irrelevance to career aspirations of many college requirements.
On the other hand, those who have trained paraprofessionals
for work in schools outside New York City, or for jobs in
other public services, report that with new forms of intensive
training focused on and directly related to on-the-job activity,
paraprofessionals have progressed more rapidly. Where
traditional requirements were modified to accept new combinations of experience and study, paraprofessionals have
been able to assume greater responsibility and to make an
important contribution.

Until recently, little local funding has been provided for
either employment or career development of paraprofessionals
in the city's schools, and a staff of only three persons has
been assigned to handle all aspects of their employment.
Early in 1971, the Board of Education made its first allocation of a significant sum to finance college education for
additional numbers, a noteworthy step because it indicates an
on-going commitment to them. But the same limited hours of
released time exist, and much more remains to be done in
regularizing, standardizing, and supervising their work so
that formal recognition can be given to experience, where
merited. Indications are that many — perhaps many of the

best qualified and most ambitious — become discouraged by the slow pace and leave the schools for jobs in other service sectors where progress is less dependent on college credits, and where released time provisions are more generous.

If these kinds of changes can be made, the paraprofessionals could be a major focus of the recruiting effort and could help to lay to rest forever the assertion that there are not enough qualified minority group candidates.

References

Luis Fuentes, "Educational Personnel Problems That Confront the Puerto Rican Community in New York City" (testimony before the U.S. Senate Select Committee on Equal Educational Opportunity, Nov. 24, 1970).

Puerto Rican Educators' Association, *Study for the New York State Commission on the Cost, Quality and Financing of Elementary and Secondary Schools* (1971).

Paul Tractenberg, ed., *Selection of Teachers and Supervisors in Urban School Systems* (Agathon Publication Services, New York, 1972).

CHAPTER 4

SELECTING THE URBAN TEACHER: THE CUSTOMARY PATTERN AND THE NEW YORK CITY MODEL

The selection process, conceived broadly, usually begins in teacher training institutions where most prospective teachers receive their professional education. Then comes the second facet of the process — recruiting — when school districts and candidates make their contacts. But the heart of the process is actual selection. The school districts take the pool of candidates which has been produced through their recruiting efforts and apply a variety of screening techniques to its members. Successful candidates are offered positions, and some of them will actually wind up in the districts' classrooms.

The final products of this process can, of course, be no better than the best people who emerge from teacher training institutions, or the best candidates recruited by the school district. Improvements in those two facets of the process should, therefore, result ultimately in better teachers and there must be unrelenting pressure in that direction. But, especially during a period of general teacher surpluses, actual selection will play an enormously important role in determining how well school districts will fare in getting the best possible teachers.

From school district to school district there are considerable variations in the selection techniques used. They range from heavy reliance on standardized written tests to heavy reliance on observed performance in the classroom. To some extent the choice of techniques depends upon the financial and personnel resources of the particular district. Some techniques undoubtedly require somewhat more money and man-hours than others. But the differences are probably not great enough in most cases to account alone for the district's choice. Rather, the choice of techniques often says something important about the district's educational value system. Is the goal of education and teaching to make certain that students have absorbed a certain amount of information? Or is it to develop a sense of self? Or is it somewhere in between?

That question — what is the goal of education and teaching — is usually answered, if at all, indirectly. And one of the best places to start is how the district chooses to choose its teachers.

Although there is considerable variety, several relatively common selection patterns emerge.

The Customary Pattern

The most widely used selection pattern involves two stages — state certification as a preliminary screening device and local school district hiring based on the application of such further techniques as the school district chooses.

In most states certification is largely a review of the applicant's record. To be certified he or she will have to present evidence of completion of the requisite academic program, student teaching, and other requirements specified by the state education department. Often certification is based more on quantitative than qualitative considerations. However, some states (and the number is increasing) do have a significant qualitative element. It may be found in "program approval," under which the state education department or an accrediting agency observes teacher training programs, approves those that meet certain qualitative standards, and then certifies graduates of approved programs. The qualitative element may also come in the form of performance on written tests. Several states utilize the National Teacher Examination of the Education Testing Service for this purpose. But the legal and practical validity of standardized written tests of all kinds is being brought sharply into question as we shall see in later chapters. Or, the qualitative element may come from the use of performance-based criteria. This rather recent development, which will also be discussed in detail, involves an evaluation of the prospective teacher's capacity to perform on the job. At least 30 states have already begun to deal with the very complicated task of developing meaningful standards and procedures for evaluating today's performance in light of what it suggests about tomorrow's performance.

As a practical matter, the more valid and reliable the state's qualitative judgments about prospective teachers, the more local school districts are likely to rely on them. This is natural and desirable. But it is hard to conceive of state certification, no matter how good and complete, ever fully supplanting local selection procedures. For statewide certification must deal with the broadest and most universal needs of school districts and the broadest and most universal qualities of prospective teachers. The very special needs of particular school districts will be all but impossible to reflect.

At the present time, school districts use a considerable array of local selection methods to make the final determination about which applicants should be offered positions. Only their ingenuity limits the possible techniques. Most school districts interview the candidates in some way. Several of New York City's community school districts have developed screening panels of parents, other community representatives, and teachers to supplement interviews by the professional staff. Some school districts require candidates to be observed while teaching in the school for some period of time. Another selection technique is a more thorough review of their records perhaps with emphasis on the detailed dossier maintained for each student by teacher training programs. Yet another in the battery of local selection devices is the written test. It can be locally created, administered, and graded. It can be geared to special local needs and conditions but created, administered, and graded by an independent testing agency. Or, the written test may be a national test such as the National Teacher Examination. In any case, it is necessary to reemphasize that written tests and the way they are being used in the employment process are under severe attack.

The pattern of selection based on state certification and local school district discretionary hiring is, of course, only as good as the actual techniques utilized and the skill with which they are applied. But, in general, this pattern has several important strengths. It does not require complicated, expensive, and time-consuming procedures. Nor does it impose elaborate central standards on individual school districts. In most cases state certification provides merely a foundation that local districts can build upon to meet their special needs. Indeed, a number of states have shown enough flexibility regarding state certification requirements so that local districts can accept alternative qualifications, such as Peace Corps or VISTA teaching experience, in lieu of the more traditional academic training.

Another significant advantage of the customary selection model is that local school officials, because they have real power in the selection process, can more effectively be held accountable for the performance of school staffs. As pressure for school accountability grows, this will be an especially important consideration.

Giving local districts broad discretion in the selection of personnel is not a phenomenon limited to education. Nor is it inconsistent with the civil service merit concept. The New Jersey Civil Service Department, for example, announced in 1971 the initation of a new system under which state agencies can conduct their own promotional tests and can make promotions, as well as take on the new responsibility of establishing promotion eligibility lists, based on job performance, experience, seniority, and oral interviews, without the traditional written examination. Previously, only the New Jersey Civil Service Department itself could conduct promotional examinations and approve promotions. According to Civil Service President, James A. Alloway, the new decentralized merit system grew out of recommendations from the department's own study of state objectives and employees needs and from the governor's Management Committee Report. [*Newark Star-Ledger,* July 14, 1971, p. 10, col. 1]

But just as the department's system reflected a trend toward vesting selection responsibility more directly in the local public employer, the response to it reflected strong resistance to changes in the civil service format. A suit was filed in the state courts by Mercer Council Number 4 of the New Jersey Civil Service Association, an organization of state employees, alleging the decentralized approach was "an open door to a new type of spoils system" with appointments no longer "made on merit and fitness but rather by favoritism and partisanship." The Appellate Division of the state's superior court overturned the decentralization system on the grounds that the Civil Service Department had transcended its "legitimate rule making power" and could not effect such a system without legislative authorization. The New Jersey Supreme Court unanimously affirmed that decision in November 1972. [*Mercer Council No. 4, N.J. Civil Service Ass'n v. Alloway,* 119 N.J. Super. 94 (App. Div. 1972), *aff'd,* 61 N.J. 516 (1972)]. Despite the fact that 718 promotions made through the decentralization system were permitted to stand, the decision has been hailed by *The Shield,* the weekly publication of the New Jersey Civil Service Association, as "the biggest thing that ever happened in Civil Service" and the salvation of state employees from "Political Serfdom." [*Newark Star-Ledger,* Nov. 19, 1972, p. 45, col. 1 and Nov. 26, 1972, p. 3–4, col. 2]. Meanwhile, Civil Service Commission President Alloway announced the creation of a substitute system which would also involve the operating departments in promotions.

As in civil service generally, the flexibility afforded local school districts by the two-stage selection process is not only a major advantage — it is the basis for the most frequent criticisms. The major weaknesses ascribed to this procedure are variations on the same theme — that local school districts will not honestly or effectively discharge their responsibilities and that state certification alone is neither a sufficient basis for assessing ability nor a sufficient safeguard against patronage and a "spoils system" or against abuses of applicants' due process rights. These are not criticisms to be treated lightly. For if there is substantial evidence that giving school districts discretion to employ teachers based only on state certification and other criteria they choose results in less competent teachers and in more patronage and violations of due process, then the worth of this selection mechanism is placed in real doubt. On the other hand, if there is no such evidence, and no other compelling reasons to commend a more elaborate and detailed process, then the criticisms can be discounted.

All of these crucial issues about the selection of teachers were raised in detail during the New York City Commission on Human Rights hearings. In this area, perhaps more than any other, the testimony has broad applicability.

The New York City Model

The New York State Legislature developed a selection procedure for the New York City school system which departs in important respects from the more customary pattern of state certification coupled with discretionary local hiring. One need only compare the pertinent provisions of the New York State Education Law sections 2569 and 2573 (10) with section 2573(9). Perhaps the main departure is that the legislature has specified the mechanism by which local hiring is to be carried out and this mechanism has taken away from the "employer" much of its discretion.

In theory there is a tripartite system for employing teachers and supervisors in New York City.

1. Eligibility Standards and Recruitment. The Office of Personnel, as the arm of the Chancellor (the successor to the Superintendent of Schools with somewhat broader powers) and the City Board of Education, is responsible for defining eligibility requirements, recruiting qualified candidates, providing the Board of Examiners with analyses of job duties on the basis of which examinations are constructed, and instructing the Board of Examiners to give examinations in particular licenses at particular times.

2. Examination and Eligibility Lists. The Board of Examiners is in turn responsible for designing and administering examinations in most of the 1,200 teaching and supervisory licenses, and for compiling eligible lists of successful candidates. Although the Board of Examiners is a part of the Board of Education for many purposes, it is required by statute to carry out its examination and eligible list functions in an independent manner. [See New York State Education Law section 2569.] The New York City Board of Examiners is the only autonomous local examining body in New York State and one of only a handful in the country. Buffalo was the only other school district in New York State expressly required by statute to have a local examination, but in 1968 the requirement was eliminated by the legislature for most supervisory positions. [See New York State Education Law section 2573(10-a.] Even in Buffalo, however, the examination process is not administered by an independent board of examiners, but by the Office of the Superintendent of Schools.

3. Appointment, Assignment, and Promotion. Until 1969, the City Board of Education made all appointments to teaching and supervisory positions, assigned the appointees to schools, supervised their activities, and granted them tenure.

The appointments to all teaching positions and to most supervisory positions were required to be from among the top three names on ranked eligible lists. The use of ranked lists, of course, substantially reduced the discretion of the appointing authority. In 1969 the legislature enacted a Decentralization Act [New York State Education Law section 2590-a*et seq.*] under which the single New York City school district was divided into 31 community school districts, each with an elected community school board. These community boards were given significant powers over the operation of elementary, intermediate, and junior high schools within their districts. Certain personnel powers were included, such as the power to appoint supervisory personnel from *unranked* eligible lists, and the power to assign all personnel to schools, to supervise them and to grant or deny them tenure. The senior high schools and special schools and their personnel remained under central authority — the Chancellor and the City Board of Education. Moreover, the Chancellor and City Board were given power to establish citywide policies, rules and regulations, and education and experience requirements for all personnel.

The division of personnel authority into three discrete areas is both theoretical and greatly oversimplified, however. In practice the division is less precise and the areas of overlap more extensive. A few examples should suffice.

In his testimony Dr. Theodore H. Lang stated that during his five and one-half years as Deputy Superintendent in charge of the Office of Personnel, no analyses of duties were prepared for any teaching licenses. [*Selection of Teachers,* 1972, p. 77] Dr. Jay E. Greene, a member of the Board of Examiners, confirmed that the board had not received such analyses. Consequently, *it,* rather than the Office of Personnel, had effectively constructed the needed descriptions of job duties by relying upon characteristics described by assorted Board of Education publications, state certification requirements, Board of Education eligibility requirements, and panels of "experts" convened in advance of each examination. [*Selection of Teachers,* 1972, p. 170–71]

Theoretically, the Board of Examiners has independence in constructing and administering examinations. There is, however, a substantial degree of interdependence with other parts of the school system. The chancellor or his designee is an *ex officio* member of the board. Much of the actual work of constructing and administering examinations is done by examination assistants, who are, for the most part, teachers and supervisors in the New York City school system selected by the Board of Examiners to assist with particular examinations. The state education law now expressly provides that no one can serve as an examination assistant unless approved by the chancellor or a community superintendent.

The Board of Examiners and the Local Examination

In the public mind selection of teachers and supervisors in New York City has long been regarded as the domain of the Board of Examiners. That has been true to an important extent even though eligibility standards, recruiting, appointment, assignment, tenure, and promotion have been outside the Board of Examiner's province. Indeed, provisions of the 1969 Decentralization Act have somewhat reduced the scope of the Board of Examiner's role. For example, eligible lists for all supervisory positions are *qualifying* rather than *ranked.* That means anyone whose name is on the list, rather than just one from the top three, can be appointed. Although it is still necessary for candidates to pass through the Board of Examiners' process, the significance of the examiners' gradations is reduced and the scope of the Board of Education's discretion to appoint is correspondingly increased.

Moreover, other provisions of the Decentralization Law authorize community boards in certain circumstances to appoint professional personnel entirely outside the framework of the Board of Examiners' system. Community boards can select their community superintendents on the basis of state certification. And when teaching vacancies occur in schools which are in the lowest 45 percentile on citywide reading tests, the community boards can appoint teachers from October 1 to May 1 on the basis of their performance on the National Teacher Examination. Teachers for those schools may also be selected from a regular ranked list but without regard to their rank, or from an unranked list based on a special qualifying examination given by the Board of Examiners.

Despite these modifications, however, the local examination is still at the heart of the selection process. Success in the examination continues to be regarded as the critical element in making it through the selection process. And the Board of Examiners, as the judge of both content and performance in relation to examinations, continues to be a central force in the selection of teachers and supervisors.

What caused the birth of this institution and the personnel system of which it is the center? Why has it been so durable in the face of mounting efforts at reform? What does the future hold for it?

The answers to these questions will reveal much about the nature of school district personnel systems and the prospects for their reform. Not just in New York City or State, but nationwide.

The New York City Board of Examiners and the personnel system of which it is the heart was largely created just before the turn of the century. Apparently it was a response to evidence of widespread patronage in the filling of teaching and supervisory jobs. The Board of Examiners is a creature of statute but the ultimate foundation for the examination process over which it presides is the New York State Constitution.

In a provision with analogs in many other state charters, the New York Constitution requires that appointments to the civil service, including teaching and supervisory positions, "be made according to merit and fitness to be ascertained, as far as practicable, by examination which, as far as practicable, shall be competitive. . . ." [N. Y. Const. art. V, sec. 6 (1894)]. The New York State Education Law, in implementing the constitutional provision, permits each city school board in the state, except Buffalo and New York City, to make appointments based on state certification and such additional or higher qualifications as it prescribes. The "merit and fitness" requirement of the state constitution may be fulfilled in all those districts by the local school board's determination that a candidate possesses the necessary qualifications prescribed by the state. And each school board has discretion to decide the practicability of determining merit and fitness by examination, competitive or noncompetitive. Only in New York City and Buffalo has the legislature determined that competitive or qualifying examinations for most teaching and supervisory positions are practicable on a citywide basis, and only in New York City has it required a Board of Examiners.

So, the legislative answer to "widespread patronage" in filling teaching and supervisory jobs was to mandate a highly structured system with substantial responsibilities outside the control of the Board of Education and its professional staff. Eliminate some of the discretion. Take exclusive control out of the hands of those who had abused it. Pattern the personnel processes after the Civil Service model by relying on an examination process administered by an impartial, objective third party.

Certainly this seemed to be a logical response to a specific problem. But why was the problem seen as so narrow? Only New York City was required to have its own Board of Examiners, and only New York City and Buffalo, the two largest cities in the state, were expressly required to rely upon an examination process. Are problems of patronage and a "spoils system" limited to the biggest cities? Are Syracuse and Rochester competent to exercise discretion in personnel selection because they are smaller, although still substantial cities? Or is the explanation unconnected with size per se? Are public officials in New York City and Buffalo just more susceptible to corrupt impulses? Is such an examination process for some reason, "practicable" in New York City and Buffalo but not in the other school districts of New York State?

Lurking beneath all these questions is the ultimate question — will developing elaborate safeguards against patronage actually ensure that better qualified teachers and supervisors are employed so that the children will receive a better education?

The answer to that question will undoubtedly be elusive. But we have to judge the performance of institutions such as the New York City Board of Examiners against that standard just as we must judge proposals for reform against it. For if the New York City model does not produce better teachers and supervisors than other less cumbersome and less expensive systems in use, the role of reform should be to devise a personnel system more likely to produce better people while, at the same time, protecting the rights of all applicants.

So, it is necessary to see how the New York City model has actually functioned, to weigh the criticisms against the defenses, to compare the future alternatives to the current procedures. And to keep always in mind the impact on the children.

The examination conducted by the Board of Examiners typically consists of a written short-answer test with essay or written English questions, an interview test, a review of academic record, and a medical examination. In a few cases there may also be a performance component.

According to the courts, however, none of these aspects is required by the state constitution or by the State Education Law. The requisite examination may consist of an unassembled examination — perhaps just a review of record. And an unassembled examination can be competitive as well as qualifying. Indeed, the Board of Examiners does create some eligible lists on the basis of unassembled examinations. Presumably it has the discretion to do so in all cases.

According to its former chairman, Gertrude E. Unser, the Board of Examiners conducts an average of 200 different examinations annually, covering as many as 50,000 applicants. Those who pass receive licenses in the particular job category and are placed on eligible lists. Overall there are about 1,200 different licenses in the school system.

A sample of results supplied by the Board of Examiners indicates that between 75% and 85% of the candidates who take examinations in teaching licenses are ultimately licensed. As that sample would suggest, the Board of Examiners sees their current examinations as having a limited purpose — "to ascertain whether the applicants have the necessary knowledge, know-how, background, record, health, and observable personality factors required of a beginning teacher." [Letter from Gertrude E. Unser, Chairman, Board of Examiners to Eleanor Holmes Norton, Chairman, New York City Commission on Human Rights, March 17, 1971, p. 3]

To carry out its responsibilities, the Board of Examiners has a full-time staff of about 170 persons. Almost all the full-time professional staff are teachers and supervisors assigned to the board on a yearly basis by the chancellor. There is also a roster of approximately 4,500 persons who are called upon as needed to prepare, conduct, and rate examinations. Approximately three-fourths of these temporary examination assistants are also employed full-time as teachers and supervisors in the New York City school system.

None of the board's personnel, full-time or temporary, except the four regular members of the Board of Examiners, is required as a condition of employment to have training or expertise in personnel administration or test construction (although some do have some such training or expertise). In fact, there are no formal requirements of any kind and no formal screening procedures, despite requests by the Board of Examiners to the Board of Education to establish such procedures. The four members of the Board of Examiners, on the other hand, take Civil Service examinations which include a written test designed to evaluate, among other things, technical competence "in the fields of education, testing and research." [New York City Civil Service Commission, Notice of Exam No. 1138, "Examiner, Board of Educ." (2d amended notice July 14, 1965)]

The Board of Examiners' budget for 1970–71, its 72nd year, was $3,528,211. A total of $3,466,911 was allocated to personnel costs and $1,911,000 of that amount to compensation of temporary examination assistants. The allocation for research personnel was, according to Dr. Jay E. Greene, a board member, $40,000.

For a variety of reasons the Board of Examiners has been a lightning rod. It has attracted the most detailed scrutiny and has been the subject of the most elaborate public criticism regarding school personnel matters. This may be because of the central role of selection in the personnel system, and the public association of the Board of Examiners with selection. It may be because written tests, such as the ones developed and administered by the board, tend to be regarded as the whole of the examination process and are being attacked along a wide legal, psychological, and personnel management front. Or it may be because the Board of Examiners has acquired the reputation for being the principal roadblock for black candidates, for Puerto Rican and other Spanish-speaking candidates, and for white candidates who are "different" from the prevailing mold at any given time. The recent crescendo of criticism probably results to a significant extent from the decentralization of the New York City school system. With locally elected boards of education installed in the 31 community school districts, there is great pressure to place more complete and unfettered responsibility for personnel selection in the hands of those boards rather than to leave substantial control over the process in the hands of distant bureaucrats.

But there have been crescendos before. For more than 20 years there has been a series of studies and evaluations recommending the abolition or substantial reorganization of the Board of Examiners. These have come from a variety of prestigious study groups and task forces appointed by the State Education Department, the Mayor of New York City, the New York City Board of Education, and the Public Education Association. In recent years, the Board of Education's own decentralization plan (which the legislature required it to submit), supported by the State Board of Regents and the State Commissioner of Education, advocated the abolition of the Board of Examiners and the end of a compulsory local examination. Some of these recommendations have resulted in serious legislative consideration. But, at best, they have resulted in minor piecemeal amendments. The Board of Examiners has also made some internal changes on its own initiative. On balance, however, it has been extraordinarily resistant to change and able to withstand pressure for serious reform. What accounts for this strength and resiliency? In many ways it is the same combination of forces that explains the continuation of traditional civil service procedures throughout the public sector. There is fear of a return to the rampant favoritism which was common many years ago. There is continuing public acceptance of things labeled "merit" and "objectivity," and continuing public suspicion of efforts to change the system.

There is the influence of the testing agency and its sizable body of examiners which forms a formidable special interest lobby. The writer of a letter to the editor of *The New York Times* said it well about another well-known New York examination, the Regents' examination:

Making competent examinations takes an army of dedicated souls. Making them for nearly a century in New York State has created a unique bureaucratic special-interest group. Educationally speaking, their arguments seem more those of Theodore Roosevelt than of John Dewey, although contemporary to both. [Letter from Henry

Miller Littlefield, Assistant Dean of Students, Amherst College, *The New York Times*, July 13, 1971, p. 32, col. 5]

There is the growing political power of public employee organizations which, by and large, prefer the known evils of a questionable personnel system to the unknown evils of a different system. And, in New York City at least, the desire of public employee organizations to retain the current centralized personnel selection system seems to have increased in direct relationship to the pressure for decentralization and community control. Many people have seen this reaction as a part of the cutting edge of racial and ethnic hostility between the largely white, largely Jewish teacher and supervisor organizations, on the one hand, and the largely black and Spanish communities on the other. Indeed, the frequent references of Albert Shanker, President of the United Federation of Teachers, to the danger of turning selection powers over to "community vigilantes" gives some credence to this view.

Are civil service principles being used then to thwart legitimate community efforts to reform the educational system? Or are they being used, as intended, to protect the integrity of the personnel system so that qualified candidates and employees are not excluded for reasons unrelated to their capacity to perform? The answers to these questions will have vast implications for civil service systems in cities across the country. For if, in their current form, those systems are remnants of a past without clear correlation to today and tomorrow, there will be increasing pressure to overturn them. And if these efforts are not successful, frustration will quickly turn either to violence or to apathy. In either case, the viability of public education in urban centers will be further jeopardized.

Thus, developing an honest, constructive answer to the question of how urban school districts should select their teachers is of the highest priority. Efforts, like those of the New York City Commission on Human Rights, to fully and publicly develop information about the functioning of the current selection processes and about the alternatives being tried or considered are an essential first step. For one important result of the commission's investigation, public hearings, and report was to spotlight a striking consensus about the need for major change in the New York City school system's selection process. This unanimity, which had been largely obscured during the earlier heated public colloquys about the Board of Examiners, was more noteworthy because it included those principally responsible for the current system and those principally affected by it. For example, in the area of test validity, such diverse witnesses as Dr. Jay E. Greene of the Board of Examiners; Isaiah Robinson, then Vice-President of the Board of Education; Albert Shanker, President of the UFT; Dr. James Deneen of the Educational Testing Service; Community Superintendents Edythe Gaines and Andrew Donaldson; a junior high school principal; and many teachers and former teachers in the New York City system, agreed that significant improvements are necessary. Indeed, early in his prepared statement to the commission, Dr. Greene listed 15 significant changes effected by the Board of Examiners in recent years. Both he and Gertrude Unser, then Chairman of the Examiners, conceded that many additional changes should be made. But, they argued, before the entire system is dismantled, its critics should establish that the alternatives being proposed will actually work better than the current system.

It is not enough to find fault with the current system, said Dr. Greene, because:

> We're naturally in the position of being a target. I know of no umpire in a baseball game who is popular per se. ... [O]ur job is such we can't be very popular. We have to be attacked and criticized because we are making important decisions to the best of our ability. We can't be everybody's friend. [*Selection of Teachers,* 1972, p. 188]

This argument did not persuade the bulk of the witnesses who believed a process of gradual change was insufficient at

this stage. Of the 140 witnesses, most urged immediate abolition of the Board of Examiners, at least in its current quasi-
independent form. Those who felt that the Board might be
continued recommended restructuring so that it could become
a service agency of the City Board and community boards
rather than the ultimate decision-maker on eligibility for appointment. Only eight witnesses, including members of the
Board of Examiners, favored retention of the board in substantially its current form.

This difference of opinion marks most reform efforts. When
advocates of reform first state their case, it is normally rejected
out of hand by the "professionals." When significant public
support is marshaled and the case is clearly too strong to be
rejected out of hand, the common bureaucratic response is to
say, "Your criticisms are valid, but we've already made many
changes designed to meet them. Of course, we're open to
further appropriate changes."

Whether or not this is a prudent response in the face of
destructively drastic demands or a bureaucratic defense
mechanism depends upon the particular circumstances. To
evaluate this question in the New York City school system
context is interesting in its own right. It should also provide
important insights about broader educational reform efforts,
especially in the personnel area, and about the increasing efforts generally to reform civil service concepts and procedures.

An analysis of the New York City school system's selection
procedures inevitably involves weighing a wide variety of
charges and counter-charges, criticisms and defenses, covering most facets of the process. Organizing the materials
around the most important categories of criticism is an effective way to convey the flavor and weight of the arguments for
dramatic reform and to compare them at the same time to
the arguments in favor of continuing substantially the current
selection process. The principal areas of criticism are: (1)
that the process is outmoded; (2) that it results in delays and

otherwise serves as a deterrent; (3) that it is rigid; (4) that it is costly and, in the name of merit and objectivity, has created its own patronage system; (5) that it is inconsistent with de-centralization of a school system; and (6) that the current New York City selection process is invalid and biased.

The first five areas are sufficiently related so that they should be considered in one chapter, and Chapter 5 is devoted to them. The nexus is that each deals with an issue which is essentially policy-oriented. That is, the criticism goes princi-pally to the wisdom of selecting personnel in the way it is currently done.

On the other hand, the sixth area, invalidity and bias, in-volves largely a consideration of the legality of the current procedures under the federal and state constitutions, and under federal, state and local law. For that reason, and because of the special importance and complexity of these questions, Chapter 6 is devoted to them. Particular emphasis is given to the use of written tests as an important part of the per-sonnel selection process.

Finally, an evaluation of the selection of teachers would not be complete without serious consideration of alternatives, and Chapter 7 undertakes this task. For, in a real sense, the current system is weak or strong in relationship to actual alternatives. This is not to say, however, that the burden should be on advocates of reform to *prove* unequivocally that other procedures will work better. If they can do so, so much the better. But it should be enough for them to demonstrate that there is a reasonable likelihood of significant improvement in the selection process and, ultimately, in the quality of education.

CHAPTER 5

SELECTING THE URBAN TEACHER: ISSUES ABOUT THE NEW YORK CITY MODEL

The ultimate test of a system for selecting personnel is how it works. And "how it works" has many levels of meaning, especially when it is teachers and school administrators who are being selected. Does it produce the best qualified candidates for the particular school district or school? Does it produce them when they're needed? Does it treat them fairly and with dignity? Do the taxpayers receive a good return on their investment? Do school personnel, candidates, parents and students, and the general public have confidence in the selection system? Whether the system meets prevailing legal and psychometric standards is implicitly raised in some of these questions. But it is also raised in more direct and discrete ways in the next chapter.

The investigation and public hearings of the New York City Commission on Human Rights evidenced strong feeling among a wide variety of witnesses that current New York City selection procedures are not working on any of these levels. The issues raised there provide a valuable check list against which other selection systems can be measured. For, these issues, raising as they do the broadest public employee selection questions, extend well beyond the particular structure of the New York City system. Most large school districts, and a considerable number of smaller ones, throughout the country have selection processes which raise many of the same issues.

The System Is Outmoded

Many witnesses testified that, although the Board of Examiners and its elaborate formal examination process may have served an important function in former years, it had ceased to do so.

Chancellor Scribner faulted "a system of licensing which, however useful it has been in helping to eliminate a spoils system since creation of the Board of Examiners more than 70 years ago, is now antiquated, outmoded, and inconsistent with both contemporary educational requirements and the concept of decentralized schools." [*Selection of Teachers,* 1972, p. 35]

A similar view was expressed by Irving Flinker, principal of the George Gershwin Junior High School in New York City:

> In industry, when a corporation president finds that his machinery is outdated and uneconomical, he is quick to change that machinery so that it is efficient and brings in the dividends. Certainly we can do no less for our children. ... The conditions of labor supply and children's needs at the turn of the century were far different from those prevailing today. The size of our system, current state certification standards, decentralized control, and the special needs of inner city children require a re-evaluation of our teacher selecting system. [*Id.* at 58]

Former Superintendent of Schools John Theobald testified further as to differences in the historical situation under which the Board of Examiners was created and the current situation in the city's public schools. In briefly sketching the history of the current system's development, he testified that at the time of the creation of the Board of Examiners the requirements to teach consisted of one year of teacher training school beyond high school. According to Dr. Theobald, the situation is materially different now.

> I think we are talking about a different kind of a teacher world. ... Right now we have moved teacher requirements up to master's degree, temporary certificate with a baccalaureate degree and some ten or twelve credits in teacher education. This is far beyond what we had when the system and the Board of Examiners [started]. We

measure in our teacher examination pretty much the same things that youngsters supposedly learned at college. ... I would like to see somebody make a correlation study between our examination in New York City and college grades ... and I think you will find the examination was not testing anything new. [*Id.* at 42]

In response to this criticism, members of the Board of Examiners contended that the examination system has been substantially modernized already and can be further changed as conditions require. Dr. Greene testified that "so far as our Board of Examiners' procedures are concerned, unfortunately many individuals and persons who have formed judgments and even those who testified here are expressing judgments that are based upon the Board of Examiners' selection procedures of ten, twenty, or thirty years ago." [*Id.* at 139]

On the other hand, Chairman Unser noted that some of the basic conditions which prompted the legislature to create a Board of Examiners still exist. She said:

Can anyone seriously believe that influence, patronage, raiding the public treasury, the desire for power are any the less operative today than they were in that time [when the Board of Examiners was established] ? If you think that, just read the daily press. [*Id.* at 16]

The System Causes Delay and Otherwise Deters Qualified Candidates

Many witnesses criticized the Board of Examiners for long delays in promulgating eligible lists that discourage many applicants from applying and that cause some who have applied to accept jobs elsewhere.

This is a major problem for those who recruit for the Board of Education and for community boards. In discussing the UFT-Board of Education Joint Recruitment Program, Daisy Hicks, a board staff member in change of the program, indicated that 1,000 minority group applicants had been identified but were, at the time of hearings, still far from actually getting into the school system. The examination process and its delays cause serious problems. Ms. Hicks testified that although written tests in some licenses were given on the campuses by examiners between January and April, the eligible lists were not expected to be promulgated until September 1. When asked whether that meant applicants interviewed and tested during that period could not be offered positions until September, Ms. Hicks said:

> Well, I have hopes. Now I can't predict what they [the Board of Examiners] are going to do, but . . . [t] his type of an examination they . . . are supposed to give . . . priority. . . . [S] o you and I can just hope. [*Id.* at 112]

Aside from the delays, Ms. Hicks testified that the examination process serves as a deterrent because so many applicants are confused by the procedures. This is especially true now that the National Teacher Examination is accepted in lieu of the New York City written test in some licenses and under certain circumstances. The Board of Examiners gives its own written test on campuses in a limited number of licenses, but other applicants must still come to New York City to take the written test.

James Watkins, who also participated in the Joint Recruitment Program, seconded Ms. Hicks' views. According to him, it has been difficult to move minority group applicants recruited by the program through the selection mechanism.

> Out of the people that we recruited last year, there were something like 124 people that I was acquainted with. There were 120 blacks and four whites, and by September 1st the Board of Examiners had finally recommended for licenses three whites. [*Id.* at 120]

This was true even though the black applicants had been interviewed in March and April and had taken the required examinations on their campuses.

Mr. Watkins testified that the form of the examination was another deterrent.

... You are sitting there and I am examining you with respect to a
teaching position, and this is another examiner over here, and we
are firing questions at you like in a third degree. Many of the teachers
will get up and walk out, for they would not want to be subjected
to this. [*Id.* at 119]

The task of assigning teachers to classrooms, as well as recruiting them, is made more difficult by the length of time it
takes to promulgate eligible lists. According to Dr. Lang, it
takes from six to eight months to bring out teachers' lists and
longer for supervisors' lists. "It is a problem when the lists are
not available when needed. Of course, the Board of Examiners
will always tell me that they are working very, very hard. ..."
[*Id.* at 79]

If vacancies cannot be filled by regularly licensed teachers,
per diem certificates can be issued within a few days and the
holders hired to fill in. Of course, in many cases, these are the
very people who have not yet been found eligible for
regular licenses.

All of this creates problems for school administrators, according to several who testified. One described the impact
on a principal:

The Board of Examiners sets up such a barrier between teacher applicant and school as to discourage the candidates from taking the test
and to frustrate the school principals who have uncovered positions.
Early in September, 1969, hundreds of teachers stormed the corridors
of the Examiners' offices protesting the delay in processing the July
3rd examinations. Aware of this situation many principals nomi-
nated these qualified applicants for per diem certificates to fill their
vacancies about five days before school opened. Because of an inefficient system, tied in knots by red tape, principals waited from
one to two weeks to fill vacancies with these teachers who had
qualified three months earlier for the jobs. In the meantime, classes
went uncovered. Results of the August, 1969 examinations were
still not available by the middle of January, 1970. When a principal
asks for an explanation he is told that more applicants took the test
than were expected, and that the processing took a long time. In my
school a substitute teacher took the regular teacher's examination in

French in November, 1968 but was not informed of passing until January 20, 1970. The processing of examinations is so cumbersome and confused that one regular examination is given before the results of the previous test are released. For example, the same applicants who took the industrial arts examination or the high school mathematics examination in October, 1969, sat for these tests again in January, 1970, because the processing of the first tests was incomplete. When a system of teacher selection requires needless second testing, the symptoms of disintegration are clear. There is evident neither consideration of applicants' morale nor regard for taxpayers' money. The result of such an uncoordinated procedure, so frustrating to teacher applicants, is to impede the natural flow of graduate students into the city's schools. . . . [*Id.* at 59]

In response to such charges, the Board of Examiners offered several defenses. Of the changes in the board's procedures enumerated by Dr. Greene, two relate to problems of delay.

There was a time when an examination for a regular license took a year, sometimes two years, and that was unconscionable. . . . But, there has been a speed-up in the processing. For example, 6,000 or so students who are lower seniors will take our common branches examination in November. The list will come out in March or early April. That's four months for the processing of 6,000 applicants. . . . I don't know any other examining body in the country or possibly in the world that can match a record of speed and a record of some comprehensiveness to that extent. [*Id.* at 142]

Thus, in addition to speedier processing, a second recent innovation made by the Board of Examiners is giving examinations to "lower seniors" so that the results may be available before they graduate. Previously, only graduates could take the examinations and this had an obvious deterrent effect, since nearby school systems without examination processes could offer positions earlier. Even under the new system, however, apparently only 6,000 of the 40,000 or more predicted teacher applicants will be tested during the fall of their senior year.

Another modernization defense presented was the use of one-day, walk-in examinations to fill emergency vacancies.

Ironically, however, testimony was received that emergency vacancies often arise because the Board of Examiners has not promulgated an eligible list by the beginning of a school term and, thus, no one can be appointed to a regular teaching position in that license (although many qualified candidates have taken the regular examination and are awaiting a formal determination of their eligibility).

In any event, some witnesses suggested that the one-day, walk-in examination may have important ramifications beyond its current use in filling emergency vacancies. Presumably, its use to determine merit for regular licenses would satisfy the state constitutional and statutory obligations imposed on the Board of Examiners. In fact, Dr. Green characterized the purpose of these much simpler examinations as checking the applicant's "minimum competence to begin teaching children the next day." [*Id.* at 145] This standard — "minimum competence" — is the same standard the board says it uses for its regular examinations.

Finally, Dr. Greene maintained that the examination process, and especially the written test, should not be a deterrent because the applicants:

> ... have taken examinations of various kinds in colleges and it is no great or horrendous thing to say that such applicants ought to be able to pass a test in their subject, ought to be able to demonstrate minimum proficiency in written English, ought to be able to converse with reasonable clarity on a professional subject. [*Id.* at 140]

The System Is Rigid

Another common theme in the testimony was that the present selection system is rigid and inflexible, unduly restricting the pool of eligibles.

Murry Bergtraum, then president of the New York City Board of Education, pointed to "the emphasis on formalistic training, formalistic requirements, long periods of service" as a reason why the New York City school system has a low per-

centage of blacks and Puerto Rican professionals. [*Id.* at 9]
He testified this emphasis was, moreover, a disservice to all
applicants for professional positions.

Chancellor Scribner spoke of the current selection system
as a "form of city certification . . . laid on top of state certification" which ". . . [i]n many respects . . . is far more intri-
cate and much less flexible than state certification." [*Id.* at
33] The chancellor amplified this point with a statement
which captures the essence of the testimony of many
other witnesses:

> Because the present system of licensing severely limits the schools
> of this city in selecting professional staff, the system in its existing
> form, I believe, is self-defeating. For example, the present list of
> eligible candidates for appointment as high school principals is com-
> prised of approximately 12 names. . . . Without deprecating the
> professional ability of the candidates on this list, it is patently absurd
> to limit the search for high school principals for New York City to
> that list. It's a decimated list of a dozen candidates who qualified
> for that list on the basis of an examination given more than two and
> a half years ago. The kind of system which sets such limits does not
> serve the best interests of youth, I believe. . . . I would also submit
> that in 99 percent of the situations in the United States, you are not
> confined, restrained to this kind of a system. I would also submit to
> you as a part of this record that we ought to take a look today at
> some of the problems we have, and ask ourselves if any of it, if any
> of it, just a bit of it, may be contributed by this particular
> situation. [*Id.* at 34–35]

Dr. Greene responded to this criticism by charging that
patronage would inevitably follow the establishment of a
more "flexible" system:

> Let's examine this phrase "flexibility" which is a public relations
> word and sounds wonderful. I think you ought to want to examine
> it rather than merely accept it. It means you have a right to choose
> anybody that you want because you say that if you are the boss . . .
> you are accountable and if you are accountable, you ought to have
> the right to choose the staff. That sounds wonderful on the face of
> it. But, this is the timeworn argument that existed before Civil Ser-

vice, because every department head in public employment said that
too. The head of a fire department might say you can't hold me responsible for the fire department unless you let me choose all the
firemen. . . . Then the new head comes in. The new head doesn't
want these people. He didn't pick them. There is no flexibility any
more. He wants them out. That's the spoils system. If you want that
flexibility, that's what it leads into. And that's one of the things the
public and legislature and, I believe, the majority of people in this
city do not want in the school system. [*Id.* at 149]

But a fair review of the testimony of those who advocated
flexibility does not suggest that any believed there should be
authority to remove competent professionals from their positions in order to replace them with new, handpicked persons.
In fact, these witnesses often emphasized that their criticism
of the current selection system for its inflexibility was not a
challenge to concepts of tenure and job security (although
questions of that sort were raised in connection with accountability and promotion of school professionals).

Dr. Greene argued further that, far from restricting the pool
of eligibles, the current selection system actually results in a
larger pool. He called attention to eligible lists, such as the
elementary school assistant principals' list, with 700 to 1,000
names. According to Dr. Greene:

. . . the reality of that so-called flexibility is that the person who
makes the choice makes it from a very small group of those he
knows or those who are recommended to him or those who are
forced upon him by influence. [*Id.* 150]

According to Dr. Greene, the persons selected under a free
choice system will be "yes men" as opposed to the many "nay
sayers," iconoclasts, and innovators, who are now included on
Board of Examiners' eligible lists.

Responding to some of these concerns, Peter Strauss, Chairman of Community School Board No. 2, testified:

I want to return to the role of community school boards in the
selection process. . . . Among the dangers is the possibility that
political or other improper criteria will be used to discriminate

against qualified professionals. This should not and need not occur if
fair and reviewable standards are developed. . . . The community
school board should be required to develop objective, rational and
reviewable — I think that is important — reviewable employment
criteria which would supplement the minimum standards.
[*Id.* at 47—48]

Still Dr. Greene's dichotomy is at the very heart of the
dialogue about the professional's relationship with the community in which he works and the parents and children to
whom he is ultimately responsible. Where is the line between
a professional who is sensitive to the special needs of a community and its children and a "yes man"? Where is the line
between an iconoclast and a professional who simply cannot
relate to or understand the children he is asked to teach or
supervise? These are difficult questions which cannot be disposed of by generalities. The test of a selection process is
whether or not it can indeed make the appropriate distinctions. There is strong evidence that New York City's system
and others like it are failing.

The System Is Costly and Has Created Its Own Patronage Process

Many witnesses criticized the high direct and indirect costs of
an elaborate local examination system. The Board of Examiners'
annual budget exceeds $3.5 million. Several witnesses argued
that since the failure rate on the most popular examinations
has been so relatively low (from 2% to 28%, but seldom as
much as 20%), the cost per "incompetent" screened out is
extremely high.

According to Jeanette Hopkins, a vice-president of Metropolitan Applied Research Center:

. . . [A]ll but approximately $66,000 is paid for salaries. If the
$32,000 paid to each examiner is subtracted, about $2.8 million is
left for the Board of Examiners to disburse to assistants and consultants of their own choosing. Overall, the budget of the Board of

Examiners has increased about 233 percent during the 10 years between 1958—59 and 1968—69. By comparison, the total budget of
the Board of Education increased 175 percent during the same period.
For other comparisons, the budget of $3 million-plus of the Board of
Examiners in the year 1968—69 approximates the money spent for
libraries in all day schools, and exceeds that spent for adult education
in evening high schools. [*Id.* at 533—34]

Several witnesses testified that the large proportion of the
budget of the Board of Examiners available for salaries of
assistants is itself a form of patronage. Peter Strauss said that
the manner in which examination assistants are selected:

... is one of the things that has always distressed me very much,
that in a system which has defended itself by arguing it was so fair
and objective, the very people who did the examinations were
chosen in a system of patronage. The way you get to earn your
$3,000 or $4,000 a year as an assistant examiner is really whom you
know downtown. I've had experiences where principals and assistant
principals have complained to me that because of some personal
run-in with somebody who made the selections, they are no longer
employed as assistant examiners. [*Id.* at 49]

Andrew Donaldson, Community Superintendent of Community District No. 9 in the Bronx, who holds a number of
licenses within the school system, spoke from his personal
experience with the examination process:

There is no merit to the Board of Examiners. It has discouraged people
from coming into the school system. The actual examination ... is
not done by the four members of the Board [of Examiners] who are
carefully examined in objective tests, but by an army of hundreds of
assistant examiners, both permanent and temporary, who are paid
and who actually create the tests, conduct them and mark them. I
would suggest that the millions of dollars spent on this endeavor
could be better spent on the children of New York City. ..... The
...political patronage and interference exists right now, and has
existed in the Board of Examiners. And what appears to be merit is
strictly a facade. [*Id.* at 203—4]

Superintendent Donaldson also referred to an indirect cost of the examination process which attracted strong criticism from many witnesses — the costly private coaching courses. And the costs are not limited to the registration fee for the coaching course (although that, by itself, can be significant). There are also costs in terms of time committed to an exercise which may have limited, if any, relevance to the performance of the job, according to witnesses who had taken and given such a course. Mr. Donaldson testified:

I think we are all aware of the examination jargon, the fact that there is a kind of language which has to be learned — rote learned — to be spewed back on the examinations whether in written form or in verbal form; the fact that people make hundreds and hundreds of dollars writing these coaching books, thousands of dollars conduct-the coaching courses, which still exist, in order to learn the jargon and spew it back. . . . [E]ven in the official coaching courses, which have just been begun in the last few years by the Board of Education to prepare candidates for the exam, the phrase is used, as has always been used, "For Examination Purposes Only." At the time I took the examination, of course, there weren't any Board of Education coaching courses. You had to pay. And when they talk about minority group candidates, if I hadn't had the G.I. Bill of Rights, I probably couldn't have afforded the coaching courses. It cost $700. There were several hundred people in it. A principal, practicing principal, was conducting it, a principal who made sure that he told us that he made it a point to play golf on weekends with some of the examiners who are on the Board of Examiners. . . . The saddest part of this entire fiasco is that it has discriminated against whites more than it has discriminated against blacks. . . . Having gone through this, having sat with the hundreds in the coaching courses and having heard the . . . anguish, I can tell you most of the people who were discriminated against were not black or Puerto Rican or Spanish. These were white people. I have heard of the men who had to take their families up to the Catskills all summer and virtually abandon them so as to retire to cabins and cram and cram and cram, to learn the nonsense material in order to be able to regurgitate it on signal at top lightning speed. . . . [In the coaching courses] you are virtually trained out of doing every single thing you learned in school. Your whole orientation is "For Examination Purposes Only." You

are told by the coach over and over again. This has nothing to do
with running the school. This has nothing to do with reality. This is
in order to pass the examination. [*Id.* at 205–7]

John King, a former Executive Deputy Superintendent of
Schools and now Professor of Education at Fordham University, testified about his experience as the operator of a private
coaching course and as the moving force behind the creation
of the Board of Education's coaching courses for supervisory
examinations — the so-called Professional Promotional Seminars:

Immediately after I was appointed an assistant principal I started
coaching courses, not out of altruism but in order to supplement
my salary as an assistant principal. . . . If one wanted to become a
supervisor or if one wanted to become a teacher, he had to match
wits with the Board of Examiners with the help of a coaching
course. . . . [The examination is a] rather extravagant examination
of a person's ability to memorize facts — and I know that it can be
done that way because in giving coaching courses over the years . . . I
could guarantee that the person would pass that examination if he
did the things that we asked him to do in memorizing the necessary
mnemonics and other devices. . . . I was preparing people to pass an
examination. I was not preparing people for the principalship.
[*Id.* at 93; 100]

According to Dr. King, the Professional Promotional
Seminars, at least initially, were designed to serve the same
function — to get people through examinations. When
questioned about whether a school system doesn't seem to
be working at cross purposes when one of its arms is creating
and administering an examination process and another is preparing people to succeed in that process, Frederick Williams,
then Assistant Superintendent in charge of the Division of
Recruitment, Training and Staff Development (subsequently
Executive Deputy Superintendent), could only answer that
other institutions have done the same.

The Board of Examiners defended itself against the
criticism about the cost of the system in several ways. First,

Dr. Greene argued that, in fact, it was less expensive to use local examinations administered by the Board of Examiners than to use an alternative written examination, such as the National Teacher Examination. To support this claim, he stated that the short-answer part of the Board of Examiners' common branches elementary school teacher examination could be prepared, conducted, and graded for $5,000. If the approximately 6,000 applicants who normally take this examination annually took the NTE instead, it would cost $78,000 ($13 registration fee per applicant). Therefore, the use of the local examination would save $73,000, according to Dr. Greene. [*Id.* at 153]

The basis for Dr. Greene's $5,000 cost figure is unclear, however. Certainly, from an overall point of view, it is difficult to conceive of how so low a cost figure could result. The Board of Examiners' annual budget is more than $3.5 million. According to Dr. Greene, roughly 50,000 applicants are examined each year. That would suggest the average cost of examining each applicant is more than $70. On that basis, the cost of the common branches examination for 6,000 applicants would be more than $420,000.

But aside from the details of how the cost of Board of Examiners' written tests is computed, many witnesses considered any mandatory written test unnecessary, if not undesirable. If written tests were eliminated entirely, the cost savings would be indisputable. The Board of Examiners' response was that decentralizing the selection system would lead to expensive duplication, whether or not a written test was used. Dr. Green said:

> ... [W]e have 50,000 teachers applying to us. What will happen in New York City if there are 30 community boards and we know there are some 50,000 people who want jobs? Are the 50,000 people going to apply to Local School Board 1 and also to Local School Board 2 and 3 and 4? Is each local school board going to screen 50,000, or a thousand who are on the principal's list ... ? [*Id.* at 158]

He did not suggest whether there were mechanisms other than the Board of Examiners, such as a central recruiting and screening system, which could perform such tasks. In any case, most of the witnesses at the hearings wanted to decentralize the decisive appointment authority rather than the ministerial referral authority.

To the charge of patronage in the Board of Examiners' selection of temporary examination assistants, Ms. Unser, Dr. Greene, and Dr. Weinstein, President of the Junior High School Principals Association and a unit head of the Board of Examiners, conceded that the procedures for selection of full-time and temporary assistant examiners were entirely informal and based largely on recommendations. All stated that for years the Board of Examiners has urged the Board of Education to require examinations for *full-time* staff members to replace the current practice of year-to-year assignment of persons licensed as teachers or supervisors. Dr. Greene stated that he and Dr. Murray Rockowitz, another member of the Board of Examiners, had been appointed as a committee to develop more formal procedures for the selection of *temporary* assistant examiners, "some procedure that will be free of any taint and fairer." [*Id.* at 174] At another point, Dr. Greene said that "if charges [of patronage] are made, if this [a more formal procedure] is believed in any way to make it better and fairer . . . that's the purpose of the committee. . . ." [*Id.* at 174] And, at yet another point, he said, "If there is public dissatisfaction with the way it is being done, then it [a more formal procedure] is worth doing. . . ." [*Id.* at 175] Clearly, the Board of Examiners is becoming sensitive to public concern about the method used to expend about $2 million of its budget for temporary assistant examiners.

The final area of criticism — coaching courses — gave rise to several interrelated defenses summarized in the following exchange:

Miss Unser: . . . [T] he Board of Examiners suggested originally that there ought to be professional seminars, not to coach people for examinations because there is no special know-how or expertise to take this kind of exam as compared to anything else. . . . We suggested that professional seminars be set up to increase the professional competence of minority group applicants so that they would be better prepared to be successful in examinations.

Mr. Tractenberg: In view of your last comment, particularly, I would like to . . . get your reaction to a page . . . from the notes handed out in one of the private coaching courses . . . last fall. . . . Some of the advice given included the following: "number one, if in doubt about any item, include it, the marking key does not provide penalties for errors, no matter how foolish."

Miss Unser: . . . [W] e are not responsible for what some coaches may be saying in an effort to drum up business.

Mr. Tractenberg: I wasn't suggesting that you were responsible for them. I think it is interesting how people who are within the system, licensed people, view the examination process. . . . Among the other hints given are, "Don't waste time erasing, simply cross out. Remember, time is of the essence." Next, "Shall I use mnemonics? Yes, these constitute an integral facet of your successful examination technique. The mnemonics we will provide, used in accordance with the techniques prescribed and the subject matter presented, will do much to insure your success in this examination." Do you have a reaction, not in terms of the Board of Examiners being responsible in any direct way . . , but simply about this as a perception of how people see your exams and ways in which they can tutor people to pass them?

Miss Unser: . . . We can't stop them if they have faith in that sort of thing. . . . I didn't think it was necessary to go through that sort of thing, but if people make money out of it and other people think it will help them, we can't stop them. I don't think it reflects our philosophy at all.

Mr. Tractenberg: Do you regard it as a wasteful by-product of the examination system?

Miss Unser: I certainly do not. I think there are coaching courses all over for people who think they should have some help. We have always refused to use anyone who was engaged in coaching as an examination assistant. . . .

Mr. Tractenberg: . . . I want to point out that your by-laws say anyone who has conducted a private coaching course in the past three
years is excluded; but presumably if a person conducted one four
years ago he would be eligible to be an assistant examiner; and
similarly, someone who is currently serving as an assistant examiner
would be fully eligible under your own by-laws to be head of a private
coaching course immediately after his connection with you is severed.

Miss Unser: If he so desired, we couldn't stop him. [*Id.* at 25—26]

Data provided the Commission by the Board of Examiners
subsequent to the hearings indicated that during the three
years between 1968 and 1971 "approximately 65 examination
assistants have been removed from service because of participation in courses preparing applicants for license examinations."
[Letter from Gertrude E. Unser, Chairman, New York City
Board of Examiners, to Eleanor Holmes Norton, Chairman,
New York City Commission on Human Rights, April 22,
1971, p. 6]

The System is Inconsistent with Decentralization

Another common theme which ran through the testimony
was that a selection process which placed such great emphasis
on a centrally created, conducted, and rated examination was
inconsistent with a decentralized school system. In January
1969, the New York City Board of Education recommended
in its *Plan for Development of a Community School District
System for the City of New York* that "maintenance of a citywide competitive examination system would be inconsistent
with giving community boards powers and duties regarding
appointment and promotion of teaching and supervisory
staff. . . ." [p. 18]

This recommendation was supported by the State Commissioner of Education and State Board of Regents. Yet, the
legislature saw fit to provide for a decentralized school system with significant personnel powers given to community
boards while continuing the Board of Examiners.

At the commission hearings, Chancellor Scribner discussed this inconsistency in some detail:

> By decentralizing management control of the elementary, inter-
> mediate and junior high schools in this city the [Decentralization]
> Act gave to parents new hope of gaining greater and more direct con-
> trol over the schools which educate their children and for which they
> pay. ... The process of decentralization is far from complete. ... It
> will be a painful process, marked by occasional battles and frustrations.
> One should not expect the carving up of long centralized power to be
> a serene act, but the significant fact is that the city has begun to move
> in the direction of high promise. ... Perhaps the most critical ele-
> ment in the process of enabling a youngster to learn is the quality of
> teaching available to him. Thus, the paramount responsibility of the
> community school boards of New York City is the same as that of
> all other school boards in this country, the selection of staff for the
> school of their districts. ... It is a power and responsibility which
> school boards ought not to take lightly and an authority which
> ought not to be unnecessarily diluted by the policies of other public
> agencies. ... In this city the selection of professional school staff is
> still, in essence, a centralized process. ... [T]he list of candidates
> from which they [community boards] make their selection is defined
> by the centralized licensing system. ... In short, the present system
> of licensing is a form of city certification by us laid on top of state
> certification.
>
> ... Nationally, I would estimate that 99 percent of all school boards
> rely on state certification and their own good judgment. It is my
> personal hope that this philosophy will soon prevail in New York
> City, for until the community school boards, those people closest to
> students and parents, are empowered to staff their schools on the
> basis of state certification and their own judgment, as to com-
> petence and professional potential, these boards will operate with
> severe and undue constraints. They will not be fully responsible for
> the total management of the schools under their jurisdiction and no
> mechanism for holding these boards fully accountable for the effec-
> tiveness of their schools can be devised. [*Selection of Teachers,*
> 1972, p. 32–33]

Chancellor Scribner contrasted the general requirement of
centralized licensing with two other provisions of the Decentralization Act. Under one, each community board can
select its community superintendent, its "educational leader"

and "top man," in Chancellor Scribner's words, solely on the basis of state certification. Under another provision, schools whose reading scores fall within the lowest 45 percent of the city's schools — schools with the greatest need for outstanding professionals — may select their teachers on the basis of the NTE. According to the chancellor, the inconsistency between the philosophy underlying centralized licensing and that underlying these two provisions should be resolved in favor of the latter

Many other witnesses echoed Chancellor Scribner's sentiments from their own perspectives. Dr. Theobald, a former Superintendent of Schools, urged that the judgments of peers and supervisors about job performance should be at the heart of the selection process rather than a written examination. "[I] t would be a very parallel certification to the State [certification] rather than an eligible list in the sense that you have to take [persons] off [it] in the traditional Civil Service fashion." [*Id.* at 43]

Peter Strauss, President of Community School Board No. 2, stressed the weighty responsibilities of community boards for education programs in their districts.

> We are elected officials, accountable to our community for the success or failure of our children. Although we are to be held accountable through the elective process for their performance we have little voice in the selection of our pedagogical staff. . . . Aside from the recent questionnaires sent out by the Board of Examiners, we have absolutely no voice in the development of the standards used by the Board of Examiners for licensing teachers. As to supervisors, while we now have some choice, the choice is limited as are the tools at our command for making an intelligent selection. [*Id.* at 46—47]

Dr. Edythe J. Gaines, the Community Superintendent of District No. 12, described the problems the current selection process poses for a community superintendent trying to staff her schools. It is a tale of frustration characterized by such handicaps as limited choices from a centralized list and ineligibility of experienced professionals recruited by the community district. Dr. Gaines summarized as follows:

> The . . . [process] is unnecessarily centralized. We can't select the
> staff we need for our unique needs. What could we do if our system
> became more open? We could recruit our own staff. Therefore, we
> could seek staff in less restrictive talent pools. We would not have to
> go to Puerto Rico or the South to find the people we are looking for.
> They are right in our own backyard. . . . I am not only talking about
> the ethnic or bilingual thing. I am talking also about people who
> understand what open learning is about and who want to be a part
> of that. . . . We could devise truly meaningful staff development
> programs locally arranged . . . by which we could optimize their
> abilities and minimize their weaknesses. . . . We could make our
> schools more human and humane institutions which would develop
> not only our children, but everybody in the system, including
> teachers, assistant principals, principals, and even community
> superintendents. [*Id.* at 55—56]

Frustration with the current highly centralized selection
mechanism and the belief that largely local selection would
operate more effectively were not limited to community
superintendents. Witnesses at other professional supervisory
levels within the system shared Dr. Gaines' views. Several
school principals who testified at the hearings said that the
present selection process was not only inconsistent with the
exercise of meaningful responsibility by elected community
boards and their superintendents, it was also inconsistent
with the principal's discharge of his or her responsibility.

Certain defenses of the current selection process which
have already been discussed — that it results in a larger pool
of eligibles and greater diversity and that it ensures due process and a system of merit and fitness — could be raised here
as well. A more pointed argument, which has also been discussed, is pertinent. Dr. Greene maintained that a completely
decentralized personnel system would be costly and duplicative.

> Is each local school board going to screen 50,000 [teacher applicants],
> or a thousand who are on the principal's list . . . ? Or, if we have City

College or Hunter College and you have 30 different school boards,
each one with a topnotch recruiting unit, two, three . . . top recruiters, high salaried people, should each of the 30 go to Hunter
College and give them pep talks to come to their unit? [*Id.* at 158]

The problem Dr. Greene foresees may be a straw man,
though. Under decentralization, the experience, thus far, suggests that in the areas where community boards have reasonably unfettered selection powers they have neither experienced
great problems in screening applicants nor wound up with
expensive and unnecessarily duplicative personnel mechanisms.
Self-selection by applicants may offer some explanation. Many
applicants have clear preferences which they make known for
particular community districts; so nowhere near the citywide
total number of applicants has to be considered by any community board. Also, the City Board's Personnel Office can
play a useful role as a coordinator and clearinghouse. For example, under the "45% provision," community boards are
free to appoint teachers to positions in schools which fall
among the lowest 45% citywide based on a special reading
test without resort to regular Board of Examiners eligible
lists. One of the alternatives is the use of the NTE. The City
Board's Personnel Office already makes available to interested
community boards information about applicants who have
achieved NTE scores which qualify them under this alternative.

*   *   *

The clear weight of informed opinion at the commission's
hearings favored elimination of elaborate, locally created,
written testing procedures. For those procedures have not recently demonstrated great worth, even toward the realization
of their most commonly stated advantages. Screening out incompetents? Eliminating patronage and a "spoils system" by
objectivity and professional development and administration?
Upgrading the professional status of teaching? All are worthy

goals certainly. But the record of mandatory, centralized
written testing procedures in helping to reach them is spotty
at best. Many witnesses went much further to argue that such
testing procedures are actually a major impediment to the
realization of an effective urban school system. Whatever their
advantages, these procedures, as epitomized by the New York
City selection model, now carry with them unacceptably
high costs in dollars, manpower, inconvenience and frustration. Moreover, as the next chapter demonstrates, the legal
and psychometric problems raised by substantial reliance
on many written tests for employment purposes are formidable. They may actually preclude the use of such tests.
Finally, as Chapter 7 indicates, the available selection of
ternatives are sufficiently promising to make dogged retention
of the existing procedures untenable.

CHAPTER 6

SELECTING THE URBAN TEACHER: TESTING THE WRITTEN TEST

The constitutions of most states contain a "civil service" provision; a requirement that appointments to civil service positions be made on the basis of "merit and fitness" for the particular position. Many of these provisions go further to require that merit and fitness be determined "to the extent practicable" by examinations, which "to the extent practicable" must be competitive. [*See, e.g.,* N.Y. Const. Art, 5, *Aff'd.* sec. 6 (18940]

Teaching and supervisory positions are in the civil service and, therefore, subject to these requirements. But a number of questions are raised by the constitutional language. How is "merit and fitness" to be determined and by whom? What is an "examination"? What is a "competitive examination"? Who determines the practicability of using an examination of any kind and of using a competitive examination?

In most states detailed statutes establish a state civil service department or commission and perhaps local counterparts as well. Moreover, the public schools often have their own parallel administrative structure to handle matters of personnel qualification and selection. These administrative agencies, state and local, typically establish detailed regulations which provide for the categories of positions in which licenses are granted, the procedures to be followed, and the criteria to be used in determining eligibility.

The determination of whether an examination is "practicable" for a particular position or class of positions is often made by

the administrative agency; those positions for which an examination is deemed not practicable are "exempt." The agency often
determines the practicability of a "competitive" examination too.
But sometimes the state legislature itself makes the judgment of
practicability. That has been the case, for example, with teachers
and supervisors in the New York City schools. The legislature
specifically provided for a system of examinations, which is administered by the Board of Examiners. The legislature also
specified that for teachers the examinations would be competitive *(i.e.,* resulting in a list of eligibles ranked by their scores
on the examination). Although supervisors' examinations by
legislative mandate also used to be competitive, that has been
changed to qualifying, or noncompetitive *(i.e.,* the eligible list
just includes in alphabetical order all who have passed the
examination).

What are these instruments for determining merit and fitness—
"examinations" and "competitive examinations"? As a matter
of law, neither category of examination is required to include a
written test component. Any reasonably objective and
quantifiable methods for determining a candidate's capacity to
perform the job in question are sufficient. Indeed, many civil
service agencies have used "unassembled examinations" as the
basis for compiling their eligible lists. An unassembled examination may consist of merely a review of record and references.

Written tests are, however, usually an integral part of the
civil service approach to merit and fitness. Together with reviews of record, oral interviews, physical examinations, and,
occasionally, performance tests, they comprise the "examination." And commonly they become the heart of the selection
process. Why is this? Probably because they create the impression of objectivity and fairness. After all, they can be given and
graded without reference to the identity of the candidate. They
result in a tangible, reviewable record. Most Americans are fully
conditioned to believe that if the same questions are asked to
all applicants for a position, and if these questions appear to

involve "objective facts," the written test is an unimpeachable way to determine "merit and fitness."

But there are other purported advantages to written tests. They are said to be relatively inexpensive to obtain and administer, and very easy and inexpensive to grade, at least if they are of the short-answer variety.

If a selection process based on written tests were really such an objective way to test merit and fitness, and, to boot, were inexpensive and easy to use, its value *would* be unassailable. And its only attackers would be those who were misguided or those who opposed appointments to civil service positions on the basis of merit. As we saw in Chapter 1, however, the kind of written test-oriented procedure used in New York City has been vigorously attacked by a broad array of educators and citizens for a broad range of reasons. For the most part they place in doubt whether such a procedure is actually easy to use and inexpensive, and whether its use facilitates the recruitment and selection of qualified personnel at all.

Important criticism of another sort is coming from another source. The courts are making increasingly clear that a selection process, especially one relying heavily on written tests, must have other attributes. It must meet legal standards imposed not only by state constitutions and statutes but by the United States Constitution and federal statutes as well. It is no longer sufficient for an employer to hold up an "objective" written test and assert that reliance on it assures that the selection process is nondiscriminatory in purpose and effect. The courts are beginning to undermine the average American's Pavlovian response to such a test. In case after case, the courts are telling us that more is required to support the legality of a selection procedure. Especially is this true of public employers and the civil service system.

This is a development of enormous importance. For years many people have argued that certain examination processes were invalid and discriminatory, but efforts at legislative or administrative reform have had little impact. The defenders of the system were usually able to wrap themselves in the cloak of "merit," "objectivity," and "purity" and to discredit their critics as advocates, witting or unwitting, of a return to the "pork barrel" and a "spoils system." The availability of the courts, and especially the federal courts, to consider and deal with the charges gives new life to these reform efforts. Indeed, court decisions rejecting some selection procedures on legal grounds will pave the way for legislative action, either because the decisions have directly invalidated statutory procedures or because the decisions have provided the legislature with some political insulation if it makes changes which are unpopular with powerful lobbying groups.

The importance of the judiciary's role may be especially great in school districts like New York City where existing selection procedures have demonstrated such impressive staying power against determined reform efforts. In the mid-1960's, when even the United Federation of Teachers was its sworn enemy (and brought suit to overturn some of its procedures), the Board of Examiners hung on. Now, with the UFT and the Council of Supervisors and Administrators firmly in its camp, the board may be even harder to budge by traditional lobbying means. But there are signs that the board may not fare so well in the courts. In July 1971, the Federal District Court for the Southern District of New York preliminarily enjoined the Board of Examiners from giving new supervisory examinations or promulgating eligible lists based on supervisory examinations already given, and preliminarily enjoined the Board of Education from making appointments from existing supervisory lists. In effect, the court shut down the whole statutory procedure for the licensing of supervisory personnel. This significant step was taken by the court, in the case of *Chance v. Board of Examiners,* after the plaintiffs had convinced the court of the likelihood that they would succeed in proving the illegality of the procedures at full trial. The Board of Education, which is after all responsible for operating the school system, did not appeal the court's decision and, instead, installed an interim procedure for appointing acting supervisors. The Board of Examiners did appeal but was unsuccessful. [330 F. Supp. 203 (S.D.N.Y. 1971), *aff'd,* 458 F. 2d 1167 (2d Cir. 1972)] This decision, the first in which a major Northern school district's selection procedures may be held unlawfully discriminatory, has enormous implications. The implications warrant and will get detailed consideration later in this chapter. But in order for that discussion and the discussion about other aspects of reliance on written tests to be meaningful, it is necessary to explore first the developing legal and psychometric contexts. (Some of the material about the legal context was drawn from the testimony of Stephen J. Pollak, former Assistant Attorney General in charge of the Civil Rights Division. [*Selection of Teachers,* 1972, pp. 422–32]

The Legal Background

The Fourteenth Amendment to the United States Constitution provides in Section 1:

> . . . nor shall any State deprive any person of life, liberty, or property without due process of law; nor deny to any person within its jurisdiction the equal protection of the laws.

Boards of education, their superintendents, principals, and other officers and employees, are agents of the state; as such they are bound by the Fourteenth Amendment and may not exclude a person from practising his or her profession "in a manner or for reasons that contravene the Due Process or Equal Protection clauses. . . ." [*Schware v. Board of Examiners,* 353 U.S. 232, 239 (1957)] The Due Process clause requires that their conduct must not be arbitrary, capricious, or unreasonable. Thus, if a school district based its selection process on a written test which had little or no relationship to the job in question, a candidate who was excluded on the basis of the written test might have been denied due process. Several recent federal court decisions support this proposition. [*See, e.g., Armstead v. Starkville Mun. Sep. School Dist.,* 325 F. Supp. 560 (N.D. Miss. 1971), *aff'd in pertinent part,* 461 F. 2d 276 (5th Cir. 1972), where the court specifically held that defendants' uses of the Graduate Record Examination violated the Due Process clause because they constituted "arbitrary and unreasonable qualifications for employment" wholly "apart from [their] discriminatory aspects" (325 F. supp. at 570); and *Baker v. Columbus Mun. Sep. School Dist.,* 329 F. Supp. 706 (N.D. Miss. 1971), *aff'd,* 462 F. 2d 1112 (5th Cir. 1972), where the court concluded that "apart from its discriminatory aspects," use of the National Teacher Examination without a demonstrated correlation between test scores and job performance violated the Due Process clause. (329 F. Supp. at 722)]

The conduct of school districts (and other public employers) must also not deny equal protection of the laws. Since *Brown v. Board of Education,* 347 U.S. 483 (1954), that has meant that school boards may not discriminate, directly or indirectly, ingeniously or ingenuously, on account of race, religion, or national origin. The use of written tests in the selection process must meet this constitutional requirement.

The increasing body of law in this area provides insights into the approach of the courts and the consequent guidelines which are being developed for public employers. The court's starting point in the equal protection analysis is whether the plaintiffs have been able to establish a *prima facie* case of unconstitutionality by demonstrating that the selection process has resulted in *de facto* racial or ethnic discrimination—that is, a racial or ethnic classification. Courts have evaluated the plaintiffs' factual evidence against several standards. Some courts have compared the racial or ethnic composition of the work force against the composition of the *general* population in that geographic area. [*See, e.g., Carter v. Gallagher,* 3 FEP

Cases 692 (D. Minn. 1971), *aff'd in pertinent part,* 452 F. 2d
315 (8th Cir. 1971), *aff'd in pertinent part en banc,* 452 F. 2d
327 (8th Cir. 1972), *cert. denied,* 406 U.S. 950 (1972)
[Minneapolis firemen] ; *Western Addition Community Organization v. Alioto,* 330 F. Supp. 536 (N.D. Cal. 1971), *prelim.
inj. granted,* 340 F. Supp. 1351 (N.D. Cal. 1972), *Supple-
mental decrees issued,* 5 FEP Cases, 221, 222, 223 (N.D. Cal. 1972)
[San Francisco firemen] ; *Penn v. Stumpf,* 308 F. Supp. 1238
(N.D. Cal. 1970) [Oakland policemen] ; *Arrington v. Mass.
Bay Transp. Auth'y,* 306 F. Supp. 1355 (D. Mass. 1969)
[transit workers] ; *Davis v. Washington,* 4 FEP Cases 1132
(D.D.C. 1972) [Washington, D.C., policemen] ; *Fowler v.
Schwarzwalder,* 5 FEP Cases 43, 270 (D. Minn. 1972) [St.
Paul firemen] See also *The New York Times,* Dec. 24, 1972,
p. 31, col. 1, regarding a decision involving Cleveland policemen.] These cases involved jobs of a relatively unskilled sort,
at least in the sense that limited educational and other special
requirements were present. Consequently, many people in
the general population would at least be eligible to compete
for the positions.

Where, however, professional skills of lawyers, doctors,
professors, engineers, architects, "and practitioners of other
learned callings" [*Castro v. Beecher,* 334 F. Supp. 930, 936,
clarified, 334 F. Supp. 947, *judgment modified,* 334 F. Supp.
950 (D. Mass. 1971), *aff'd in part, rev'd in part, op. modified,
remanded,* 459 F. 2d 725 (1st Cir. 1972)] are involved, some
courts are less willing to use the general population standard.
Instead, they may compare the percentage of minority group
employees in one school district with the percentages in other
comparable districts. That was one of the bases of the court's
finding of a *de facto* racial classification in the *Chance* case,
where New York City's figures for supervisory personnel were
far below those of the next four largest districts in the country.
Or, the court may look to the pass-fail rates of different ethnic
groups on the examinations under scrutiny. The courts in

Chance, Western Addition Community Organization, and *Castro* all considered this factor.

Whichever standard the court uses, the plaintiffs must be able to demonstrate that the representation of blacks, or Spanish-Americans, or Mexican-Americans, or other minority groups in defendants' work force falls substantially below the yardstick. For the difference must create an inference that something in the selection process works to screen out disproportionately more minority group members.

If the plaintiffs fail to demonstrate this to the court's satisfaction, they cannot establish a violation of the Equal Protection clause. As we have seen, they may still be able to demonstrate a violation of the Due Process clause. Or, they may be able to prevail under state law. A state constitution which requires appointments based on "merit and fitness" may be violated by the use of a written test which has no proven job-relatedness, a concept which will be explored shortly. Moreover, some state laws, like New York's, expressly require the testing body to "periodically review the validity and reliability of examinations as well as examination procedures. . . ." [N.Y. State Educ. Law Sec. 2569(1)]

If the plaintiffs *are* able to demonstrate *de facto* racial or ethnic discrimination, the court will move to the second part of the equal protection analysis—is there sufficient basis for the defendants' use of the particular selection procedure despite its effect of creating a *de facto* racial or ethnic classification? The federal courts which have considered this question in connection with employers' selection processes agree at least that the employers, public and private, have a heavy burden to justify the use of such selection devices. But that does not answer the question of what the defendants must actually demonstrate. It seems clear that evidence of a lack of discriminatory intent is necessary but not sufficient. For ingenuous discrimination can violate the Equal Protection clause. And it is unintended discrimination that seems principally at issue in the recent cases. [But see *Allen v. City of Mobile*, 4 FEP Cases 1290 (5th Cir. 1972), *dissenting op.*, Goldberg, J., for a critique of the traditional approach to determining intent.]

If defendants must show more than simply a lack of malice, what is it? There are two approaches to proving a violation of the Equal Protection clause; the "rational relationship" test and the "compelling state interest" test. The former has typically been used in areas of economic regulation and the latter where either the classification involved was "suspect," as in the case of racial classifications, or where the interest asserted by the plaintiffs was a "fundamental" interest, as the right to vote.

According to the Court of Appeals for the Second Circuit in the *Chance* case, "Although state action invidiously discriminating on the basis of race has long called for the 'most rigid scrutiny' . . ., the Supreme Court has yet to apply that stringent test to a case such as this, in which the allegedly unconstitutional action unintentionally resulted in discriminatory effects. . . ." [458 F. 2d at 1177] While that may be so, a number of lower federal courts seem to be applying that or an equivalent standard in employment testing cases. Thus, in the *Baker* case, the Court of Appeals for the Fifth Circuit said that "in order to withstand an equal protection attack it [the selection process] must be justified by an overriding purpose independent of its racial effects." [462 F. 2d at 1114]. And in the *Carter* case the court quoted and applied the "business necessity" standard laid down by the Supreme Court in *Griggs v. Duke Power Co.*, 401 U.S. 424 (1971), *reversing,* 420 F. 2d 1225 (4th Cir. 1970) [452 F. 2d at 326], and upheld various aspects of the district court's decision based on the compelling state interest test. In *Arrington* the court held that tests resulting in unintended discrimination were "constitutionally suspect," requiring for justification a "demonstrated correlation between scores . . . and ability to perform." [306 F.

Supp. at 1358]. In *Pickens v. Okolona Mun. Sep. School Dist.*,
No. EC. 6956-K (N.D. Miss., Aug. 11, 1971) (mimeo. op.), the
court found that use of the National Teacher Examination,
where it had a discriminatory impact, placed the burden on
the employer to show an "absolute, overwhelming necessity.
. . . [I] t would have to be shown that [it was] the only way
it was possible to obtain competent and worthy teachers."
[Slip op. at 17–18]

A similar strict test has been applied in cases arising under
Title VII of the Civil Rights Act of 1964. Until recently, Title
VII covered only private employers, but the Equal Protection
clause of the Fourteenth Amendment may impose at least as
strict an obligation on public employers. (Some commentators
believe, however, that proof of discriminatory effect may be
less burdensome in Title VII cases as a result of *Griggs*
decision.) Indeed, many federal courts considering alleged employment discrimination by governmental bodies have applied
either directly or by analogy the Title VII cases. Now of course
there is an even clearer basis for applying those cases. The
Equal Employment Opportunity Act of 1972 [Pub. L. 92–
261, Mar. 24, 1972, 86 Stat. 103] extended Title VII's cover-
age to governmental agencies and political subdivisions, including school districts.

The leading Title VII case is *Griggs*. There the Supreme
Court ruled that "the touchstone is business necessity. If an
employment practice which operates to exclude Negroes cannot be shown to be related to job performance, the practice is
prohibited." [401 U.S. at 431]. Cases since *Griggs* have made
it clear that for an employer to support a claim of "business
necessity" it must make a very strong showing that test scores
are correlated with job performance and that there is no less
discriminatory alternative. For example, in *Robinson v.
Lorillard Corp.*, 444 F. 2d 791, 798 and n. 7 (4th Cir. 1971),
the court defined *Griggs'* business necessity test as follows:

... The test is whether there exists an overriding legitimate business purpose such that the practice is necessary to the safe and efficient operation of the business. Thus, the business purpose must be sufficiently compelling to override any racial impact; the challenged practice must effectively carry out the business purpose it is alleged to serve; and there must be available no acceptable alternative policies or practices which would better accomplish the business purpose advanced, or accomplish it equally well with a lesser differential racial impact.

Certainly no less can be expected of a public employer under the Equal Protection clause's compelling state interest test. So, if a court finds that to be the appropriate test, the school district will have to demonstrate the job-relatedness of the selection procedure, that it is necessary to the accomplishment of the district's personnel policies, and that there is no less discriminatory alternative. It is difficult to conceive of circumstances under which a school district or other public employer could demonstrate such a compelling state interest. The Court of Appeals in *Baker* suggested that a "school district's desire to improve its faculty may be such an overriding purpose, providing the policies and procedures employed to implement this goal are clearly related to it." [462 F. 2d at 1114] But, the court went on quickly to add that the case before it was not such a case. Neither are most of the cases thus far presented to other courts.

But even if the less stringent rational interest test is applied, the school district will still have a heavy burden to discharge, one that few public employers have succeeded with in recent cases. The Court of Appeals in *Chance,* for example, was able to avoid deciding whether the compelling interest test should be applied because it determined that the defendants failed under the rational interest test. According to the court, both tests require that the defendants prove the job-relatedness of their selection process. The difference between them is that the compelling state interest test also would require the defendants "to demonstrate that no less discriminatory means of obtaining its supervisory personnel were available." [458 F. 2d at 1177]

In most cases, as in *Chance,* proving job-relatedness is a bigger hurdle than the defendants can deal with. Before we consider the legal principles in this area, however, it is necessary to have some understanding of the basic psychometric concepts which relate to the validity of an examination process. Therefore, a short psychometric primer is in order. The information which follows was extracted principally from testimony of expert witnesses participating in the segment of the Human Rights Commission hearings devoted to test validity. [*Selection of Teachers,* 1972, pp. 401–33]

A Psychometric Primer

An examination process is evaluated by three principal criteria— objectivity, reliability, and validity. *Objectivity* signifies that, to the extent possible, each applicant is evaluated on the basis of criteria and by means which are applied uniformly to all applicants; that is, there is no bias or discrimination against any applicant or group of applicants. Accordingly, every effort must be made to neutralize the subjectivity of those who construct, administer and grade the examinations.

Reliability refers to the consistency with which an examination measures what it purports to measure. An optimally reliable examination, therefore, is one on which each applicant will achieve the same score no matter how many times he takes it.

Finally, *validity* expresses the degree to which an examination actually measures what it is used to measure. In the case of examinations used for employment purposes, validity is often referred to as "job-relatedness." Two types of validity dominated the testimony on this subject—content validity and predictive validity. (Other types include face and construct validity.)

According to Dr. Robert Thorndike, Professor of Psychology and Education at Columbia Teachers College and a testing consultant to the Board of Examiners, content validity is assessed in terms of how well the examination tasks match specific parts of the performance required on the job and how important those parts are to total performance. This assessment generally is made both by those familiar with the particular job and by those expert in creating examination tasks to reflect important parts of job performance.

Predictive validity, on the other hand, is an examination's ability to identify who is likely to perform well on the job. This type of validity usually is evaluated by empirical studies to determine whether examination scores are closely related to appropriate measures of success on the job.

Two examples should be sufficient to illustrate the meaning of these two types of validity and the difference between them. The most common example of a content valid examination is a typing test for prospective typists. The examination task, typing, is identical with the major job task and, therefore, is obviously job-related. But the typing test may have limited predictive validity. The fastest and most accurate typist may not necessarily be the best employee if he or she lacks diligence, good judgment, knowledge of grammar, or other skills that may be important in a particular job setting. Moreover, this kind of obvious content valid test is less readily available as the job in question becomes more sophisticated and requires less tangible skills. A teacher's job, for example, does not directly involve writing answers to questions; so determining the level of content validity of a written test for teachers involves a more detailed inquiry, as we shall see later in this chapter.

Another example may indicate how these validity principles apply in the teacher context. A portion of an examination for elementary school teachers might be designed to test knowledge of English grammar. (This is like most Board of Examiners' written tests which, according to Drs. Greene and Thorndike, are proficiency tests designed to measure acquired knowledge, rather than aptitude tests.) Because most elementary school teachers teach English grammar, this subject matter knowledge may relate to an appropriate job task. Whether or not it is sufficiently important to warrant being singled out as a part of the selection process must be assessed by those completely familiar with teaching in the schools today. On the other hand, whether or not the test items designed to determine if applicants know English grammar are likely to do so must be assessed by test experts. Only then can the content validity of this portion of the written test be determined. But even if it validly tests applicants' knowledge of English grammar, success on it is no assurance of success in actually teaching students English grammar. The only prediction about performance made by a test designed to be content valid is the negative prediction that a person without a minimum knowledge of English grammar will probably not be a good teacher of it.

A determination of predictive validity does not depend on this kind of judgment. Rather, it requires identifying criteria of good English grammar *teaching*. Then, an empirical study must be conducted to see whether high scorers on these test items tend to be better at teaching English grammar than low scorers.

Because a proficiency test assesses the extent to which an applicant has certain specific skills or knowledge required on a job, according to Dr. Thorndike, it is usually validated by a content validity study. An aptitude test, on the other hand, determines whether or not a person has the underlying abilities that are necessary if he or she is to acquire the knowledge and skills of a job. A predictive validity study is normally used in this case.

Some testing experts state, however, that predictive validity studies are appropriate, if not necessary, for proficiency tests as well. Dr. Thorndike considered such a study to have "supplementary relevance." [*Selection of Teachers,* 1972, p. 403] Another Board of Examiners' testing consultant, Dr. Aaron Carton, Professor of Education at Stony Brook, went further, stating in an affidavit that "without studies of *predictive validity (i.e.,* assessments as to how well the tests select individuals who function successfully on the job) the very assumptions as to what constitutes expertise in any given field cannot be fully tested." [*Id.* at 166]

This is important testimony because, as we have seen, Drs. Greene and Thorndike have said that most Board of Examiners' written tests are primarily proficiency tests (although Dr. Richard Barrett, another psychometric expert who has reviewed these tests, testified that they are aptitude tests because a teacher's or supervisor's job does not involve writing answers to questions but rather using skills or communicating knowledge). Much of the criticism of the Board of Examiners' tests was based on the lack of predictive validity studies.

A final background item is important. Validity, considered in its broader, lay sense, has several components. One, the psychometrician's (testing expert's) concept of validity just discussed. Two, the lawyer's concept of legality under constitutional, statutory or regulatory standards. Three, the layman's concept of general relevance to the school system and the education of children.

*   *   *

With this brief background, we can now return to the equal protection analysis. What is sufficient evidence that an employment test is job-related to permit an employer to discharge its heavy burden?

The courts of course rely substantially on the testimony of psychometric experts. For job-relatedness is just another way of saying validated. If the employer is unable to find a responsible test expert to state that the test procedures are valid, there should be no way for the court to rule in favor of the employer. [*See, e.g., Western Addition Community Organization, supra.*] Some courts will inject their own "common sense" view of whether or not the test seems job-related but that is usually to assist the court in resolving a conflict between experts. [*See, e.g., Chance, supra.*] If no previous validation studies had been carried out, even expert supporting testimony at the trial may not be sufficient to carry the day for the employer. [*See, e.g., Arrington, supra; Armstead, supra.*] Similarly, if a test validated for a limited purpose or a particular type of job is used for a broader purpose or a different type of job, its validity is severely compromised. A perfect example of that is the overreliance of several Southern school districts on the National Teacher Examination. [*See, e.g., Baker, supra.*] The validity of the National Teacher Examination has also been undercut in another manner—by the establishment of arbitrary, unreasonable, or discriminatory pass marks. The test's creator, Educational Testing Service, has become very careful now in defining the scope of its usefulness and validity.

Evidence that the employer is making improvements in the test seldom causes the court to stay its hand. Indeed, it may accomplish exactly the opposite result. A number of courts have reacted to such evidence by stating that it represents recognition by the employer that the test has been invalid or discriminatory. [*See, e.g., Carter, supra.*]

The court may have a relatively easy task under these sorts of circumstances. But what if the defendants do produce substantial evidence of validation? As the court said in *Arrington, supra:*

> The difficult issue in situations such as these is the determination of the level of business relevance necessary to justify the utilization of a test. It is one thing to demand that a test be designed to measure abilities relevant to job performance and be an accurate determinant of those abilities, but quite another to decide what showing is

adequate to indicate that a particular test is performing that function successfully. [306 F. Supp. at 1358–59].

A number of federal courts have looked for guidance to the Equal Employment Opportunity Commission's *Guidelines on Employee Selection Procedures,* 29 C.F.R. Sec. 1607. Although they are not legally binding, the *Guidelines* are entitled to considerable weight. [*Hicks v. Crown Zellerbach Corp.,* 319 F. Supp. 314 (E.D. La. 1970), *modified,* 321 F. Supp. 1241 (E.D. La. 1971)] They offer guidance in an area which will increasingly come before the courts—what kind of validation is the employer required to undertake to discharge his burden? The two main contenders are likely to be content validity and predictive validity. Thus far, the courts have given limited guidance in this area.

In *Chance,* the Court of Appeals said, "We also need not decide whether, upon a showing of invidious discriminatory impact in a case such as this, the State is required to establish predictive validity as well as content validity for its job testing procedures." [458 F. 2d at 1177, n.16] Some courts have said that predictive, empirical, or criterion-related, validity may be preferable but none has yet expressly required it. The approach of the *EEOC Guidelines* is to require predictive validation except where it "is not feasible" [29 C.F.R. Sec. 1607.5], in which case content validation may be appropriate. The *Guidelines* add yet another wrinkle—differential validation. Where technically feasible (that is, where there are sufficient numbers of minority group individuals to achieve findings of statistical and practical significance and where unbiased job criteria exist), a test should be validated for each minority group for which it is used. Any differential rejection rates must be relevant to performance on the job or the test can't be used for minority groups it discriminated against. With EEOC's jurisdiction expanded to include public employees, its testing *Guidelines* will inevitably be given more weight by the courts in teacher selection and other public employee cases; differential validation is, therefore, likely to be increasingly before the courts in public employment cases. In fact, the Justice Department has already begun to file suits charging public agencies with discrimination against racial minorities in filling public jobs. The first two suits were against Montgomery, Alabama and Los Angeles, California [*New York Times,* Aug. 8, 1972, p. 12, col. 3]

If, after weighing the employer's justification by these kinds of standards, the court concludes that the examination is not sufficiently job-related to explain and warrant its racially discriminatory effect, the court must conclude that the selection process violates the constitutional right of minority group applicants to the equal protection of the laws. Other difficult legal questions remain, however. What remedies should the court order to correct the situation?

A host of possibilities exists. For the federal courts have broad equity powers to fashion appropriate remedies, especially in cases where the plaintiff's constitutional rights have been infringed. The most difficult remedial issues grow out of the judiciary's efforts to eliminate the present effects of past discrimination. These may go well beyond the remedies necessary to prevent future discrimination.

Thus, a number of federal courts have totally enjoined the operation of the existing system *and* have either ordered substantial changes before it could be used again or ordered the development of a totally new and validated system. [*See, e.g., Castro, supra; Western Addition Community Organization, supra; Chance, supra; Vogler v. McCarty, Inc.,* 2 FEP Cases 491 (C.D. La. 1970), *modified,* 4 FEP Cases 11 (E.D. La. 1971), *aff'd,* 451 F. 2d 1236 (5th Cir. 1971) [Title VII case involving discrimination by a union].] Other courts have enjoined the operation of the existing system, too, but have ordered the hiring of minority group candidates on some specified basis. [*See, e.g., Arrington, supra; NAACP v. Allen, supra; Carter, supra.*] This so-called preferential hiring of

minority group candidates may accompany or be in lieu of the
development of a new or markedly improved selection process.
Its implications are being heatedly debated and will be discussed later in this chapter.

In some cases, federal courts have exercised their discretion
in fashioning remedies by permitting the existing examination
process to continue (usually because of the time and expense
involved in developing a new and validated system, or because
of uncertainty about whether or not there was a clearly valid
alternative) but with some important modifications. For example, in *Carter* the court authorized the continued administration of a written test but stipulated that it be used as a
qualifying rather than competitive device. And there, the
court went further to order that appointments from the en-
suing "qualified" pool be on the basis of one minority appointee for every three vacancies. Other court-ordered modifications of the existing system may include lowering of the
pass rate, giving heavier weight to supervisors' ratings, reducing physical qualifications or educational background requirements, or adding a wholly new factor. Each raises obvious problems. But each reflects the growing sense of the
federal courts that employment discrimination, especially
of the unintentional kind, will not be eliminated simply by a
judicial determination that the old system is no good.

Indeed, there is already much evidence that if the courts
do not require specific corrective measures, and a selection
process of questionable validity is permitted to continue in
existence, there will be increasing efforts to find ways to make
appointments without reference to that process. The most
common end run is the use of "acting" appointments. The
theory is that the appointment is only an interim one and,
therefore, does not require use of the formal selection process. In fact, however, in school districts such as New York
City the acting appointment strategy has long been used to
place in supervisory positions persons who could not or would

not be licensed under the formal Board of Examiners' process. Frequently, these persons "act" as principals and other supervisors year after year. The courts are increasingly being asked to rule on the propriety of such arrangements and the extent to which they are prepared to accept them as valid exercises of school board discretion is revealing. In one case, *Board of Education v. Nyquist,* 322 N.Y.S. 2d 370 (App. Div. 3d Dept. 1971), the court did decide that an acting principal cannot be reappointed indefinitely. At the moment, however, that seems a stricter approach than most. In an almost contemporaneous New York State court decision, for example, *Application of Council of Supervisors and Administrators,* 324 N.Y.S. 2d 778 (Sup. Ct. N.Y. Co. 1971), the court sustained a community board's appointment of an acting elementary school principal although there were 215 candidates on the official eligible list. The person appointed had a state certificate but not a New York City license. Nevertheless, the court said it was permissible for the community board to appoint him after it found none of the 215 "eligible" people suitable. And this was so despite the fact that a rather transparent subterfuge had to be used. Under New York State law a "regular" vacancy, one which is permanent or complete in nature, has to be filled by a permanent appointment if there are persons eligible. On the other hand, an acting principal can be appointed if the vacancy is temporary. Through the cooperation of the city board of education, the community board was able to convert a regular vacancy into a temporary one. The sleight of hand necessary to accomplish this was based on the technical assignment to the vacant position of a regular principal who was on extended medical leave. So, there was need for a replacement, but it could be an acting person.

The court ruled that this was not a sufficiently "flagrant and arbitrary flouting of the law that a temporary injunction should issue." [324 N.Y.S. 2d at 781] The court was obviously influenced by the fact that the New York Court of Appeals, the state's highest court, had earlier upheld another route around formal licensing procedures. In *Council of Supervisors and Administrators v. Board of Education,* 23 N.Y. 2d 458 (1969), the court permitted the Ocean Hill/Brownsville Demonstration District to create the position of "Elementary School Principal, Demonstration District" and fill it without reference to existing eligible lists for elementary school principals on the ground that it was a new and different position. The court supported its decision by indicating that the courts should narrowly confine their review of school authorities' decisions and, further, that there must be broad discretion for educational experimentation. The court did suggest, however, that if the new position became a permanent position, it would have to be filled by means of the formal selection process.

Lower courts in New York have followed the lead of the Court of Appeals by giving substantial discretion to school boards, especially in New York City, to appoint candidates on an acting basis if no one on the eligible list for the position was judged to be "qualified." [*See, e.g., Matter of Council of Supervisors and Administrators v. Board of Education,* 318 N.Y.S. 2d 220 (1971); *Matter of Council of Supervisors and Administrators* (Kings Co., N.Y., Law Journal, Dec. 29, 1970).]

Of course, the impact of the federal courts' opinions in *Chance* is being felt too. As we will discuss in Chapter 7, all New York City supervisory appointments have been on an acting basis since the preliminary injuction issued in *Chance* in July 1971.

Efforts to avoid the harshness of a competitive examination system are not limited to school personnel. The much criti-, cized New York City civil service system is a case in point. Mayor Lindsay has been under fire for using provisional appointments outside of the civil service to hire or advance chosen aides. In October 1972, Deputy Mayor Edward K. Hamilton announced a frontal assault—a number of major changes aimed at expanding the mayor's ability to select and promote new employees. Some of the changes require legislative action — lateral entry into middle- and upper-level jobs so that qualified persons, especially scientists and managers, would not have to start at the bottom of the system; and qualifying rather than competitive examinations for higher-level jobs. But other changes, according to the deputy mayor, will be carried out administratively. They include widening of the "examination" concept to give greater weight to "training and experience," and widening the marking system on tests by rounding scores to the nearest whole number rather than carrying it out to two decimal places. The effect of the first administrative change is expected to be greater correlation between successful performance on the job and promotion. Under the present approach there is no effective linkage, according to Mr. Hamilton. The second administrative change is also expected to have a substantial effect. In a large civil service system, the consequence of rounding to the nearest whole number is to "increase enormously the number of ties." [*New York Times*, Oct. 15, 1972, p. 1, col. 2] That would result, in turn, in an eligible pool of a substantial number of persons grouped at every whole number score. The discretion of the appointing officer is therefore vastly increased.

The willingness of Mayor Lindsay to press for restructuring of the city's civil service system may be based at least partially on the threat or fact of litigation. For legal challenges to public agency selection processes, and particularly their reliance on standardized written tests, are not limited to the selection of school professionals. In March 1972, the NAACP Legal Defense and Educational Fund, Inc., had filed suit against the New York City Civil Service Commission charging that the written tests used to select and promote policemen unconstitutionally discriminated against black and Spanish-speaking candidates. A similar suit has also been brought against the examinations used to select firemen. The legal theories advanced in both were similar to those relied on in the *Chance* case (which is not surprising since the Legal Defense Fund also represented Boston Chance and Louis Mercado there). [*New York Times,* Mar. 4, 1972, p. 21, col. 5, and Jan. 12, 1973, p. 30, col. 5]

Attacks against civil service examinations and modifications of them are by no means limited to New York City, however. A suit was brought in the U.S. District Court in Newark on behalf of black policemen from East Orange charging that a computer-scored promotional examination invidiously discriminated against black candidates. [*The Evening News,* Apr. 28, 1972, p. 2, col. 1] A suit attacking both written tests and general civil service selection procedures has been filed by black and Spanish policemen in Newark. [*New York Times,* Dec. 29, 1972, p. 29, col. 1] The Connecticut State Personnel Policy Board proposed to reduce education and age requirements for state policemen. [*New York Times,* Aug. 8, 1972, p. 40, col. 7] The Detroit Police Department has revamped its examination procedures for new recruits. The thrust of the new test, developed by the Industrial Relations Center at the University of Chicago, is to put less emphasis on general intelligence and more on ability to operate under stress. According to the police department, the new battery of tests, taking four and a half hours to complete against 45 minutes for the old intelligence tests, "measures an applicant's motivation, occupational interests, ability to size up a situation, aptitude in dealing with problems involving people, tolerance under pressure, and personal and emotional adjustment, in addition to determining an applicant's intelligence." [*New York Times,* Oct. 4, 1971, p. 41, col. 1] The first time the new tests were given to applicants 60% of the minority group candidates passed as compared to 34% on the old intelligence tests.

Of all the efforts, through the courts, the legislatures and the administrative agencies, to reform selection processes for public employees, one kind has raised the greatest and most serious resistance. It is the effort to require preferential hiring of minority group candidates. Give it whatever name you like—quotas, goals, reverse discrimination, compensatory hiring, absolute preferences—and apply it to whatever level of public or private employment you wish—university professors, policemen, firemen, train conductors, assembly line workers—it is still certain to lead to an emotional response and bitter disagreement.

The nature of the response makes it all the more essential to understand what the courts and other agencies are doing, why they are doing it, what alternatives may be available to them, and how constitutional principles bear on the situation.

The starting point is, of course, a finding that the selection process has in fact invidiously discriminated against members of certain racial and ethnic groups. Consequently, those groups now have disproportionately few members among the work forces in question. Virtually everyone would agree that if particular minority group members can demonstrate that they *personally* were rejected for discriminatory reasons, a court can and should order that they be given jobs or other compensation for their unlawful rejection. [But see the opinions of the district and circuit courts in *Castro, supra.*] The difficulty and controversy arise when courts and legislatures and administrative agencies move beyond this traditional type of remedy to consider whether members of minority groups discriminated against should be given some "preferential" treatment simply because they are members of those racial or ethnic *groups,* whether or not they *personally* had been discriminated against in connection with the particular job.

This treatment is usually sought to be justified on the ground that it is necessary to effectively erase the present effects of past discrimination. Its roots are imbedded principally in the soil of school desegregation litigation where courts frequently have exercised sweeping equity powers to eliminate segregation "root and branch." A commitment not to unlawfully segregate more students in the future clearly would be insufficient to accomplish that end.

Similar reasoning is applied to employment discrimination cases. But for the unconstitutional discrimination, minority groups could have constituted "x" % of the particular work force; instead they constitute only "y" %. Therefore, the way to undo the present effects of past discrimination is to require that as quickly as possible the percentage of minority group employees be brought up to "x" %.

But, it is argued, the analogy breaks down. In the school desegregation area no student has a constitutional right to attend a segregated school or even a neighborhood school. So long as the state treats all children according to rational and proper considerations, the constitution is satisfied. Therefore, busing or other remedies rationally designed to root out the present effects of unlawful segregation infringes no conceivable constitutional right of any individual white student. That may not be true in the employment discrimination case, however. The way for minority group employment to reach the "x" % level most quickly is to require that *all* vacancies be filled by minority group candidates until that level is reached. But what of individual white candidates who may be equally or better qualified for the particular jobs? Do they have any constitutional rights which would be violated by such a requirement? Certainly they as individual citizens have the same due process and equal protection rights under the Fourteenth Amendment as black citizens. That means the state, whether acting through the judicial, legislative, or executive branch, cannot act arbitrarily or capriciously with reference to any citizen and cannot intentionally create a racial or ethnic classification unless it is necessary to promote a compelling state interest. If the purpose of the state's action is to bring minority group employment to the level it would have been but for past discrimination, is there a compelling state interest in doing so by means of an absolute preference for minority group candidates?

At least one federal court has had to consider that question. In *Carter v. Gallagher, supra,* the District Court ordered that the next 20 vacancies in the Minneapolis Fire Department be filled by minority group candidates who passed the civil service examination. On appeal the Circuit Court, in an unfortunately imprecise opinion, ruled that:

> The absolute preference of 20 minority persons who qualify has gone further than any of the reported appellate court cases in granting preference to overcome the effects of past discriminatory practices and does appear to violate the constitutional right of Equal Protection of the Law to white persons who are superiorly qualified. [452 F. 2d at 328]

The court seemed to base its conclusion in large part on the language of the Supreme Court in *Griggs v. Duke Power Co., supra,* to the effect that a court cannot guarantee a person a job without regard to qualifications because he was the subject of past discrimination or is a member of a minority group whose members have generally been subjected to employment discrimination. Said the Supreme Court, "Discriminatory preference for any group, minority or majority, is precisely and only what Congress proscribed." [401 U.S. at 430]   [But see *Vogler v. McCarty, Inc., supra,* for a broader approach to preferential treatment under Title VII.]

Griggs must be applied carefully, however. It was decided under Title VII of the Civil Rights Act of 1964, which then covered only *private* employment. Public employment cases, on the other hand, have been and will continue to be considered under the Fourteenth Amendment. Thus, what Congress intended to proscribe under Title VII may have limited pertinence. Moreover, the Supreme Court made clear in the *Griggs* opinion that it was speaking about the preference of unqualified, or at least less qualified, minority group candidates.

It is not at all clear that the Court of Appeals in *Carter* had before it a case involving either of these situations. Certainly the Fourteenth Amendment rather than Title VII provided the relevant legal standards. And whether the preference would actually prefer unqualified or less qualified minority group candidates over *"superiorly"* qualified white candidates was dubious. The minority candidates had to *pass* the same examination as white candidates and the Court of Appeals itself recognized that the tests were imprecise and unvalidated so that their ability to *rank* candidates in order of relative qualifications was suspect. One might therefore assume that the pool of eligibles consisted of people of *equal* qualifications insofar as the qualifications had been measured by the selection process. Is it, nevertheless, a violation of the constitutional rights of white members of that pool to be passed over in favor of equally qualified minority group members to the extent of 20 vacancies?

The court never really gets this far in the analysis. [But see *Southern Illinois Builders Ass'n v. Ogilvie,* 327 F. Supp. 1154 (S.D. Ill. 1971), *appeal pending,* 7th Cir., where the court, balancing basic self-interest of the individual against social interests, concluded that there might be no alternative to minority preferences to overcome decades of discrimination against blacks, and that such preferences were constitutional as a part of affirmative action programs.] Indeed, its conclusion may suggest it never even started the analysis. After rejecting an absolute preference as unconstitutional, the court proceeded to authorize a limited preference.

> . . .[W]e think some reasonable ratio for hiring minority persons who can qualify under the revised qualification standards is in order for a limited period of time, or until there is a fair approximation of minority representation consistent with the population mix in the area. Such a procedure does not constitute a "quota" system because as soon as the trial court's order is fully implemented, all hirings will be on a racially nondiscriminatory basis, and it could well be that many more minority persons or less, as compared to the population

at large, over a long period of time would apply and qualify for the positions. However, as a method of presently eliminating the effects of past racial discriminatory practices and in making meaningful in the immediate future the constitutional guarantees against racial discrimination, more than a token representation should be afforded. For these reasons we believe the trial court is possessed of the authority to order the hiring of 20 qualified minority persons, but this should be done without denying the constitutional rights of others by granting an absolute preference. [452 F. 2d at 330—31]

The reasonable ratio suggested by the court is one minority group appointment for every three vacancies. In accepting the concept of a limited preference, the court was acting consistently with substantial federal court precedent in employment or labor union discrimination cases. For example, a one-to-one formula has been applied by several courts of appeals and many district courts under Title VII. [*See, e.g., Local 53, Asbestos Workers v. Vogel,* 407 F. 2d 1047 (5th Cir. 1969); *U.S. v. Ironworkers Local 86,* 443 F. 2d 544 (9th Cir. 1971), *cert. denied,* 404 U.S. 984 (1971); *U.S. v. Central Motor Lines, Inc.,* 325 F. Supp. 478 (W.D.N.C. 1970).] The one-to-one formula has also been incorporated into many consent orders under Title VII. Moreover, the same formula has been sustained as a "goal" or a requirement in cases involving federal contractors under Executive Order 11246. [For citations and generally, *see* Note, "Constitutionality of Remedial Minority Preferences in Employment," 56 MINN. L.R. 842 (1972).] Finally, the one-to-one approach has been adopted in at least two public employment cases under the Fourteenth Amendment. [*NAACP v. Allen,* 340 F. Supp. 703 (M.D. Ala. 1972) [until minority group employees constitute 25% of the state troopers] ; *U.S. v. Frazer,* 317 F. Supp. 1079 (M.D. Ala. 1970) [until the percentage of minority group employees is proportionate to the percentage of the general population].]

The *Carter* court refused to adopt a one-to-one ratio only because the minority population of Minneapolis was so relatively small — less than 6.5%. But it accepted the essential theory of those cases. [Similarly, the Court of Appeals for the Third Circuit reversed a district court pre-trial order requiring a one-to-three hiring ratio on the ground that there was insufficient evidence to support the ratio chosen, but specifically stated that by this ruling it "in no way suggests that imposing a quota system is unconstitutional as a judicial remedy for discrimination." *Commonwealth of Pennsylvania v. O'Neill,* 4 FEP Cases 1286, 1289 (3d Cir. 1972), *rev'g,* 345 F. Supp. 305 and 348 F. Supp. 1084 (E.D. Pa. 1972), *further orders,* 5 FEP Cases 277, 280 (E.D. Pa. 1970) [Philadelphia policemen].] How does that theory relate to our equal protection analysis? Is a *little bit* of discrimination against "better qualified" or "equally qualified" white candidates constitutionally permissible? That is exactly what the dissenting judges in *Carter* say is the import of the majority decision. And it is this conception of minority preferences as a violation of the constitutional rights of *other* job applicants which has spawned an increasing amount of critical essays, complaints and litigation. The tensions and conflicts generated by this issue are especially unfortunate when, as is frequently the case, they pit members of different ethnic minorities against one another. [*See, e.g.,* a class action by non-Indian employees of the U.S. Bureau of Indian Affairs [*New York Times,* Oct. 23, 1972, p. 20, col. 3]; information revealed during public hearings of the U.S. Civil Rights Commission in Albuquerque to the effect that Federal and state agencies have implemented affirmative action programs usually by hiring mainly Spanish-Americans to the detriment of Indians (*New York Times,* Nov. 17, 1972, p. 52, col. 1); the ruling of a federal judge halting a minority hiring program of the San Francisco Board of Education (*New York Times,* Nov. 5, 1972, p. 76, col. 4); the complaints to the Secretary of H.E.W. by a number of Jewish organizations about discrimination against white males by many colleges and universities acting pursuant to Federal guidelines (*The Jewish News,* June 29, 1972, p. 14, col. 1);

and the split among members of the New York City Board of
Education over a community board resolution calling for affirmative hiring of teachers in "an ethnic distribution that is
more nearly representative of the student population in the
district" (*New York Times,* July 9, 1972, p. 19, col. 3). See
also, among the many recent articles addressed to this issue,
Anthony Lewis, "The Future of Equality," *New York Times,*
Nov. 26, 1972, p. 35, col. 7; J. Stanley Pottinger, "Race, Sex
and Jobs: The Drive Toward Equality," *Change,* Oct. 1972.
p. 24; and John H. Bunzel, "Race, Sex and Jobs: The Politics
of Quotas," *Change,* Oct. 1972, p. 25.]

But there may be a way to square the distinction *Carter*
draws between absolute and limited preferences with equal
protection analysis. Perhaps implicit in the court's approach
is the view that a compelling state interest does support the
kind of racial classification involved in granting a preference
to minority group candidates—the interest of the state in
equalizing the employment situation, especially in *public* employment, of minority *groups* which have been discriminated
against. But there must also be a reasonable relationship between the way in which the racially determined class is treated
and that compelling state interest. Perhaps the *Carter* court is
saying that an absolute preference is not clearly necessary to
the realization of that compelling state interest, but that a
limited preference is. If so, the decision may rest on a reasonable constitutional foundation, even though the constitutional
rights of individual white cnadidates may appear to be infringed.
Unfortunately, we have to speculate about the basis of the
court's decision since it never really discloses its reasoning beyond the generalities quoted above.

In the case of the employment of school personnel, another
constitutional justification may be offered for giving preference to minority candidates. Some courts, including the Court
of Appeals for the Third Circuit, have found a constitutional
requirement that school boards achieve racially balanced facul-

ties. This requirement stems from equal opportunity considerations in the employment and education areas. Thus, in
Porcelli v. Titus, 302 F. Supp. 726 (D.N.J. 1969), *aff'd,* 431F.
2d 1254 (3d Cir. 1970), *cert. denied,* 402 U.S. 944 (1971),
the court sustained the Newark Board of Education's uni-
lateral abrogation of a contractually imposed civil service
selection process and its replacement with a less formal system expressly designed to increase the percentage of minority
supervisors in the schools. The board justified its action in
terms of its overriding obligation to provide for the education
of the children. In its judgment, a school system with almost
75% minority group students needed more than 10% minority
supervisors for *educational* reasons. The State Commissioner
of Education, the State Board of Education, and the federal
courts all agreed. Indeed, the Court of Appeals seemed to go
out of its way to state that the board had a constitutional
obligation to do something about the racial imbalance among
supervisors. Doesn't that result in discrimination against those
white applicants deemed better qualified at least on the basis
of the old selection mechanism? But there was no *express requirement* that any black candidates be hired. The theory was
that a new merit system had replaced the old and those who
ranked high on the old had no continuing vested right. The
court concluded that if this constituted discrimination at all,
it didn't rise to the level of an actionable constitutional
violation.

Two aspects of *Porcelli* are especially interesting. As was
true of *Carter,* the Supreme Court denied certiorari. But,
unlike *Carter,* there was no determination that the old selection process was itself unconstitutional. At least the *Carter*
court could draw support for its "preferential" hiring from its
conclusion that the old examination was not capable of determining relative qualifications of the candidates. In *Porcelli*
the court simply had to rely on the compelling need for more
minority supervisors to justify any preference (although

implicit in its conclusion may have been the belief that the
new system was more valid).

Porcelli may suggest that if a school district wants to increase its minority representation among teachers and supervisors, it can constitutionally do so so long as it doesn't establish an explicit mandatory preference for minority group
members. This view may be supported by a recent New York
case, *Jackson v. Poston,* 328 N.Y.S. 2d 279 (Sup. Ct. Albany
Co. 1971). There the State Civil Service Commission sought
to give a preference in hiring, much like the statutory veterans'
preference, to those "who are successful in the examination
and who have recognizable identification with black or Spanish-
speaking minority communities." [328 N.Y.S. 2d at 280]
The court invalidated this preference on several grounds: that
there had been no showing that the positions covered were
presently racially imbalanced; that there had been no showing
that competitive examinations were impracticable for the
positions; and that it was inappropriate to replace ranking on
a list with some administrator's determination of which candidates had "recognizable identification."

Even assuming a preference can be justified on some theory,
another remedial issue remains—how long should the preference remain in effect? The analysis is similar to the first one
we considered in this chapter: how do we determine whether
or not the plaintiff has established a *prima facie* case by showing a *de facto* racial classification? Is the standard the percentage of minority group members in the general population?
In the prospective work force? In the group of applicants?
Essentially the same considerations bear on the question of
determining the goal for preferential hiring. And, as in the
other area, courts have gone all over the board. They have
used all of the above standards, as well as a flat percent or
number cutoff, if they have determined to order some form
of preferential hiring. Or, they have rejected preferential hiring because, in their judgment, it was too difficult to set the
cutoff point.

In a sense, then, we have come full circle in this discussion of the legal standards applicable to employee selection, especially where there is heavy reliance on written tests. Significant as the judicial developments are, however, they should not obscure the related movement in the area of professional test development. Perhaps largely because of the legal challenges, the professionals have begun to refine their thinking about the proper use and reliance on their written tests. They have begun working to eliminate cultural bias. They are preparing tests which focus more precisely on the special needs of urban school districts. For example, the Educational Testing Service is offering a special form of the NTE called, "Teaching in an Urban Setting," and it is developing tests which focus on candidates for bilingual teaching positions. New York City, too, is moving in that direction. [*See* N.Y. State Education Law Sec 2569(1), which now provides that "for purposes of qualifying teachers for service exclusively within a school district wherein instruction is given bilingually, all written and oral examinations . . . shall be given in the English and Spanish language and the applicant at the time of application shall designate the language of his choice, except that a written composition shall be given in English determined by the chancellor of education of the City of New York under the policies of the city board of education."]

To understand more fully the broad impact of these developments, and to consider how an actual selection process measures up to the legal and psychometric standards, it is important to return to the New York City model as revealed at the commission's hearings. For the most frequent and serious of the criticisms leveled against that selection process is that it fails to achieve the objectivity and evenhandedness claimed to be one of its cornerstones and that it lacks validity from legal and psychometric points of view.

CRITICISM AND DEFENSES OF THE NEW YORK CITY SYSTEM

Criticisms of the New York City selection system have focused on two of the three main criteria for evaluating examinations — its lack of objectivity and its lack of validity. The reliability of the examinations apparently has not been a significant issue.

Lack of Objectivity or Bias

Many witnesses charged that the system was discriminatory, if not in purpose, certainly in effect, and not alone on racial or ethnic grounds. It operates against outsiders, against all who are different, against all who do not reflect the conventional wisdom, it was alleged. Dr. Laurence Iannacone, Professor of Educational Administration at the University of Toronto and senior researcher on a study of the Board of Examiners, testified that the personnel practices of the school system "function to protect the vested interest of earlier arrivals, more established ethnic populations . . . at the expense of more recent in-migrants or newer upwardly mobile groups. The city schools' personnel system is so inbred as to be sociological incest." [*Selection of Teachers,* 1972, p. 518] Ultimately, said a number of witnesses, it discriminates against the children by being an "antimerit" system.

The tendency to protect the "vested interest of earlier arrivals" is not limited to the New York City school system. It is probably characteristic of most civil service type systems whose bulwarks are themselves products of the system. For those who play key roles in selecting personnel quite naturally tend to select people in their own image. Applicants who depart most dramatically from the prevailing image are likely to have the most difficulty with the process. This tendency is undoubtedly reflected in the interview and review of record facets of the selection process where the most room for personal, subjective reactions exists despite efforts to build in safeguards. But it may exist in the written test facet as well.

The opportunities are self-evident in essay questions. But even short-answer, "objective" questions are not free of doubt. The selection and wording of these questions, and decisions about the "correct" answers provide ample possibilites for unconscious bias in favor of applicants who react as the testers do. Any of us who have wrestled with multiple choice questions know the frustration of trying to answer a question with no answer which is wholly right or with several which may be right. How you answer and whether or not you are "right" depends often on how closely you identify with the tester's underlying assumptions and point of view.

A tendency to unconsciously favor candidates who reflect the conventional wisdom and who react the way the testers do is especially likely to be found in a system such as New York City's. Great reliance in test construction, administration, and grading is placed on persons presently holding teaching or supervising positions for which the examinations are being given. It is well recognized that people regard as the most important duties of their jobs those they do well, and that they regard as the proper way of carrying out those duties the way they have been doing them.

Favoring candidates who reflect the conventional wisdom and who react as the testers do may also unconsciously favor candidates who come from or reflect the characteristics of "earlier and more established ethnic populations . . . at the expense of more recent in-migrants" (in Dr. Iannacone's words). Where teachers are involved, this tendency could have particularly devastating effects. Pupils from the more recent in-migrant groups tend to predominate in urban school systems. And their need for both sensitivity and role models in their teachers makes it especially important for otherwise qualified candidates of their ethnic or socioeconomic group to have every reasonable opportunity in the selection process.

Because of the seriousness of these questions, it should be made absolutely clear that what was at issue in New York

City and what is at issue in many other cases where selection
systems are being challenged is *unconscious* discrimination—
discriminatory effect rather than discriminatory intent. From
the inception of its investigation, the New York City Human
Rights Commission stressed that, while the law required it to
uncover discriminatory intent as well as effect, complaints
presented to the commission concerning the public school
system raised questions only of discriminatory effect. In opening the hearings Chairman Norton said:

> ... [T] he search for scapegoats has no place here, for no complex
> phenomenon of long duration can be explained by a select list of
> villains. This problem is systemic, not dependent upon any set of
> personalities. We must spend this week in trying to understand the
> intricacies and origins of a system which—no doubt without malicious
> intent—has taken on the trappings of exclusiveness. ... [T] he im-
> plication that we are concerned with bigotry is equally simplistic and
> false. The problem is far more complicated than that. It is time that
> Northerners ceased judging their actions with regard to minority peo-
> ple by standards developed in the South where exclusion based ex-
> pressly and overtly on race has been the rule. The courts have long
> made it clear that practices which have the effect of excluding groups,
> even if that is not their intent, fall within the purview of the law.
> ... [W] e seek the common end of educating children while being
> fair to those who teach and supervise them. I ... know that a school
> system based on merit and fitness will not tolerate any but the high-
> est and most objective standards for selecting personnel. [*Selection
> of Teachers,* 1972, pp. 2—4]

This theme was echoed by a number of the witnesses. Dr.
John King said he thought the small number of black and
Puerto Rican professionals was not a result of deliberate,
planned discrimination. "I think that it's worse. It is not unfairness. It is indifference. ..." [*Id.* at 102]

Other witnesses saw the examination process as having two
main sources of bias—cultural and geographic bias in the written
test and an opportunity for highly subjective reactions in the
oral interview and review of record.

Recently there has been a nationwide crescendo of criticism

about many kinds of written tests on the ground they are culturally biased. For example, Dr. Henry S. Dyer, Vice-President of the Educational Testing Service, attacked I.Q. and grade equivalency tests as "psychological and statistical monstrosities," stating as one of the reasons that, "[the sampling upon which the average is based] is very frequently biased against blacks. . . ." [*New York Times,* Mar. 23, 1971, p. 19, col. 1 The President of the National Bar Association cited studies indicating that state bar examinations are culturally biased against blacks because they gauge memory and test-taking ability more than the capacity to practice law. A special committee of the Philadelphia Bar Association concluded, after a detailed study, that the state bar examination had a clearly discriminatory effect. A law suit has been filed charging that the principal test by which college graduates qualify for federal employment and promotion, the Federal Service Entrance Examination, is culturally and racially discriminatory. As we have seen, the federal government itself, through the Equal Employment Opportunity Commission, has established stringent guidelines for employers with regard to testing. The United States Supreme Court, in March 1971, held in the case of *Griff v. Duke Power Co.* that a private employer's reliance on standardized general intelligence tests violated the Civil Rights Act of 1964 when the tests had the effect of disqualifying a disproportionate number of black applicants and were not shown to be significantly related to successful job performance. Chief Justice Burger, speaking for a unanimous court, said:

> The Act proscribes not only overt discrimination but also practices that are fair in form, but discriminatory in operation. . . . [G]ood intent or absence of discriminatory intent does not redeem employment procedures or testing mechanisms that operate as 'built-in headwinds' for minority groups. . . . The facts of this case demonstrate the inadequacy of broad and general testing devices. . . . [401 U.S. at 431–33].

Finally, the closest analog to the Board of Examiners' written tests, the National Teacher Examination, has often been charged with being culturally biased. During his testimony, Dr. James Deneen of the Educational Testing Service reported:

> The question of a test's validity is often raised in relation to its appropriateness for minority groups. The prevalence of low test scores within a given population may be an indication that the test is unfair for that population. [*Selection of Teachers,* 1972, p. 414]

On the other hand, said Dr. Deneen, the prevalence of low test scores within a given population may result from a validly designed test which measures college preparation and thereby reflects the poorer preparation of some groups of students, such as those attending black institutions in the South. In that case, "the test scores attest not to differential ability but to the often separate and almost invariably unequal education that is offered to blacks and whites in this country." [*Id.* at 415]

To ensure that its tests are as free from cultural bias as possible, ETS has undertaken an on-going program of review and revision. According to Dr. Deneen,

> Our tests have been subject to at least three reviews in the last year by minority group persons. We had a panel of black educators a year and a half ago, and they cleaned up—I don't think that is too strong a word—some of what they perceived as perhaps subtly racist items in the test. We are conducting currently two studies in bias ... [to measure whether there is] bias against blacks or other minority groups contained somewhere in the items in those tests. ... I could go on and on. This is a problem of enormous importance to us. [*Id.* at 421]

The Educational Testing Service says significant modifications of the NTE have resulted from this program and that an even more fundamental reaction to possible test bias is in the offing. According to Dr. Deneen, ETS has reacted to criticism of the NTE as a test for suburban teachers by designing a special test for those intending to teach in urban settings. Moreover, ETS has moved toward development of a Spanish version of its test which could adequately test applicants for bilingual teaching positions. Dr. Deneen agreed that the present NTE is not a valid test for applicants who are either more comfortable taking tests in Spanish or whose preparation programs were taken in Puerto Rican or other Spanish-speaking universities. But the success of these efforts to eliminate bias was placed in some doubt by the March 1972 resignation from ETS of C. Sumner Stone, its director of minority affairs. In resigning, he expressed doubt about the organization's ability "to commit itself to the change necessary to make tests more humanistic and relative to the minority experience. . . In the last three years we didn't achieve the kind of success I felt was imperative. . . ."[*The New York Times,* Mar. 28, 1972, p. 39, co. 1]

The criticism of the Board of Examiners' written tests on the grounds of bias (as well as invalidity) must be considered in this context of widespread criticism of written testing. Indeed, many of the charges against the board parallel the criticisms of Dr. Deneen, discussed above. A number of witnesses complained that the written tests were so oriented to New York City school practices that it was virtually impossible for someone not fully acquainted with the school system to do well. Others criticized the white, middle-class orientation of the tests. Some of the recent tests have contained questions dealing with black history or culture but there was testimony dismissing these efforts as inadequate.

Dr. Barrett raised an even broader issue by referring to a study by Professor Irwin Katz, formerly of New York University, which concluded that the element of threat in an examination process had a more harmful effect on blacks than on whites. According to Dr. Barrett:

> I have talked to various principals about how . . . [the Board of Examiners'] testing procedure works, and it is loaded with threat. There are cram courses. . . . [The applicants] meet and test each other. They practice writing out tests. . . . [I] f Professor Katz' generalization is true . . . this whole system is going to dis-

criminate against those people who will take the test poorly regardless of how well they would have done on the job. [*Selection of Teachers*, 1972, p. 410]

This concern was also expressed in the testimony of Wendy Lehrman, a teacher at P.S. 87 in Manhattan, describing her experience with the examination process:

> I thought, all those examiners were white, they were all my people. . . . They were . . . City College people, the kind of people who talked the way I did; and that made me less afraid of them. I suppose if I was faced by a black or Puerto Rican board, I might not feel as comfortable as I felt then. . . . [*Id.* at 231]

Some of the most compelling testimony regarding alleged bias came from Spanish-speaking witnesses. Among them were a number of applicants for licenses as Spanish teachers who said they had failed the examination because of an inadequate performance on the written English test. This is an essay portion which is graded for English spelling and grammar but not content. The following testimony of Jorge Maldonado exemplifies these charges:

> I am a graduate from the University of Puerto Rico. In addition, I have taken both graduate courses in the University of Puerto Rico and in the City University of New York. For salary purposes I am considered to have a master's degree equivalency in social studies. I have had experience as a teacher in Puerto Rico and in New York City. I have been working as a teacher for the Board of Education of the City of New York since September 1964 on a regular substitute basis. I have applied, so far, for eight licenses, of which I have six. It is the eighth license that I applied for that I want to tell you about tonight. This is the license for regular Spanish Teacher. . . . The written part of the test, all in English, consisted of questions about Spanish and Latin American history and culture. . . . The test consisted of three parts. First there was a short answer test, followed by a written essay. Then I was called for an oral interview, which was conducted in Spanish and English. In my opinion, the interviewer did not master the Spanish very well. The test, in general, was an advantage for any applicant whose vernacular was English. . . . In my opinion, just the knowledge of a few words in Spanish would have

been enough for any applicant whose vernacular was not Spanish to pass the short part of the interview conducted in Spanish. Sometime in May 1970 I got the result of the test. I had passed the short-answer test and interview. But I was disqualified for the license because my written English in the essay was found unacceptable. . . . To require of prospective Spanish teachers an exam which tests written ability in English but not written ability in Spanish is not only foolish but discriminatory against native Spanish-speaking people, mostly Puerto Ricans. . . . The method and standards employed by the Board of Examiners to grade my examination paper have the effect of discriminating against me because of a written Spanish accent. It is true that I may make grammatical errors, but these errors are no proof I cannot communicate with English-speaking students and parents. In addition, the grading method and standards apparently provided no credit for the quality or the competence of the content or the color, tone and expressiveness of language used by the applicant. . . . I don't insist that when the tests of the Board of Education were created they were intended to discriminate against Puerto Ricans, but that is their effect today. [*Id.* at 480–81]

If, in fact, the examination process discriminates against Spanish-speaking and other bilingual teachers, this would be an extremely serious indictment of the system. As Chapter 3 showed, many witnesses stressed the critical need for more bilingual professionals. The figures speak for themselves. With the number of Puerto Rican and other Spanish-speaking pupils fast approaching the 300,000 mark, there are reportedly only several hundred bilingual teachers. Some witnesses spoke of community districts with more than 20,000 Spanish-speaking pupils and five bilingual professionals. While the problem may be more acute in New York City, it is of national scope.

Testimony concerning the Chinese community was also devastating. This community has recently experienced phenomenal growth because of the reforms effected in the immigration laws in 1965. Yet, the public school system has almost completely failed to take account of the increased need for bilingual teachers to accommodate many youngsters who speak only Chinese. According to testimony, the resulting dropout rate and other school problems among Chinese youth is perhaps the most important ingredient in the developing ghetto pathology in a community that has traditionally been free of such trends.

Although Mr. Maldonado's charge of bias did not relate to the oral interview, many witnesses told of disqualification because of speech patterns or "traceable foreignisms" in their speech. And this is not a problem limited to black and Puerto Rican applicants. Among the white witnesses who told of failure for these reasons were Albert Shanker, President of the UFT, and Dr. Martin Frye, Community Superintendent of District No. 4

The charges of discrimination do not stop with the oral interviews, however. The examination process includes a review of record, and Ira Glasser, Executive Director of the New York Civil Liberties Union, charged the Board of Examiners with discrimination here, too. He testified that the Civil Liberties Union had evidence that licenses have been denied for the following reasons, among others:

1. Controversial political beliefs.

2. Refusal to release confidential Selective Service records.

3. Youthful offender convictions where supposedly sealed records have been obtained by the Board of Examiners.

4. Illegal arrests, where no conviction occurred, in civil rights demonstrations. (According to Mr. Glasser, the NYCLU at the time of the hearings was representing a teacher denied her license because of an arrest during a civil rights march in the South years ago.)

Against this range of criticism, the Board of Examiners made two principal defenses, defenses that are typical of civil service supporters — that the examination process now has many safeguards against bias (including a number added recently in response to public criticism) and that the alternatives to the examination process would be fraught with much greater danger of bias.

Former Chairman Gertrude Unser listed as essential features of a merit system a number which relate to preventing discrimination:

1. Absolute openness in terms of announcements of examinations, qualifications required, the scope of the examination, the pass marks and the opportunity to file.

2. Full documentation and reviewability of all procedures, including a documented statement of the reasons for rejection.

3. Right of appeal to higher authority.

4. Confidentiality to keep the examination process free from undue pressures.

5. Professional development and administration of examination.

6. Selection of members of the Board of Examiners itself, solely on the basis of merit and with tenure so they can be protected from undue influence and pressure.

Presumably, this has been the credo of the Board of Examiners for many years. And none of the witnesses objected to any of these features. What they maintained was that these criteria were not being fully met, not because of conscious prejudice but largely because the process was ill-conceived to ensure their full implementation. Even Dr. Greene's testimony about recent changes in the process reflected expressly, or by implication, that opportunities for bias existed notwithstanding this credo. For instance, he testified that:

> The separate oral English test was abandoned. . . . This is a city where immigrants came and so perhaps the standards were unreasonable. . . . Our goal now is an interview test of ability to communicate so that children will clearly understand the teacher, so adults will clearly understand. There is no bar on an accent. At one time there were all sorts of hazards in the oral English test. That is no longer true. [*Selection of Teachers,* 1972, p. 142]

Another change he referred to was the institution of the critical score concept, which involves the averaging of examination components so that a particularly strong performance on one part can offset a weak performance on another. "In other words, we recognize the written test itself has weaknesses and that to screen people out on a written test at 60 percent instead of 55 or instead of 50 may not be justified because personal factors are important." [*Id.* at 142–43]

Finally, Dr. Greene described with pride that oral interviews are now tape recorded and the tapes are available to applicants. He asked rhetorically whether any other school district provides such selection safeguards. But the later testimony of Dr. Alfred Weinstein, a unit head of the Board of Examiners and President of the Junior High School Principals Association, made clear that the recording of oral interviews was begun only in 1969 in response to an express mandate of the state legislature. When asked whether the Board of Examiners had not been urged for years to make such recordings, Dr. Weinstein said it had. In fact, he reported:

> ... [A] number of years ago, as a co-litigant in a suit, we asked for that through our lawyer. Many people who believe in the examination process believe that that would have made it much more valid. ... [*Id.* at 446]

Why did the Board of Examiners resist so long until they were required by law to record the oral interviews? Dr. Weinstein said he understood it was because they ". . . had these huge tape recorders, and it was a question of expense, too. But I think it should have been done." [*Id.* at 447]

Developments in the *Chance* case, *supra,* persuasively add to the evidence of discriminatory effect. On July 14, 1971, Judge Walter R. Mansfield, a federal court judge (he heard the case as a district judge, and although he was subsequently elevated to the Circuit Court of Appeals, he was designated to sit on the district court to complete this phase of the case), issued a lengthy opinion granting the plaintiffs, black and Puerto Rican acting principals who have all the qualifications for permanent appointment except the license issued upon passage of the Board of Examiners' examination, preliminary injunctive relief against the defendants, the Board of Examiners, the Board of Education and their respective members, the chancellor, and the deputy superintendent in charge of personnel. [330 F. Supp. 203 (S.D. N.Y. 1971)] The order of the court was issued on July 23. It provided that:

> . . . pending the settlement of a preliminary injunction, defendants, their agents, servants, employees, attorneys, and all persons in active concert and participation with them be and they hereby are:
>
> (1) restrained from announcing or conducting further examinations for supervisory service positions in the New York City School System;
>
> (2) restrained from promulgating or otherwise publishing any new eligible lists for supervisory service positions in the New York City School System;
>
> (3) restrained from using or permitting to be used outstanding eligible lists for supervisory service positions in the New York City School System in making appointments or assignments to vacant supervisory service positions, provided, however, that this order shall not affect the validity of any other requirements for appointment or assignment to supervisory service positions established pursuant to law. . . .

Thus, that order and the September 20, 1971, preliminary injunction effectively suspend the entire selection process for permanent supervisory positions pending further court proceedings, and Judge Mansfield's order has been sustained by the Court of Appeals. This is obviously a serious step. What convinced the court to take it?

According to Judge Mansfield's detailed opinion, it was a conclusion that "a sufficient showing has been made of violation of the Equal Protection Clause of the Fourteenth Amendment to warrant the issuance of preliminary injunctive relief." [330 F. Supp. at 205] The "sufficient showing" was, in turn, based on (1) adequate evidence from the plaintiffs of a discriminatory effect, and (2) inadequate evidence from the defendants of a job related justification for that discrimination. The issue of job relatedness will be discussed further in the section on "Lack of Validity." The issue of discriminatory effect is, of course, directly pertinent to whether the examination process is objective.

Starting in 1966, the New York City Board of Education has conducted several ethnic surveys of its teachers and supervisors. They show strikingly low percentages of blacks and Puerto Ricans in all categories and relatively little improvement. For example, according to Judge Mansfield's opinion:

> There are approximately 1,000 licensed Principals of New York public schools of varying levels (e.g., elementary day, junior high school, high school, etc.), of whom some act as the heads of schools and others function in administrative positions. Of the 1,000 only 11 (or approximately 1%) are Black and only 1 is Puerto Rican. Furthermore of the 750 licenses Principals of New York elementary schools only 5 (or less than 1%) are Black and none is Puerto Rican. Of the 180 high school administrative assistants, none is Black or Puerto Rican.

> Of the 1,610 licensed Assistant Principals of New York City junior high and elementary schools only 7% are Black and only .2% are Puerto Rican. When the list for the position of Principal, elementary school, was originally promulgated, only 6 out of the 340 persons (or about 1.8%) were Black and none was Puerto Rican; and when the list for Principal, high school, was promulgated, none of the 22 licensed people was Black or Puerto Rican. The promulgated list of licensed Assistant Principals for junior high schools reveals that only 55 out of 690 persons (or 8%) were Black and none was Puerto Rican. [330 F. Supp. at 208]

Many people, including Boston M. Chance and Louis C. Mercado, have argued that the examination process is a major factor in the extremely poor record of the New York City school system in attracting black and Puerto Rican supervisors. Yet, despite these charges and the system's often-stated frustration at its failure to significantly improve the record in recent years, there had never been a statistical study dealing with the impact of the examination process until the *Chance*

case. Judge Mansfield ordered the Board of Examiners and
Board of Education to compile the necessary racial statistics.
The court's description of the survey and its analysis of the
results bear careful study for they provide a framework within
which any public employer can begin to evaluate the legality
of its selection process.

> The result has been that after months of research we have been pre-
> sented with the pass-fail statistics for the relevant racial and ethnic
> groupings of candidates for 50 supervisory examinations given over
> the past few years. In view of plaintiffs' claims that the examinations
> had a "chilling effect" inhibiting Blacks and Puerto Ricans from be-
> coming candidates, this statistical survey ("the Survey") also includes
> figures as to those candidates who "Did Not Appear" to take the
> written test, which commenced the examination process, or who
> "Withdrew," *i.e.*, took the written test but did not appear for sub-
> sequent parts of the examination. . . .
>
> All parties and amici have submitted briefs as to the relevance of
> the statistics thus adduced and the inferences that may be drawn from
> them. The parties also submitted affidavits by statistical experts. A
> hearing was held, at which each side's expert testified and was subject
> to cross-examination; and we heard more oral argument on the
> statistical data. After declining the opportunity to examine and cross-
> examine any other witnesses, including those presented by affidavit,
> both sides rested on the record thus adduced. . . .
>
> Upon the evidence thus presented we find that the examinations
> and testing procedures prepared and administered by the Board for
> the purpose of determining which candidates will be licensed as super-
> visory personnel have the effect of discriminating against Black and
> Puerto Rican candidates.
>
> The Survey reveals that out of 6,201 candidates taking most of the
> supervisory examinations given in the last seven (7) years, including
> all such examinations within the last three (3) years, 5,910 were
> identified by race. Of the 5,910 thus identified, 818 were Black or
> Puerto Rican and 5,092 were Caucasian. Analysis of the aggregate
> pass-fail statistics for the entire group reveals that only 31.4% of the
> 818 Black and Puerto Rican candidates passed as compared with 44.3%
> of the 5,092 white candidates. . . . Thus on an overall basis, white
> candidates passed at almost 1½ times the rate of Black and Puerto
> Rican candidates. These overall figures, however, tell only part of

the story. Of greater significance are the results of two examinations which had by far the largest number of candidates, those for Assistant Principal of Day Elementary School and Assistant Principal of Junior High School, which revealed the following:

	Assistant Principal, Day Elementary Schools, 1965 Examination (PF-03)	Assistant Principal, Junior High Schools, 1968 Examination (PF-43)
Caucasian		
Total	1171	1319
% Pass	**61.3**	**48.82**
Black		
Total	278	236
% Pass	**45.68**	**26.27**
Puerto Rican		
Total	7	14
% Pass	**28.57**	**14.29**
Black and Puerto Rican		
Total	285	250
% Pass	**45.26**	**25.60**
Probability* of Chance Result Less Than—	1/1 million	1/1 million

*Table adapted from affidavit of plaintiffs' expert, Professor Jacob Cohen, May 6, 1971, para. 5. The computations of probability are his; the racial statistics come directly from the Survey.

Thus white candidates passed the examination for Assistant
Principal of Junior High School at almost double the rate of Black
and Puerto Rican candidates, and passed the examination for Assistant
Principal of Day Elementary School at a rate one-third greater than
Black and Puerto Rican candidates. The gross disparity in passing rates
on these two examinations is of particular significance not only because they were taken by far more candidates than those taking any
other examinations conducted in at least the last seven years, resulting in licensing of the largest number of supervisors, but also because
the assistant principalship has traditionally been the route to and
prerequisite for the most important supervisory position, Principal.
To the extent that Blacks and Pureto Ricans are screened out by the
examination for Assistant Principal they are not only prevented from
becoming Assistant Principals but are kept out of the pool of eligibles
for future examinations for the position of Principal as well. The fact
that the process involves a series of examinations and that to reach
the top one must pass several examinations at different times in his
or her career serves to magnify the statistical differences between the
white and non-white pass-fail rates. For instance, if we take a group
of 100 Black and Puerto Rican candidates, on the one hand, and
1,000 white candidates, on the other, and assume a passing rate of 25%
for the former and of 50% for the latter on a given assistant principal's
examination (as was approximately the case in the examination for
Assistant Principal of Junior High School), the results would be
as follows:

Black & Puerto Rican	25% x 100	=	25)	Licensed Assistant
White	50% x 1,000	=	500)	Principals

The group of 525 licensed assistant principals would then form
the pool of eligibles for the related principal's examination. Assuming
the same relative pass rates, we have the following results:

Black & Puerto Rican	25% x 25	=	6.25)	
				) Principals
White	50% x 500	=	250	)

Thus the true resulting difference between the Black and Puerto
Rican versus the white pass rates would be even more substantial:
only 6.25% of the Blacks and Puerto Ricans would pass the two
successive examinations as against 25% of the whites.

When we look at all 50 examinations which were the subject of
the Survey, we find that only 34 were taken by at least one member

of both the white and Black-Puerto Rican racial groups. One of these
examinations (Assistant Administrative Director, given Dec. 1967,
PF-17) was passed by everyone taking it. Another (Director, Bureau
for Children with Retarded Mental Development, given Jan. 1968,
PF-18) was not completed successfully by anyone taking it. . . . There
remain 32 examinations where one or the other of the two main racial
groups — Black and Puerto Rican in one group and white in the other —
had a larger percentage passing than did the other group. *Of these 32
examinations the white group had a larger percentage passing in 25
examinations and the non-white group had a larger percentage passing in only 7 examinations.* Thus the whites passed at a proportionately higher rate in *three times* as many examinations as the non-
whites. The probability of these results occurring by chance is less
than 1.05 in 1,000.

Finally we are impressed with the revealing statistics comparing
the percentage of Black and Puerto Rican Principals to White Principals in the five largest school systems in the country:

City	Total No. of Principals	% Black	% Puerto Rican	% Black and Puerto Rican
Detroit	281	16.7	––	16.7
Philadelphia	267	16.7	––	16.7
Los Angeles	1,012	8.0	1.7	9.7
Chicago	479	6.9	––	6.9
NEW YORK	862	1.3	0.1	1.4

Thus, New York City has by far the lowest percentage of minority
representation. The next lowest city, Chicago, has almost *5 times*
the percentage of minority principals found in New York City,
and as the following table shows there is a similar imbalance of
minority Assistant Principals:

City	Total No. of Assistant Principals	% Black	% Puerto Rican	% Black and Puerto Rican
Detroit	360	24.7	0.2	24.9
Philadelphia	325	37.0	––	37.0
Los Angeles	––	––	––	––
Chicago	714	32.5	––	32.5
NEW YORK	1,610	7.0	0.2	7.2

[330 F. Supp. at 209–13]

Interestingly, the court rejected the plaintiffs' argument that
discrimination could be inferred from the great discrepancy
between the percentages of black and Puerto Rican supervisors,
on the one hand, and the percentages of black and Puerto
Rican students in the school system or the percentages of black
and Puerto Rican members of the general New York City population, on the other hand. The court explained its position by
stating that supervisors are drawn from the pool of qualified
teachers and not from either present-day students or the
general population. The issue before it, said the court, was
whether "New York City's examination system discriminates
against *minority candidates* who have already qualified as
licensed teachers." [*Id.* at 214]

In taking this position, the court expressly stated that
"statistics as to the current dearth of qualified minority
teachers do not have probative value." [*Id.*] The court did
speculate, however, that a part of the reason for there being
so few licensed minority teachers must be that 10 or 15 years
ago the percentage of minority students who went on to
college and qualified for a teaching career was much smaller
than that for white students. But the court left open the
question of whether the teacher examinations conducted by
the Board of Examiners might be discriminatory, too. Many
people have charged that they are. Another law suit is almost
certain to be filed moving the charges about teacher examinations to the judicial forum. In some respects the suit would
seem to be potentially stronger than the *Chance* case. For the
teacher examinations are the foot in the door for all future
progress up the school system's career ladder and the multi-
plier effect, which Judge Mansfield found significant for
lower supervisory level examinations, is even more significant.
Moreover, evidence of any chilling effect on black and Puerto
Rican candidates caused by the examination process ought to
be entitled to serious weight. But, absent the ethnic pass-fail
data which was prepared for supervisory positions, there can

be no serious prediction about the success of such a suit.

Finding that "the examinations prepared and administered by the Board [of Examiners] for the licensing of supervisory personnel in New York City schools do have the *de facto* effect of discriminating significantly and substantially against qualified black and Puerto Rican applicants" did not complete the court's inquiry.

> . . . [T] he existence of such discrimination, standing alone, would not necessarily entitle plaintiffs to relief. The Constitution does not require that minority group candidates be licensed as supervisors in the same proportion as white candidates. The goal of examination procedures should be to provide the best qualified supervisors, regardless of their race, and if the examinations appear reasonably constructive to measure knowledge, skills and abilities essential to a particular position, they should not be nullified because of a *defacto* discriminatory impact. We accordingly pass on to the question of whether the examinations under attack can be validated as relevant to the requirements of the positions for which they are given, *i.e.*, whether they are "job related." [*Id.*]

And we must pass on to that question, too.

Lack of Validity

Many witnesses at the commission's public hearings spoke to the issue of validity. And the predominant reaction was that there is insufficient evidence of validity to warrant continued reliance on the current examination process. No proof exists that applicants who score well on the examinations actually perform better on the job than others or that the examinations accurately test whether applicants have important job skills.

The Federal District Court, in the *Chance* case, agreed that when there is evidence of discriminatory effect, the burden of proof as to job relatedness is on the public employer. It said:

> . . . Where, as here, plaintiffs show that the examinations result in *substantial* discrimination against a minority racial group qualified to take them, a strong showing must be made by the Board [of

Examiners] that the examinations are required to measure abilities
essential to performance of the supervisory positions for which they
are given. [*Id.* at 216]

This is a heavy burden. It is no surprise that the court concluded the Board of Examiners had failed to discharge the
burden; at least not to the many critics of the examination
system who testified at the commission's hearings. Indeed,
many of them maintained that the system did not just fall
short of adequate job relatedness, but actually was antimerit,
that it screens in those who know or care to learn the lingo
and orthodox test knowledge, but screens out many who
could be more effective teachers and supervisors. Albert
Shanker, President of the UFT, testified, "I would think that
an examination which takes the amount of time to cram for,
which some of the examinations have . . . , [is] counterproductive. In many cases, it might actually tend to attract a person who is . . . less qualified for a job. . . . " [*Selection of
Teachers,* 1972, p. 350]

Criticism about invalidity was voiced in the main not by
those whose careers had been impeded by problems with the
examination process. Deans and professors of schools of education, community board chairmen, community superintendents, current and former Board of Education officials,
teachers and supervisors who had been successful in the process, educational consultants and testing experts — most expressed the same concerns.

The consensus is striking for two reasons. It may, of course,
point to an actual lack of validity. And that is a real possibility
in light of Judge Mansfield's careful opinion in the *Chance*
case and the affirmance by the Court of Appeals. But even if
the examination process could be demonstrated by test experts to have a satisfactory level of content validity, the fact
that so many responsible people involved in so many facets of
education react to it as they do might compromise its actual
value as a testing instrument. Test experts have a term for it.

They speak of face validity — a limited kind of validity based on whether the test-takers *believe* the test validly measures some job-related characteristics.

Wendy Lehrman, a teacher at P.S. 87 in Manhattan, told of her reaction to the test:

> ...I was told where to go for this coaching. . . . [I]t was memorizing. They gave us old examinations and told us old answers and we were told that we mustn't stray from or challenge the status quo. There were certain answers to be expected from us. We weren't to use multi-syllabic words or complex sentences . . . because we might misspell them, or do anything to increase the statistical chance of error. We were given the key vocabulary in fad that year in order to incorporate it into as many answers as possible. I spent two weeks memorizing meaningless phrases. . . . It was apparent that I was neither expected to be intellectually or morally committed to, or capable of carrying out, any of the answers. . . . I passed the examination, and there was no way they could tell whether I could communicate with children. . . . [*Id.* at 230–31]

The criticism that there is no evidence of a correlation between good performance on the test and good performance on the job goes largely to an absence of predictive validity. Even assuming the Board of Examiners' tests are proficiency rather than aptitude-type tests, a number of testing experts believe, as we have seen, that predictive validity studies are important and useful. Designing such studies is admittedly difficult. But Dr. Greene testified that the Board of Examiners had never attempted such a study with respect to its teachers' examinations. (Apparently there had been a minor predictive validity study of a supervisory level examination.) By way of comparison, the Educational Testing Service has carried out several predictive validity studies of the National Teacher Examination, according to Dr. James Deneen's testimony, and the Philadelphia school system has recently begun a predictive validity study of its own selection process.

The Board of Examiners responds to criticism about the lack of predictive validity evidence in two ways. First, that it relies on *content* validity rather than predictive validity. Second, that there is a shortage of funds, as described in the following exchange:

> Dr. Greene: . . . [D] id we imply that we believed the first three people . . . on the list . . . are better than the next four in terms of teaching ability or supervisory ability? I don't believe we have.
>
> Mr. Tractenberg: Then the record ought to be clear that the ranking of people on the exam, insofar as the Board of Examiners is concerned, has no correlation to their likely performance on the job.
>
> Dr. Greene: . . . I have said that the ranking indicates that on the tests we have used . . . these are the people who did best.
>
> Mr. Tractenberg: This does not represent a prediction on your part?
>
> Dr. Greene: We don't have evidence on that.
>
> Mr. Tractenberg: I gather you don't plan to acquire that evidence.
>
> Dr. Greene: We have tried. We didn't have a research staff at all until three years ago. We pleaded for one every year. Now we have two people. . . . Hardly enough in today's climate. Hardly enough to do more than get guidance from the colleges.
>
> Mr. Tractenberg: You agree if you had a larger staff through more budget funds, you could have made more extensive efforts to validate the tests?
>
> Dr. Greene: We have pleaded for that. There are so many problems that we really ought to go into. The percentage of our budget allocated for research is abysmal as compared to other organizations.
>
> Mr. Tractenberg: What is your budget for this current year?
>
> Dr. Greene: We have one research associate and one assistant. I would say, therefore, it's about $40,000.
>
> Mr. Tractenberg: Out of a total budget of how much?
>
> Dr. Greene: About three million.
>
> Mr. Tractenberg: Doesn't it seem the proportions are a little askew? Wouldn't it make more sense to spend more to find out whether the tests are valid and a little less on giving them?
>
> Dr. Greene: I agree we should have more research and go into matters of validity whether predictive or content. . . . [*Id.* at 168—69]

Dr. Greene's statement that more research is necessary regarding even content validity leads to the second main area of criticism — that the examination process lacks even content validity.

As noted above, content validity depends principally upon two ingredients. There must be adequate job descriptions, prepared by persons fully familiar with the current demands of the positions, on the basis of which the test items are constructed. And the construction of the test items must be done by persons with the necessary expertise. Many witnesses charged that neither of these ingredients was present in the New York City school system's examination process.

Theodore Lang, formerly Deputy Superintendent in charge of the Office of Personnel, testified that during his five and one-half years in that position he was unaware of any updating of the description of duties for any teaching license.

> Mr. Tractenberg: But isn't it your responsibility . . . to devise that statement of duties?
>
> Dr. Lang: I would say that we do have a responsibility to devise the statement of responsibilities and send it down, yes.
>
> Mr. Tractenberg: But you have not felt that responsibility involved updating any of the teacher statements of duties in at least the last five years?
>
> Dr. Lang: That's correct. That doesn't mean it shouldn't be done now, but I have not up to this point. [*Id.* at 78]

Dr. Greene explained how the Board of Examiners compensates for this lack of a job description. "When an examination is prepared, we bring in experienced principals, college personnel, and we often begin by saying what are the problems that teachers will be facing. . . . Let us prepare questions based upon the problems teachers face and the knowledge that they should have in today's climate. . . ." [*Id.* at 170] But Dr. Greene conceded that this was an informal procedure — a "shortcut" in his words. "I don't believe we have been derelict in getting the facts, but we haven't gone through a procedure and they [the Office of Personnel] haven't bothered sending it." [*Id.* at 171] Dr. Greene testified, "Every time they ask us for an examination, they should send us such a statement [of duties]." [*Id.*] When asked whether he was satisfied that the panels of experts were sufficiently in touch with the real needs of the school system, Dr. Greene replied, "We hope so." [*Id.*]

During the testimony of Stephen Pollak, former Assistant Attorney General in charge of the Civil Rights Division of the Justice Department, a statement by William Enneis, staff psychologist at the U.S. Equal Employment Opportunity Commission, was quoted. It is relevant to the composition of such panels. Dr. Enneis cautioned against using job analyses developed by people serving in the position for which the examination is being given, saying:

> The job analyses should be conducted by independent persons trained in this activity. . . . Otherwise, the results may be seriously biased by self reports which are completed by the incumbent. . . . The reason for this potential bias is that many employees . . . tend to report as important those work aspects which they most enjoy or those which they do well. . . . Therefore, some critical components of the job may be slighted, even though they are matters of the greatest concern. . . . [*Id.* at 431–32]

This is one way in which the deficiencies of the system tend to be multiplied by the examination process.

The absence of updated job descriptions for teaching positions was a source of concern to some witnesses. Dr. Robert Thorndike, who has been an expert testing witness for the Board of Examiners in litigation, testified, "Assuming the job has substantially changed, if the description refers to a previous job which is obsolete, it would not be very useful." [*Selection of Teachers,* 1972, p. 404] (Dr. Thorndike did question whether the passage of five and a half years necessarily meant the earlier description was obsolete.) Dr. Richard

Barrett, who specializes in the impact of testing on minority groups, criticized the job description facet of the process for reasons other than failure to update. He said:

> The first and, I think, most crucial step in developing a selection procedure is a job description. The job description should tell what a person does, why he does it, how he does it, what skills are involved, what kind of performance is likely to lead to success, what kind of performance is likely to lead to failure. Once there is a good job description, and this could take months for a complicated job such as that of a principal, the description will serve as a guide in the development of the rest of the selection procedures. [*Id.* at 406]

Dr. Barrett characterized even the formal job descriptions which the Board of Examiners relies on in constructing some examinations as mere skeletons, referring specifically to a recent job description for high school principals.

> One item is "to work to build and maintain high teacher morale." That is the end of the statement. As it stands there, it is simply a platitude. Everybody wants high morale of the people that work for him. . . . [T]his is the skeleton of a job description that does not give the kind of information that is useful for a person who is going to develop a test. . . . The problem that comes up first, if we don't have an adequate job description, is that the person who is developing and scoring the tests, interviewing people, or giving them an observation, must then fall back on his experience. This means we have some senior person who has been in the system for a long time, whose experience is rapidly becoming out-of-date as circumstances change, who has probably had a very limited experience. In a system of 900 schools, he cannot have seen all of it. He falls back on his own experience and tends to perpetuate the conventional wisdom of the existing establishment. It is difficult for him to conceive of . . . different kinds of people coming into the kind of job that he has been used to. [*Id.* at 407–08]

This testimony states essentially the approach of the District Court in the *Chance* case. The court found the techniques and procedures adopted in principle by the Board of Examiners, and approved by independent experts, to be adequate. But,

according to the court, ". . . a major stumbling block — and in
our view a fatal weakness in the Board's system — lies in the
methods used by the Board to implement the techniques and
procedures. . . . Despite its professed aims the Board has not
in practice taken sufficient steps to insure that its examinations will be valid as to content, much less to predictiveness."
[330 F. Supp. at 219] Moreover, the board's own research
reports failed to demonstrate the content validity of its examinations. "Many of the reports are irrelevant. . . ; or they
deal with objectivity or consistency; or they are mere proposals, not studies." [*Id.* at 220]

The court's conclusion regarding the board's failure to adequately test content validity was reinforced by its own study
of some of the examinations. Many of the short-answer mul-
tiple-choice tests struck the court "as having little relevance to
the qualities expected of a school supervisor." [*Id.*] Among
the questions singled out by the court were the following:

1961 Examination for Principal, Day Elementary School

64. Of the following characters in the nursery rhyme, *The Burial
of Poor Cock Robin,* the one who killed Cock Robin is the

1. Lark
2. Thrush
3. Bull
4. Sparrow

1965 Examination for Assistant Principal, Junior High School

211. *I've Got a Little List,* from the *Mikado,* is sung by

1. Nanki-poo   2. Pish-Tush   3. Ko-Ko   4. Pooh-Bah

212. Arthur Sullivan, of the team of Gilbert and Sullivan, wrote

1. Gypsy Love Song   2. The Lost Chord
3. Ah, Sweet Mystery of Life   4. A Kiss in the Dark

218. Which one of the following violin makers is NOT of the great
triumvirate of Cremona?

1. Amati   2. Stradivarius   3. Guarnerius   4. Maggini

1968 Examination for Assistant Principal, Junior High School

63. The author of *Dodsworth* is also the author of:

   1. *Daisy Miller*
   2. *Elmer Gantry*
   3. *Henry Esmond*
   4. *Mrs. Dalloway*

*   *   *   *   *

74. The author of *Tender is the Night* also wrote:

   1. *The Great Gatsby*
   2. *Butterfield 8*
   3. *The Sun Also Rises*
   4. *Sanctuary*

75. A contemporary play in which one of the characters seems to turn into a rhinoceros was written by:

   1. Beckett
   2. Pinter
   3. Ionesco
   4. Shaw   [330 F. Supp. at 220–21, n. 23]

    The court also concluded that both the short-answer and essay questions "appear to be aimed at testing the candidate's ability to memorize rather than the qualities normally associated with a school administrator." [*Id.* at 225] Confirmation of this was drawn by the court from a "well known publication widely used by candidates to prepare for supervisory examinations, which is entitled *Principal, Assistant-to-Principal* by Paul Treatman, Ph.D., Principal, New York City Public Schools (Teacher License Series, ARCO)." [*Id.*] This manual advocates a course of training in "memorization" or "superficial memories." In a footnote to its opinion, the court listed the following samples of "mnemonic methods and professional jargon" suggested by Dr. Treatman:

Objectives of Elementary Education — *Cohetkase*

Character
Our American Heritage
Health
Exploration
Thinking
Knowledges and Skills
Appreciation and Expression
Social Relationships
Economic Relationships

Developing a Learning Experience — *Rice*

Readiness
Instructional materials provided
Carrying out experience
Evaluating the experience

Kinds of Learning Experiences — *U.S.O.*

Unit
Short-term
Ongoing (centers of interest)

Areas for Evaluation — *I Am Same*

Interaction among children
Atmosphere of classroom
Materials
Status (health, social, interests)
Achievement
Methods and procedures
Experiences, worth of

Uses of Evaluation — *Pragg*

Process and grade placement
Reports to parents
Analysis of pupil difficulties
Guidance
Grouping

Improving School Discipline — *Pert Cages*

Planning of standards and rules
Environment, improvement of
Routines, training in

Teaching, improvement of
Conferences
Analysis of difficulties
Guidance procedures
Evaluation and follow-up
Self-control emphasis [*Id.* at 222, n. 24]

Finally, the court found the oral interview portion of the examination also wanting in practice. It based its conclusion not on content validity standing alone but on " . . . the hard, cold facts . . . that all members of the Board of Examiners are white, the great majority of the oral examiners or examination assistants are white, and white candidates have passed the combined oral and written tests at a much higher rate than Black and Puerto Rican candidates, resulting in *de facto* discrimination against the latter." [*Id.* at 223]   According to the court, "This raises a 'serious and substantial question' as to whether discrimination against Blacks and Puerto Ricans is not being *unconsciously* practiced by white interview examiners." [*Id.*]

Since the court's decision, several members of the Board of Examiners have retired and their acting replacements have been black and Puerto Rican. There has been an effort to increase the number of minority examination assistants and interviewers. But these efforts would not seem sufficient to undermine seriously the court's overall conclusion — that the Board of Examiners had failed to discharge its heavy burden of establishing the job-relatedness or the content validity of its examinations. The court's conclusion was reinforced by much of the critical testimony at the commission's hearing. Thus, the adequacy of job descriptions, the selection of job tasks, and their translation into appropriate test items was severely criticized, largely on the grounds of insufficient care and expertness.

The need for substantial expertise in the areas of psychometrics and personnel management was well-recognized by the expert witnesses. Dr. Deneen agreed that the input of psychometricians and other experts in test construction was indispensible to the construction of a valid examination. Dr. Thorndike said that if the personnel constructing examinations had familiarity only with the demands of the particular job, ". . . this is only one-half of the kind of competence that would be needed. . . ." [*Selection of Teachers,* 1972, p. 405] Indeed, he said he would be "uncomfortable" if those who played the principal role in constructing examinations were examination assistants for whom there were "no job descriptions . . . employed . . . [by] a rather informal process of recommendation" without written standards. [*Id.*]

Yet, according to members of the Board of Examiners, that is the way their entire permanent staff, except for the four members themselves, is selected. The staff consists of licensed pedagogical personnel already in the school system who are assigned to the Board of Examiners. According to the testimony of then Board Chairman Gertrude E. Unser, they are not required to have any background or training in test construction (although some of them may have had some such background or training). Indeed, there are no written requirements at all and apparently no written procedures regarding who among the school system's licensed personnel will be assigned to the Board of Examiners. The process by which temporary examination assistants are selected is, if anything, even more informal. As the earlier discussion of patronage within the system indicated, many witnesses see this process as totally inconsistent with a merit system, and members of the Board of Examiners agreed that substantial changes should be made.

It may also be inconsistent with validity, according to a number of witnesses. For example, Irving Flinker, a junior high school principal, said:

> Assistant examiners are chosen to help administer the tests on the basis of the license held. . . . The license to serve as teacher or supervisor in a special field is considered, ipso facto, enough qualification

to construct and administer tests to teacher and supervisory applicants. No inquiry is made into the actual competence, personal qualities, or special skills of the assistant examiners. A very small percentage of these assistant examiners has ever had a single graduate course in personnel selection or management. The preliminary briefing given to the assistant examiners is minimal and leaves much to be desired for administering an objective examination. It is my belief that among a group of assistant examiners . . . the variability of expectancy and standards is so wide as to negate the reliability, validity and objectivity of the entire examination process. [*Id.* at 60]

Dr. Greene said that although temporary examination assistants are "selected on an informal basis by recommendation," their competence is insured by an initial informal screening process and by removal from the approved list if their services prove unsatisfactory. The adequacy of these procedures has apparently been questioned within the school system for some time. The Board of Examiners provided the commission with a copy of a letter from Dr. Greene to Dr. Lang, dated March 21, 1969, in which Dr. Greene, responding to a request, provided a statement of how the Board of Examiners' staff was selected. Among other things, he said:

The work of each examination assistant on the job is reviewed and from time to time changes are made if the work is less than satisfactory. Since careers of individuals are determined by the recommendations of examining panels, it is important that the individuals who are chosen to serve on panels be people of good judgment, of substantial experience, of breadth of vision and understanding, informed in their fields and able to maintain the confidentiality of the process.

Later in the letter, Dr. Greene said, "In the past 3 years the compensation for examination assistants has increased considerably and we have had a number of requests from individuals who are desirous of serving. . . . [W]e anticipate a need for formalizing the procedures." Yet, at the commission hearings almost two years later Dr. Greene said that he and Dr. Rockowitz had only recently been appointed a committee to develop more formal procedures. How did the informal procedures work in the interim? According to information provided by the Board of Examiners, of the 4,500 examination assistants "approximately 8 examination assistants have been removed from the approved list in the past three years for cause. Removal is based on an evaluation of their services by examiners and Unit Heads."

Thus, about 3,500 of the 4,500 persons used as temporary examination assistants come from within the school system and are not required to have any special background or skill in test construction. Among the other 1,000 assistants there may be some with testing expertise. Ms. Unser stated that:

> We have a range of expertise available to us that is far greater than our permanent staff members. We have thousands of persons within and without the school system in state education departments, in universities, from other disciplines, from the social sciences, from psychologists, from industry, whom we call upon. [*Selection of Teachers*, 1972, p. 28]

Exactly how many of the 1,000 qualify as test experts and how often they are employed by the Board of Examiners would be important information in assessing the adequacy of the board's test construction. But the board has taken the position that the identity of temporary examination assistants is confidential information and has not provided it to the commission.

The final place to seek expertness in test construction is among the four regular members of the Board of Examiners (the chancellor or his designee is the fifth member). Contrary to their permanent and temporary staff, the four regular members are required to take a civil service examination which they say was "probably the most difficult Civil Service examination ever given." [*Selection of Teachers*, 1972. p. 27] Test construction is one of the subjects covered. Yet, the four members at the time of the hearings were all former English teachers who had moved up the supervisory ladder. When asked whether she regarded herself as a test expert, Ms. Unser replied, "I don't regard myself as a psychometric expert because I don't know what that really means. . . ." [*Id.*]

Taken together, the evidence of invalidity is convincing. But, it is of course drawn from the New York City experience. To what extent is it applicable to other school districts or to public employers outside of education? A considerable extent, according to some witnesses at the commission hearings. For the criteria and standards discussed apply to all selection procedures not just those with substantial written test components. And there is reason to believe that the New York City school system is not alone in having difficulty satisfying these criteria and standards. According to Stephen Pollak, former Assistant Attorney General in charge of the Civil Rights Division, if any examination is not sufficiently related to a careful, complete, and current job description, its job relatedness is clearly at issue and a serious legal question is raised.

> If a board refuses to hire, retain, or promote a teacher because of his score on a test, the board should be able to show that the test is a reliable predictor of the capacity of those taking the test to perform on the job in that system. If the board cannot make this showing, its action, if challenged, will not be sustained. To fulfill the mandate of the Equal Protection Clause, the standardized test must not burden or benefit candidates because of their race, economic class, or religion. . . . Further, where a test measures only a portion of the qualifications required for successful performance on the job — and that is really true with all tests that I know of — and where members of a minority group uniformly score lower on the test, the Equal Protection Clause would preclude a school board from acting solely on the basis of the test. . . . There is no requirement on plaintiffs to show that the school board has used the test purposefully to discriminate. . . . In determining whether a test discriminates against members of a minority group who will be in the test population, the school board should make its own study using expert help as necessary. . . . Where a test makes valid predictions for members of a majority group, but not for members of a minority, it should not be used in evaluating the latter group. . . . Where the test measures minor traits of teachers rather than major ones, it should not be given significant weight, particularly if members of a minority group score

below members of a majority group. Alternatives which measure
critical traits should be sought and weighed more heavily. Moreover,
this process of validation and review for non-discrimination should
not be conducted once and then forgotten. Analysis of the effect of
the test on minority applicants and review of the relationship of the
test to the skills considered necessary to top performance on the job
must be a continuing responsibility of the school administrators. . . .
I fear that few, if any, school boards have made . . . the studies neces-
sary to insure that a test serves their legitimate needs without dis-
crimination. These studies must be made and repeated as needs
change, if tests are to be the servant of the boards, rather than their
master. . . . Unless used within proper and careful limits, a test
adopted as a part will become the whole of a selection process in
what I believe will be serious risks of violations of the Constitution.
[*Selection of Teachers,* 1972, pp. 424–28] (Italics added)

Mr. Pollak spoke from broad experience in setting forth
these guidelines for all school districts. In addition to his
tenure as Assistant Attorney General in charge of the Civil
Rights Division, he has served as counsel to the plaintiffs in a
suit brought against the Columbus, Mississippi, school district,
which resulted in a federal court decision barring the use of
test-score requirements that markedly reduce the ratio of black
teachers. The school district there had required that all its
black teachers being integrated into a unitary system score at
least 1,000 on the National Teacher Examination. The result
was that 17 of the 18 first-year black teachers and only 8 of
the 73 first-year white teachers were eliminated. The judge
found that, "under this standard, 90 per cent of the white
graduates from Mississippi institutions of higher education are
eligible to teach in the Columbus school district and 89 per
cent of the black graduates from Mississippi institutions are
disqualified. This amounts to racial classification." [329 F.
Supp. at 720] And the judge concluded that the school district had failed to sustain its "very heavy burden" of proving
that the imposition of the new test-score requirement did not
constitute "an unconstitutional racial classification." [*Id.* at
721] Consequently, the court ordered the school system to

reinstate for the 1971–72 school year the eight black teachers who brought the action. It also ordered the district to establish for 1971–72 the same racial ratio among teachers that existed in 1969–70 before the test-score requirement was imposed.

This case involved a somewhat different issue than the *Chance* case—improper use of an otherwise valid test through the imposition of a racially discriminatory cutoff score. But it suggests the varied ways in which school districts can run afoul of the legal requirements governing selection procedures.

Moreover, taken in conjunction with the *Chance* case, it illustrates the national implications of these legal standards. They apply to the largest urban school district in the country and to a small, rural school district. They apply in the North where unitary school systems have always been legally required and in the South where unitary school systems are in many places just being created. They apply to situations where the best intentions may prevail and to situations where the intentions may be questionable.

Despite all these and more differences, a common thread emerges. Selection processes which rely to a substantial degree on examinations that in fact eliminate more black and Puerto Rican candidates than white candidates will be increasingly difficult to sustain in the courts. And this result is not based on the application of some legalistic formula. For what the law is saying through the courts is that school districts, and other public and private employees for that matter, must open their doors fully to all candidates who show sufficient promise of being able teachers, supervisors, and other employees without regard to traditional selection devices which cannot themselves meet the test of relevance. What the courts are doing here is cutting through the long accepted trappings of a merit system to try to reach the bedrock of true merit. The challenge of the seventies will be to build a structure for fully implementing this renewed concept of merit in fair and meaningful ways.

CHAPTER 7

ALTERNATIVES TO CURRENT SELECTION SYSTEMS

If a court rules that a selection process denies the constitutional rights of some candidates, or if a legislature restructures statutory selection requirements, or if the administrative agency in charge of actually carrying out the process decides to modify its procedures, the result is that an alternative system must be fashioned. Indeed, the decision about whether or not to replace the current selection process, in whole or in part, may turn upon whether alternatives promise to be better.

Thus, exploring possible alternatives is an essential part of any school district's review of its personnel practices and it was an important goal of the New York City Commission on Human Rights' hearings. It was a clear commitment of the hearings not only to identify and analyze existing procedures but to serve as a basis for sound recommendations. Toward this end, a wide range of expert witnesses were called because of their leadership in teacher education; in selection techniques, especially testing; and in new and innovative programs preparing school personnel on all levels. Or they were called because they represented state education departments and city school systems actively engaged in developing new forms of personnel selection. In addition, all witnesses who testified, and especially those serving in leadership roles within the New York City school system, were asked to assess the merits of possible alternatives.

The result of this inquiry was a range of alternatives. They

covered the spectrum between a minimally revised procedure which would continue heavy reliance on standardized
written tests and a totally revamped process which would
focus principally on performance in the classroom. This chapter will outline the major proposals and put them into some
perspective. It will also describe reform efforts already in progress around the country.

Although many alternatives were suggested, a number of
them, usually the ones at the conservative end of the spectrum,
received little support. And, even this limited support generally
came from those directly involved in administering the current
system. A broad consensus emerged; one of general discontent
with traditional selection methods, all of which rely heavily on
pre-employment preparation and give little attention to effective
measurement of actual performance. Screening based on knowledge or skills, presumably developed in formal academic course
work, was considered by virtually all witnesses to be an unre-
liable or at least incomplete measure of subsequent performance.
To date, most of licensure has been based on the questionable
assumption that knowledge can automatically be converted
into appropriate behavior.

Such a consensus underscores the need for major change in
the current system. But, the alternatives must be carefully
weighed against the special educational needs of a particular
state or school district before transition to a new system.
This is not to say, however, that the supporters of a particular
reform must sustain a heavy burden in proving the clear
superiority of their system over the current system. This
would result in great delay and might prove inconclusive if
the reform were tried only on a small, pilot basis. Indeed, in
federal court litigation testing the legality of various selection
procedures, the courts have uniformly placed a heavy burden
upon the defenders of the system once it has been determined
that the system operates to screen out disproportionate numbers of black and Puerto Rican candidates. Their failure to

fully justify the current system often has resulted in court ordered institution of a different selection process.

Improved State Certification for Preliminary Screening and Local Selection

The majority of the witnesses testifying at the hearings recommended a combination of state certification for initial screening and local selection as the most logical and preferable alternative because it would simplify the screening of potential candidates, minimize exclusionary aspects, and separate more clearly the professional certification (or licensing) stage from the actual employment stage of the personnel system.

Although far from perfect in its current form in New York or most other states, state certification meets the primary objectives demanded by progressive educators of opening up the system to a broader spectrum of candidates and allowing those closest to the scene, local school boards, to make the ultimate hiring decisions. In other words, it would offer to New York City's decentralized districts the same degree of flexibility and responsibility in selecting staff now enjoyed by almost all other school districts in the state and country. In exercising their selection responsibilities—and selection proper begins only after initial screening through state certification—community boards could use any selection technique they thought suited their particular needs. Freedom of the boards to experiment, according to a number of witnesses, could result in valuable data about different selection instruments.

Opponents of this alternative contend that, at present in New York and many other states, state certification is merely a perfunctory review of a candidate's transcript, testifying only to the completion of an arbitrary number and kind of college courses. As such it is no assurance of competence. Moreover, they say the administration of certification has often been snarled by bureaucratic delays.

Criticism was also directed at the second level of this alternative—the community school boards' capacity to do an effective and objective job in selection. A number of witnesses expressed fear that removal of a centralized merit system would cause the resurgence of the historic problems of patronage and political pressure which the Board of Examiners' system was designed to prevent. This is the major argument raised against serious reform of civil service systems and it is not to be taken lightly. Yet, we cannot simply react emotionally to it.

The National Civil Service League's *Model Public Personnel Administration Law* (Jan. 1971), mindful of the great need to overhaul antiquated civil service systems to fulfill the merit system intent, considered and rejected exactly that argument. The introduction to the Model Law stated:

> Depression and spoils psychology both have left their mark on current personnel systems. Therefore, perhaps the overriding characteristic needed for a law to guide the development of a viable personnel system . . . is that it be a *positive* tool with which public administrators can improve the quality of their jurisdiction's personnel, and—as a result—its services. State and local governments can no longer afford the luxury, nor in most instances do they need, a personnel statute that is grounded on a negative philosophy . . . . [M]any of the methods by which governments have continued to assure merit employment and protect the service against past abuses have also served to exclude many well-qualified persons, severely limit the flexibility of responsible elected officials, and curtail the overall effectiveness of the public service. [p. 2]

In particular, the League rejected the concept of independent "watch-dog" commissions. They have "outlived their usefulness and their continuation is incompatible with sound administrative concepts. . . . The claim that these commissions are insulating the system against pressures is often unfounded. . . . [T]he deliberations of so-called independent commissions frequently reflect political expediency rather than the requirements of good public personnel administration." [p. 3] The answer, according to the National Civil Service League, is to vest selection responsibility in the agency's chief executive.

Advocates of a system based on state certification and local selection were, nevertheless, not unaware of possible problems with this alternative. None claimed that current certification criteria are entirely satisfactory, nor that community school boards have at hand all the resources to make appropriate selection. Indeed, a sizable portion of the hearings' testimony was addressed to needed reforms in certification and to the added capabilities required by community school boards.

State certification has a limited objective—it is not claimed to be a valid predictor of teacher performance nor is it generally regarded as such. Because state certification is only a first screening, it is no guarantee of employment. According to several witnesses, this distinguishes it from the Board of Examiners' system. For many years placement on an eligible list by the Board of Examiners was tantamount to a guaranteed job in the city's schools. Under a system where state certification serves as the only mandatory, uniform screening device, determination of fitness for a particular job becomes the province of the actual employers who are free to superimpose any combination of testing, interviewing, observation, review of records, or any other objective device considered effective to meet their needs. For both initial hiring and promotion to higher levels, the combination of state certification and local selection extends hiring beyond the confines of those who have successfully passed a particular examination at a given time and allows employers to weigh qualities of training, experience, and personality in accordance with the demands of a particular role.

What is the likely effect of changing from a system like the current New York City one to a system based on state certification and freer local selection? The testimony of Superintendent Joseph Manch of Buffalo, where a change in state law freed the appointment of principals and supervisors from the examination process, was particularly pertinent. The change in the law was secured, according to Dr. Manch, because of the recognition ". . . that we were not getting capable employees as a result of our examination procedure and were unable to appoint and assign persons and most particularly of the minority community, black teachers and administrators, in a way in which we . . . [could maintain] a good balance. . . ." [*Selection of Teachers,* 1972, p. 633]. The law was changed in 1968 and in two years the ratio of minority personnel in the exempt categories was raised substantially, without any discernible lowering of standards. According to his testimony, this experience has reinforced Dr. Manch's conviction that a separate citywide examination for all categories of personnel is an unnecessary restriction.

State certification plus local selection would be less cumbersome and costly than the present New York City system, according to a number of witnesses. At this point, state certification focuses on the relevance of college preparation as demonstrated mainly by courses taken. In New York City, where the majority of applicants have attended local institutions, the relevance and the quality of college preparation could be assessed by observation and accreditation of the primary training sources, rather than by evaluation of individual graduates. But this is not to suggest that the focus of state certification should remain unchanged. The New York State Commissioner of Education Ewald B. Nyquist clearly recognized this when he said:

> There are two basic criticisms of certification as we now know it. First of all, judging fitness for licensure is based on input—courses taken—rather than output—classroom performance. Second, the decision about certification is made by agents far removed from the candidate for licensure himself. The decisions should be made, using a State approved process, by persons closer to the candidates. [*Id.* at 609]

In New York State, in common with other states, in both the State Education Department and in teacher training institutions, there is an increasing awareness of the deficiencies of traditional training and licensing practices. Indications are that New York is lessening dependence on formal criteria and moving toward a program approval approach, evidenced by growing state sponsorship and support of innovative programs. Indeed, a strong argument for reliance on state certification in a selection process is that the state education authorities appear to be more change oriented and ready to adopt new forms of training and new criteria for certification.

An array of educational experts testified to the desirability of developing performance-based criteria for certifying, selecting, and evaluating staff. As we have seen, this development is reaching the teacher training programs as well. An overview of activity on the national scene, presented by Dr. Robert Poppendieck of the U.S. Office of Education and Mr. Roy Edelfeldt of the National Education Association, disclosed an active interest in at least 30 states. Many states are engaged in defining the specific competencies that teachers should possess and that training programs should develop. Although no state, as yet, has fully developed the concepts and mechanisms needed to move to performance-based criteria, a number, including New Jersey, Washington, Minnesota, Oregon, California, Michigan, Pennsylvania, Texas, and Florida, are in the forefront. A good overview of state certification requirements can be found in Stinnett, *Manual on Certification Requirements for School Personnel in the United States,* NEA, 1970.

Representatives of the state education departments of New Jersey, Washington, and Minnesota testified at the hearings. The three states were in the midst of developing performance-based criteria and, in effect, seeking to change the role of the state in the certification or licensing process. The three exemplify some of the possible variations in approach to a common goal.

In New Jersey, 16 statewide task forces, each composed of school administrators, teachers, representatives of higher education—including schools of education and other related academic fields, curriculum specialists, and measurement and evaluation specialists—have been focusing on different teaching areas. The task forces were supplemented by advisory committees composed of representatives of the schools, civic organizations, and the community, to assure backing for task force recommendations. While developments at the time of the hearings were limited to initial teacher certification, similar studies were to be conducted for all job levels and types within the schools. The intent is to free certification from dependence on any single form of preparation, permitting assessment of pertinent skills developed in any relevant training or experience, including the Peace Corps, VISTA, Teacher Corps, or community work. The timetable looked to field testing of new criteria by the fall of 1972 and formal institution by the following summer but that schedule seems to have been overly optimistic.

Minnesota, with a tradition of certification based on program approval, also reported that it was modifying the state role, shifting it from a regulatory to an enabling function. Under this approach, the state would make available the training local needs require. This is consistent with the view that professional competence is best determined at the local level. Program accreditation task forces, working toward establishment of standards, have been composed of local representatives of all interested parties, including members of the local community. Major changes in certification, both in form and in content, are underway as a part of this whole new thrust. Life certification was abolished by an act of the legislature in 1970. Two types of certificates were envisioned — entrance and continuing—with the latter to run a maximum of five years. Committees in each school district, composed of professional and community representatives, will recommend candidates for renewal. As we will see in Chapter 8, this development may signal an important new direction. Under the Minnesota plan, a state committee will also coordinate local activity and set such broad standards as evolve out of local training plans. It is anticipated that new legislation will require, for example, that all teacher training institutions offer a human relations program in conjunction with community groups, have a plan to develop and evaluate specific competencies, and design a program of self-evaluation. Performance-based criteria, it is hoped, will open promotional sequences beyond the usual single hierarchy, permitting flexible horizontal and vertical career patterns. Ultimately, all distinctions in title and rank will be functional, and such arbitrary distinctions, as for example the difference between paraprofessional and teacher, now reflecting formal education, will disappear.

In the state of Washington, the focus has been on redesigning teacher education. Consortiums composed of representatives of professional associations, school personnel, parents, and colleges and universities have been engaged in framing new programs and recommending standards against which performance can be assessed. Performance standards were adopted in 1968 for school support personnel—including counselors—and it was expected that plans for all staff levels would be completed by the fall of 1971. Here the emphasis is on involvement at the local level. Each consortium is to recommend standards to be applied in programs within a specific locale. Once the plans are approved, the state function will be to monitor programs to insure fulfillment of the standards set. The essential ingredient is to change the role of the state and, as has been true in Minnesota, to shift the responsibility for developing criteria to the local level, thereby allowing considerable leeway to individual colleges and local groups. The expectation is that without any across-the-board state requirements, training and certification standards will be more responsive to local needs and far less resistant to change. The state will certify all personnel in three stages—preparatory, initial and continuing—to insure the involvement of all relevant agencies throughout the careers of school personnel.

It is noteworthy that written examinations are not envisioned by any of these states as a part of the certification process. All three plans call for colleges to attest to the part of teaching skill that can be measured outside of the job setting. Any college whose graduates proved deficient in literacy or subject matter knowledge, according to Dr. Ward Sinclair of the New Jersey State Education Department, would be unable to place candidates and would lose state approval. The appropriate role of the state will be to stimulate and evaluate programs, rather than stipulate their form, and to automatically certify graduates of approved programs.

Although New York State may not have progressed as far as some other states toward actually developing new criteria, it has become increasingly flexible in the administration of standard criteria and has established some alternative routes to certification through proficiency examinations and experimental training programs. Sample programs now in force in New York City colleges were presented at the hearing, including field-based teacher training, training for open-corridor teaching, and nondegree training of leaders in fields outside of education for managerial roles in schools.

Freeing the New York City school system—which has about one-third of the state's pupils—from preoccupation with the process of written tests for 1,200 licenses, would be a powerful stimulant to accelerated development of these new standards and approaches throughout the state. New York City, with its enormous and varied school population and its array of colleges and universities, could be a fertile source of new ideas and programs. Decentralization, if more fully utilized, would offer a unique opportunity to measure and compare differing selection techniques.

Indeed, since the commission's hearings, the State Education Department's Division of Teacher Education and Certification has issued a document, entitled "A New Style of Certification," which begins this way:

In a rapidly changing society in which "old ways" are continually challenged for their relevance and validity, questions are being raised concerning the appropriateness of tradional education patterns. Some of the questions which particularly concern the Division of Teacher Education and Certification focus on the relevance of teacher preparation and certification to teaching competence, and the accommodations to admit to teaching persons whose knowledge and teaching ability are achieved through a different set of experiences than those now prescribed for certification. Support continues to grow for the concept that certification should be based on a teacher's demonstrated abilities instead of being based solely on his completion of a formal collegiate program. This concept is nurtured by recently developed methods for analyzing a teacher's classroom performance, e.g., Flanders, etc., and further supported by the growing concern for accountability. Believing that the above mentioned questions and developments are worthy of serious consideration and careful response, the Department is proposing a set of process standards to be followed in developing trial projects in teacher education which will lead to a certification that signifies a measure of competence. [*A New Style of Certification,* Mar. 15, 1971, p. 1]

The pilot project outlined by the division's document provides for a number of educational agencies to combine their resources and efforts to "evolve acceptable criteria for teacher certification," [*Id.* at 2] of either the initial or continuing kind. Overall responsibility for the planning, development, monitoring, and evaluation of the project will be vested in a policy board composed of representatives of the board of education and teachers in the participating district, and of the institutions of higher education and teacher education students involved. Community representatives may also be included.

The standards established by the State Education Department for the project require the "cooperating agencies" to consider the objectives and priorities of the particular school system and the competencies a teacher should have to serve in its schools. These competencies are, in turn, to be related to the objective and become the criteria for obtaining a certificate. According to the document, "In dealing with the competencies necessary for the initial certificate, the cooperating agencies should focus on the performance expected of beginning teachers. The competencies for the continuing certificate should focus on the performance expected of the experienced teachers." [*Id.* at 8–9]

Once the criteria are established, the "cooperating agencies must specify the evidence that they will accept and the manner in which they will ascertain that the prospective teacher has reached an acceptable level of competence." [*Id.* at 10] In developing evidence of competency, consideration is to be given to:

1. Command of subject matter (knowledge criteria)

2. Teaching behavior (performance criteria)

3. Achievement of pupils (product criteria)

But, according to the document, "the emphasis is on what the teacher must be able to do rather than on any courses completed." [*Id.*]

An essential part of the project is the development of appropriate methods for helping teachers to meet the competency criteria if they are unable to do so initially. This assistance must be constantly revised as evaluation reports suggest.

Finally, a management system must be established to provide continuous data on student progress, to determine accountability for each aspect of the project, and to serve as a basis for evaluation.

Despite the broad discretion given to policy boards for the pilot projects, ultimate legal responsibility for certification remains with the State Education Department. So, it will play an active role in evaluating and approving the projects. In discussing the prospects for widespread implementation of this "new style of certification," Vincent C. Gazzetta, director of the Division of Teacher Education and Certification, said it would take at least two or three years from the introduction of the pilot projects for any significant change to be made. The reason, according to Mr. Gazzetta, was that a lot of proselytizing had to be done because "we want to bring the teaching community along with us on this." [*New York Times,* Jan. 10, 1971, p. 1, col. 3]

By October 25, 1972, when Mr. Gazzetta spoke at a Public Education Association Forum on "New Directions in the Selection and Evaluation of School Supervisors," he was already able to be more specific. The State Board of Regents had defined the purpose of certification as ensuring "that all professional staff possess and maintain demonstrated competence to enable children to learn." [Gazzetta, "Performance Based Certification and Evaluation of Supervisors," a paper presented at the PEA Forum, Oct. 25, 1972, p. 2]. To carry out that purpose, the State Education Department will focus on activities on three fronts: the accreditation of preparatory programs, the actual certification policy and procedure, and the need for a statewide system of continued education.

Beginning September 1, 1973, any new preparatory program submitted for approval, or existing programs requiring reapproval, must be "competency-based and field-centered." Mr. Gazzetta defined such a program in terms of the following characteristics:

1. The skills, knowledge, and attitudes (competencies) which are deemed necessary are announced in advance and are made public.

2. The criteria for assessing the attainment of the competencies are announced in advance and are made public.

3. There is a strong research and corrective action procedure which will permit: (1) validation of the competencies, and (2) modification of the competencies and/or assessment criteria where necessary.

4. Provides evidence that the planning, development, implementation, and evaluation of the program is a collaborative effort between higher institutions, school districts and the professional staff of the districts.

5. The preparatory program is one which facilitates the attainment of

the competencies and relates to the student's capability and learning style. [*Id.* at 3–4]

The State Department, in exercising its approval responsibility, will use three questions as the focal points: What skills, knowledge, and attitudes should the student demonstrate at the completion of the program? What evidence will be acceptable to verify that they have been achieved? What evidence is available to indicate that the desired skills, knowledge, and attitudes are appropriate?

This marked departure from the traditional program approval approach—principally, reviews of training and experience of staff, curriculum components, physical facilities and supporting services, and admission and grading practices—is easier stated than accomplished. And Mr. Gazzetta recognized the difficulties. He said:

> The problems and difficulties inherent in a new system are not being denied nor are they to be downgraded. Thus, while the long range plan identifies September 1, 1973 as the initiating date we are not expecting to see highly sophisticated programs at that point. The process must be a developmental one. The important aspect is that from an identified starting point corrective action can be taken to guide the development of highly sophisticated programs.
>
> The answer is not in grappling with what constitutes a strong program of preparation. The answer more appropriately lies in grappling with what the professional needs in terms of skills, knowledge, and attitudes. On that basis, then, the preparatory program should be developed to facilitate the attainment of the competencies. [*Id.* at 4–5]

But a new approach to approval of teacher education programs is only the first step. The second and equally necessary step is changes in certification itself. "When all preparatory programs are competency-based and field-centered," said Mr. Gazzetta, "certification will be granted only on the recommendation of an approved preparatory program. The individual evaluation of credentials will be halted." [*Id.* at 5]. This is expected to happen by September 1, 1980, but the actual date will be dependent upon the rate of progress. Another fundamental proposed change in certification is the elimination of a permanent certificate. To emphasize the *maintenance* of demonstrated competence to enable children to learn, a periodic assessment requirement would be imposed beginning also September 1, 1980. Mr. Gazzetta stressed that this new approach would have to relate to individual staff members' particular situations rather than to statewide normative data. But the details have yet to be developed.

Finally, substantial attention will be given to continuing education of teachers and supervisors. "Increasing knowledge in both content areas and in learning theory, changing curriculum, new patterns of organization, etc., call for a continued effort to not only maintain, but enhance staff capabilities." [*Id.* at 6]. Career Development Centers and Teachers Centers, which will be discussed later in this chapter, were mentioned as possible models for New York State's program of continuing staff training and education.

One important result of this kind of performance-oriented approach is that it may open the door to much faster advancement of paraprofessionals to teaching certificates based principally upon their performance in the schools. Indeed, the paraprofessionals might be an ideal control group in an experiment testing the significance of traditional qualifications to successful classroom performance. Broad implementation of this type of performance-based certification would also provide local boards of education with more meaningful assistance in its employment process. The holder of a certificate would have to be more than just the recipient of a college degree with the requisite number of education credits. He or she would even have to be more than a good test-taker.

The New York State pilot program includes a variant of improved state certification mentioned by a number of witnesses at the commission's hearings—initial or provisional certification. The theory is that the initial period of teaching or supervisory service should be a continuation of professional training as well as an evaluation opportunity. To recognize it as such would encourage the development of more meaningful in-service training programs and other professionally supportive efforts. Also, to structure the period as an internship would encourage careful evaluation before the granting of more permanent status. The overriding question of how fully and objectively a teacher's or supervisor's competence can be evaluated on the basis of performance will be discussed in Chapter 8.

The Public Education Association, a New York City-based organization, has formally proposed the institution of a two-stage state certification system for the reasons expressed above, among others. In its proposal, PEA said that "New York State, like most states, has allowed to develop over the years a licensing system for public school personnel which is not only wrong in detail but wrong in basic design. We need a radical reexamination of what we are trying to accomplish, and we must design a new system on premises which are valid for today's world." [PEA Proposal for a Two-Step System for State Certification of Teachers and School Administrators, 1971, p. 1]

Thus, PEA proposed the following basic premises for the development of a viable new system of state certification or licensing:

(1) A teacher is a person who helps other people learn.

(2) A school administrator is primarily a person who helps teachers teach.

(3) Among the most important qualities of teachers and school administrators are personal qualities, such as leadership, integrity, ability to communicate with others, commitment to children, and dedication to learning. Today's call for a more "human" education will depend upon the human qualities of those who work with children.

(4) The combinations of qualities that make for a good teacher or administrator are complex, and not uniform in all candidates.

Some kinds of teachers perform well in some situations and not others, under some learning styles and not others, with some children and not others, at one period of a child's life and not others, or with some aspects of a child's learning and not others. The same is true of school administrators.

(5) *Mechanical or mass-administered certification requirements or examinations can not adequately evaluate the kinds of personal qualities most important to teaching and administering schools;* even less do they have the sensitivity or flexibility for precise assignments for specific needs.

(6) The most reliable test of the competence of teachers and school administrators is through evaluation of their performance on the job.

(7) Teachers and teacher organizations should play a greater role than they now do in setting standards for professional competence and in evaluating performance.

(8) The assessment of performance on the job must be fair and objective. It should not be left solely to the subjective judgments of an immediate supervisor or any other group. It should involve the observation and perspectives of teachers, supervisors, parents, students, and others. [*Id.* at 1–2] (Italics added)

The PEA plan is to have a provisional license available to the widest range of "high quality candidates." Thus, provisional licenses could be granted to candidates who complete an approved program of preparation, or receive at least a certain score on the NTE, or pass any other special examination, test or experimental evaluation program approved by the commissioner. Traditional teacher training would, therefore, be only one of several routes to a provisional license.

Holding a provisional license would qualify a candidate to be hired by any school district in the state. Of course, the school district could use additional criteria of its own choosing to further assess the candidates' potential for successful performance.

Once a person is appointed on a provisional license, the granting of a regular license would depend upon an evaluation of his or her job performance. According to the PEA proposal:

Good school systems have always relied on evaluation of performance in hiring, promoting, and granting tenure, but such evaluation has not been used for the granting of licenses. The two operations admittedly have a different legal significance: Decisions by an individual school system to hire, promote, or grant tenure to teachers or school administrators all relate to their employment status with the particular school system. A license, on the other hand, is a certification from the state as to the competence of the candidate.

The idea of the two-step licensing procedure is to use on-the-job performance evaluation, which school districts must undertake during the probationary period in any case, as the last step in the licensing process: "Let's see how well he performs on the job before we give him a license." The performance evaluation would be tied in with improved supervision and in-service training for beginning teachers and administrators, which are badly needed in their own right.

Since a license is valid state-wide, the evaluation of performance, although carried out by local school districts, would have to be done on behalf of the state and would have to be periodically inspected and supervised by the state to ensure uniformity of standards. The process would also have to be formalized, with written evaluations and procedures to ensure the objectivity and fairness that have been the laudable aims of the New York City merit system, and to permit appeal. [*Id.* at 4]

Objectivity would be obtained primarily through publicly stated criteria and evaluations which incorporated the judgments not only of the candidate's supervisors but of other teachers, students, and parents. Representatives of nearby universities and other outside agencies might also be involved to reduce the possibilities of parochial judgments. And this is an important point.

For despite the broad consensus favoring a selection system based on improved state certification and local selection, two concerns relating to "parochial judgments" warrant careful consideration. Fears were expressed at the commission's hearings that the process will degenerate into pure patronage and that vigilante action by special interest groups will control decision-making. Proponents of the citywide examination see it as a protection against such abuses.

Little evidence was presented to support this assumption, and extensive testimony at the hearings by supporters of the examination system failed to lend credibility to fears of corruption and disorder. Nonetheless, these fears can never be taken lightly, because they have often been linked to valid issues of due process.

The essence of due process in the American system is that law, rules, and custom should err always on the side of zealous protection of individual rights. The Bill of Rights is not just important in case of massive threats to civil liberty; it is important as a constant safeguard against the slightest possible abridgement of any citizen's rights. Proof of possible large scale abuses in a school system is not, therefore, necessary to justify strict safeguards to ensure fairness and due process. Adequate safeguards should be an integral part of any selection process whatever its potential for bias or corruption. This is essential even though testimony at the hearings generally failed to support the oft-stated fears that local selection actually leads to bias or corruption.

In communities where local selection, unhampered by elaborate written tests, is the rule, patronage and related problems have not become serious problems. Witnesses from other cities and states reported that they were not plagued by such problems. Teachers in districts which do not use local written examinations are neither demonstrably inferior nor less secure in their jobs. Here again, the appraisal of Dr. Joseph Manch, Superintendent of Schools of Buffalo, which has the only system in the state comparable to New York City's, was most persuasive. He reported that there have been no instances of undue interference in Buffalo since examinations were eliminated for supervisors and principals.

Despite such reassurances based on the experiences of other school systems, a few witnesses expressed the view that New York City presents a fundamentally different situation. Albert Shanker, President of the UFT, considers what is feasible in more homogeneous and stable communities impossible in New York. He and the UFT favored abolition of the Board of Examiners until just five years ago, but now regard it or some other examination system as a necessary bulwark against "a process of confrontation and probably a process of selection extremely unrepresentative of the communities and New York." [*Selection of Teachers,* 1972, p. 343]

New York does face undercurrents of racial and ethnic tension which have in the past spilled over into dangerous and frightening conflicts. It would help little, however, in efforts to prevent future conflicts, if fear or speculation were sufficient reason to perpetuate a system which has had other harmful effects. It is not asking too much of an employment system that it *both* select teachers of the highest demonstrated competence to educate that district's children *and* assure freedom from bias and unfairness.

To be sure, change carries some unpredictability or risk. The unpredictability must be reduced by conscientious appraisal of the facts and experiences at hand, and the actual risks must be dealt with forthrightly.

The experience of other communities is not the only evidence contradicting fears that favoritism and a spoils system would follow hard on the heels of adoption of a less regimented selection process. New York City's own experience to date with decentralization has generally indicated that concern with the quality and effectiveness of education is high among many citizens. This was manifested not only by the widespread and high quality participation and interest in the hearings, but also in the testimony of witnesses, including community board members, community superintendents, and parent and community spokesmen.

In Community Superintendent Andrew Donaldson's words:

> The public is in there watching. The mothers and fathers are at those schools nearly every day. These community school boards have been elected by a very aroused populace. The children themselves are aware

how well the school is run or misrun. And for us to assume that simple political patronage will move people into these positions and that no questions will be asked, I think is to assume the ridiculous. [*Selection of Teachers*, 1972, p. 210]

Less explicit, but clearly present in the minds of those who oppose decentralized selection, is the possibility that race or ethnic identity may become the overriding factor in selection. This would be persuasive indeed if the fear were realistic. But aside from some generalized charges of racism, the actual experience indicates otherwise.

Dr. Marilyn Gittell, Director of Queens College's Institute for Community Studies, reported that a study of New York City's three demonstration districts showed that screening of staff was thorough and careful and those selected were generally superior candidates. Parents who participated in screening were concerned with teaching ability and not race and ethnic background. In fact, in answer to the question, "Do you think more black personnel should be hired?" the basic response of the parents interviewed was negative and a number of parents actually wrote in, "We don't care whether teachers are black or white; we just want them to teach our children." [*Id.* at 574]

A study of parental attitudes in the choice of principals conducted by the Center for Community Studies at Columbia Teachers College found a majority of parents—62% of those surveyed—ready to identify qualities they considered essential, but with no opinion on whether or not principals should share the same ethnic background as a majority of the students. [*Id.* at 462]

This finding was confirmed by Public Education Association studies of individual schools, cited by David Seeley, its director. His opinion, supported by an analysis of numerous individual schools' procedures, was this:

The cry that "We want a black principal for black kids" is made by a few spokesmen in certain cases, but this seems to be mostly a generalized expression of dissatisfaction with the kind of staff that has been produced by the "white controlled system." Once the actual selection procedure begins filling a particular vacancy, we have seen in every case examined that the parents' prime concern is to find the candidate who will do the best job for their children. As often as not, the person selected is white. [*Id.* at 334]

Thus, empirical studies suggest that neither corruption nor racism has become a factor in the school system as decision-making has gravitated to the local level.

Clearly, however, race or ethnic background is not a matter which the school system may ignore. Assuring both equal opportunity and effective education may require affirmative action to upgrade the role of minorities in the system—the kind of affirmative action routinely required of private employers by federal, state, and local law. This does not necessarily imply the establishment of onerous quotas or preferential hiring. It does acknowledge the importance of achieving better racial representation as a goal of all personnel policies and practices in a country where such equalization has been tragically delayed.

Race has been an explicit factor in making the school personnel policies fairer in such cities as Detroit and Buffalo, where significant improvements in providing equal employment opportunities have occurred. In addition, numerous witnesses testified to the deficiencies in the education of Spanish-speaking and Chinese-speaking children, a case where ethnic factors as they relate to the ability to speak a language in addition to English attain particular significance.

If commitment to teach children (especially those who have difficulties in the school system), sensitivity to the needs of a community, ability to communicate effectively with children and their parents, were accorded appropriate weight, along with subject matter knowledge, literacy, and the like, undoubtedly a higher proportion of those selected would come from minority groups. Under such an approach, the number of bilingual persons on the professional staff of the school system would surely increase significantly. Also, other serious problems arising from undue restriction of eligibility would be alleviated. Lists of eligibles, especially in the case of principals, have frequently offered few choices to many schools, since those on the lists often declined to consider schools where openings existed. Inexperienced teachers have often been "drafted" to fill assignments considered difficult, where they mark time until they are eligible for transfer. Several community superintendents and principals testified of their ability to find well-qualified persons, eager to serve in the very assignments rejected by many of those on the eligible lists. Often, however, the Board of Examiners' procedures have stood squarely in the way of the appointment of such candidates. Flexible local selection would lift many barriers of the kind that now further disadvantage the disadvantaged schools.

This does not mean that race or origin, standing by itself as a qualification, or any form of arbitrary exclusion, can ever be tolerated. The aim of change must be to improve the quality and effectiveness of personnel and to equalize employment opportunity through greater openness and flexibility. Any resort to the exclusive criterion of race or origin would not only do violence to basic concepts of human rights but would undermine the purpose of reform. Adequate safeguards against this kind of abuse must accompany any new system.

Members of community boards were among the first at the hearings to recognize the need for a range of supportive services to permit them to adequately discharge their obligations to all their contituents. They pointed to their need for assistance in developing sound recruitment and selection practices and to their need for expertise in evaluating performance. Several recommended specifically that local selection be required to be open and readily reviewable and that adequate protection against favoritism be developed.

Some protection already exists in most state laws. The New York City Board of Education and the chancellor, in common with their counterparts in most school districts, have statutory

powers which can be used to afford candidates protection
against arbitrary or unfair treatment. For example, the chancellor
has the power and duty to establish minimum education and
experience requirements for professional personnel. The Board
of Education has the authority to develop citywide personnel
procedures and policies which the chancellor has the power
and duty to enforce. Moreover, the State Commissioner
of Education has broad authority to hear controversies arising
in the schools. And, of course, recourse to the courts is always
possible and frequently used in school matters.

A Continuing Role for the Board of Examiners?

But, if selection were based on improved state certification
and local hiring, and if the due process rights of candidates
were protected by state and citywide requirements enforced
by the Commissioner of Education, and, ultimately, the courts,
what role would remain for the Board of Examiners in New
York City and its counterparts in other school districts (as well
as the licensing agencies in other areas of public employment)?
Many critics would say, "none," and have already said so. Beginning in the 1940's with the Strayer-Yavner Report, at least
half a dozen detailed studies commissioned by the State Education Department, the New York City Board of Education,
and private agencies have concluded that the Board of Examiners
should be eliminated. In recent years that conclusion has been
reached by the City Board of Education, the Regents of the
State of New York, the New York City Commission on Human
Rights, and the Fleischmann Commission, among others. The
last is perhaps especially noteworthy. As a part of its elaborate,
three-year study of the New York State education system, the
18-member commission appointed by Governor Rockefeller
concluded that the Board of Examiners should be abolished;
community boards should have "sole responsibility" for the
appointment of all personnel working in schools under their
jurisdiction (except that school principals should be selected

by parent advisory councils from lists prepared by superintendents and school boards and some voice in the selection process should be given to school faculties and to students at the high school level); local boards, in turn, should give principals "the major voice in the selection of teachers and in setting the educational tone of the school." [*New York Times,* Oct. 19, 1972, p. 1, col. 6]   Interestingly, the Fleischmann Commission also recommended sweeping changes in the way teachers are trained, certified, hired, and paid. In particular, the commission proposed that all new teachers should be required to complete satisfactorily a two-year internship before they became certified as classroom teachers, and that more paraprofessionals, volunteers—even older students—and supervisors should be used in the classroom.

Elimination of the Board of Examiners in New York City, and perhaps comparable bodies in other cities, requires legislative action. As we have seen, that has not been easy to accomplish in the past and it may not be appreciably easier in the future, even with the judicial and administrative developments discussed in Chapter 6 and earlier in this chapter. There are political problems, largely represented by the increasingly vigorous lobbying activities of the teacher and supervisor organizations (and other public employee unions). And there are practical problems. What happens to the personnel of these agencies? In the case of the Board of Examiners this should not be a serious problem since only the four regular members of the Board of Examiners are permanent employees of the board. All the rest are teachers and supervisors in the school system who are assigned to the board for periods of one or two years.

But a compromise may be necessary, at least until a new decentralized system could prove its worth. Fortunately there is a rational basis for a compromise. Although the needs of individual schools vary, even under a local selection system there would be elements common to all districts and all schools that could be handled most efficiently by a central body. For this reason, many witnesses saw a new role for the Board of Education or the Board of Examiners as an advisory and review agent. This central agency could provide information to all applicants interested in New York City, help to put them in contact with community boards whose needs matched the applicant's skills and interests, investigate and review basic data concerning all applicants, develop guidelines for selection procedures, train community board members in interviewing and observation techniques, design performance criteria and measurements for evaluation, and supply outside experts in training, selection, and evaluation to consult with community boards. In addition, such a central agency might design internships and in-service training programs, and conduct systematic research to measure the effectiveness of personnel and to compare different selection and training techniques. This is a challenging assignment, far more demanding than designing and administering standardized written tests. Upgrading selection procedures will require not only greater flexibility and innovation but also careful research and evaluation. The Board of Examiners, or some successor agency in the city board's Office of Personnel, could serve as a valuable service agency to the city board and community boards.

But even if the legislature refused to modify the statutory responsibilities of the Board of Examiners, there are important ways in which the selection process could be improved. Whether this revised process, or even a process based on state certification and local hiring, should involve continued substantial reliance on a written test is an important question.

Continued Reliance on Written Tests

As more reliable performance-based criteria for selection are developed, both state certification and local selection will rely on them. Hopefully, if the Board of Examiners remained in existence, its procedures too would reflect this development.

The extent to which there should be continued reliance on written tests was discussed by many witnesses. Most of them criticized substantial reliance on written tests which focus on acquired knowledge. In their judgment, written proficiency tests generally do no more than confirm college grades. In New York City—where approximately 65% of new teachers are graduates of City University and many more come from other local institutions—such confirmation would seem especially unnecessary. Moreover, since New York City promotions are generally awarded to those with substantial years of experience in the city's schools, reliance on written tests for supervisory and administrative positions is perhaps even less appropriate than for teacher applicants.

In the view of many experts, written tests are actually costly to administer and process and require continual assessment and revision to assure validity. In addition, even if intended as only one facet of the selection process, written tests frequently become the whole of it because test scores appear more conclusive and incontrovertible than the judgment of peers, supervisors, or observers. Evidence of this tendency is manifest in New York City where the probationary period—ostensibly a critical element in selection of personnel—is grossly underutilized and, in fact, serves only to disqualify those who display totally unacceptable behavior. Other witnesses said formal written tests may actually be counterproductive in assessing capacity if they place undue emphasis on test-taking skills at the expense of qualities such as ability to communicate knowledge, creativity, commitment, and the ability to grow in sensitivity to the needs of children and parents. Studies of test performance, according to one expert witness, suggest this may pose special problems for minority candidates. And, more generally, witnesses stressed that standardized written tests create a clear potential for discrimination, whether intentional or not, against minorities or "outsiders" to any given locality or system. Finally, according to witnesses, even partial reliance on a written test would impede the development of more valid performance-based selection criteria.

Some witnesses suggested, however, that written tests may have a continuing place in well-conceived selection procedures in conjunction with other selection techniques, but only to the extent that test scores can be demonstrated to have a clear and consistent relationship to performance. As Chapter 6 demonstrated, a written test will have to meet increasingly precise validation standards.

(a)   Locally Created Tests. The locally created tests of the New York City Board of Examiners have thus far failed to meet the legal standards applied by the Federal District Court and Court of Appeals in the *Chance* case. This fact, together with the lack of evidence that the few school systems in the country using locally developed written tests have superior teacher quality or pupil achievement, has led some critics to favor elimination of such tests from the selection process. For the process of revision and validation would be a lengthy one, even if work were begun on the necessary changes immediately. And the result of this process would likely be heavier reliance on aspects of the selection machinery other than the written test anyway.

Walter Degnan, President of the Council of Supervisors and Administrators, which represents most of New York City's 4,000 school administrators, has been one of the Board of Examiners' strongest supporters. Yet, even he urged that the licensing procedures be revamped immediately to comply with Judge Mansfield's objections in the *Chance* case. Degnan said:

> I'm not saying the examiners shouldn't fight this court ruling, but the school system will be in a state of limbo if there are years of litigation and the children will be the losers. I agree that changes and modifications must be made in the tests if they are to be viable and if the merit system is to be preserved. I hope something can be worked

out that's mutually acceptable to the court and the examiners. [*New York Times*, July 16, 1971, p. 32, col. 2]

As of October 1972, the Board of Examiners seemed amenable to working out a new set of procedures with the *Chance* plantiffs, for the approval of the court, rather than doggedly playing out the legal string. A ten-member task force, five representing the plaintiffs and five the defendants, was convened to develop the new plan and to consider what legislative changes would be necessary. Although one can only speculate about this, the replacement on the Board of Ms. Unser and Dr. Greene, two of its staunchest spokesmen, with Sylvester King, a black man, and Nathan Quinones, a Puerto Rican, may help to explain the Board's rather more conciliatory posture.

Albert Shanker, another strong, albeit relatively recent, supporter of the Board of Examiners, was noticeably and uncharacteristically silent about the implications of the *Chance* decision. Shanker has taken the position that some form of written test is necessary as a buffer against "unrepresentative" community groups and to upgrade the status of the teaching profession. He stated at the hearings, however, that either the National Teacher Examination or a statewide licensing examination would be acceptable alternatives to the current locally created test. And these may be the more fruitful directions to explore for those who share Mr. Shanker's view about the continuing need for a mandatory, written test. Even given the present spirit of cooperation, the likelihood that the Board of Examiners' procedures can be adequately restructured in a relatively short time is not great. The prospect of a lengthy hiatus with only interim selection procedures in effect, although they have worked quite well, leaves open many questions for the school system, the candidates, and the children.

(b)   The National Teacher Examination. If the use of any written test is to be required, the National Teacher Examination appears to be a logical instrument. Developed by the

Educational Testing Service and initiated in 1940, it is already used by four states for all their school districts, and in 1,100 additional school districts. Moreover, New York City itself currently makes use of the NTE under the 45% provision of the Decentralization Law and as an alternative examination in outreach recruiting activities conducted by the Office of Personnel. Thousands of teacher candidates for the city school system have used the NTE alternative. The NTE offers the advantage of broader application, permitting nationwide recruiting. The test is given four times a year in some 400 centers and candidates' scores are readily available. The test, however, has some practical disadvantages when compared with the Board of Examiners' test. It is more costly to the individual applicant (although presumably less costly to the school system as a whole) and covers only a relatively few teaching subject areas (especially as compared to the 1,200 licenses for which the Board of Examiners examines).

In terms of validity as a selection instrument, the NTE appears to have some elements of superiority over the Board of Examiners' tests, for it is prepared by a permanent staff of experts in both job analysis and test design, and is subject to regular review and revision, twice a year in common branches and annually in teaching areas. (Every three to four years it is completely redone.) The examination is carefully studied for content validity to insure that it tests only knowledge gained in college programs. The chief value of the National Teacher Examination, according to its developers, is to supplement and, to some extent, standardize academic records of prospective candidates.

There are, however, two fundamental limitations of the NTE in common with any standardized written examination: first, the question of predictive validity, and, second, the impact on minority selection. With respect to the former, the Educational Testing Service itself makes clear the limitations of the NTE as a predictive instrument. According to Dr. James

R. Deneen, Senior Program Director for Teacher Examinations at Educational Testing Service, content-validated tests are predictive only to the extent that competent performance requires the kind of knowledge gained in teacher-training programs. ETS operates on the assumption that a test that measures college training can make a contribution to the selection process but makes no claim beyond that. In Dr. Deneen's words:

> To evaluate, for example, a prospective high school mathematics teacher's knowledge of math is surely reasonable, but to predict his overall performance as a mathematics teacher on the basis of test score alone is not reasonable. . . . Results from the NTE say nothing about other factors which are absolutely critical to success in teaching, for example, physical skills, motivation, attitudes, ability to communicate with children, and so on. [*Selection of Teachers,* 1972, pp. 414; 416]

Thus, according to its designers, the NTE should only be used as one of several selection criteria.

The consensus of the test experts who testified was that the development of tests to measure effective teacher capacity is hampered by the unavailability of good measures of performance. Efforts in this direction offer some hope that practical and stable measures of demonstrated ability will soon materialize. [See Rosenshine and Furst, "Current and Future Research on Teacher Performance Criteria," in Smith (ed.), *Research on Teacher Education: A Symposium,* Prentice-Hall, 1971, ch. 2.] When such measures do exist, they, together with tests of subject area knowledge, will upgrade substantially the selection process and, thereby, the quality of teaching. In the meanwhile, Dr. Deneen said that he believed NTE scores could be given significant weight in initial screening. But he cautioned that overreliance on test scores even now must be avoided.

How the NTE is used, therefore, is the critical consideration, even if it is used as only one of several criteria. That is particularly true when one objective is to give equal opportunity to minority candidates. The NTE itself sets no passing scores. Test scores are equated to a percentile rank comparing individual scores with national norms. The test is an achievement test directly reflecting college training and not an aptitude or intelligence test. The scores are more accurately indicative of the content of graduate programs than individual capacity. The decision of how to use test scores, whether to set cutoff points and at what level they are set, is left to the determination of employers. And these decisions are the significant ones, especially in relation to minority candidates. [*See, e.g., Baker v. Columbus Mun. Sep. School Dist., supra.*]

The NTE, in common with other standardized tests, has been charged with being discriminatory. Statements ascribing bias to the NTE were made at the hearings. Daisy Hicks, a New York City Board of Education recruiting official, said, ". . . the National Teacher Examination is another examination based on things like all examinations we had to face . . . [and] not based on norms where the Black man or the Puerto Rican American were included." [*Selection of Teachers,* 1972, p. 114] She reported that many schools which used the examination in an effort "to integrate their staff are getting rid of the NTE because they found that it really screens out Blacks." [*Id.*] James Watkins, a teacher and consultant on recruiting, agreed that the NTE was as discouraging to minority groups as other tests.

According to the test designers, however, any discriminatory effect is not a product of the test; rather it results from the establishment of required passing scores. Low test scores for a given group, noted Dr. Deneen, are not necessarily an indicator of poor test construction. Test scores may confirm the disparity of educational opportunity but do not indicate individual deficiency. Moreover, the creators of the NTE do not claim that it adequately examines persons with limited facility in English or those trained in other settings such as Puerto Rican colleges. The Educational Testing Service, cognizant of these limitations, has been actively working with panels of

black educators to scrutinize the National Teacher Examination
for manifestations of subtle bias, and is constructing a Spanish
version, as well as a new test focused on teaching in urban setting
    This suggests that the use of rigid cutoff scores may dis-
qualify disproportionate numbers of minority applicants. Consequently, school boards must use other selection methods
either in substitution for or as supplements to the NTE. In Dr.
Deneen's words, "precisely because teaching competence cannot be predicted on the basis of college achievement alone,
measures of such achievement should never be the only criteria
for selection of beginning teachers." [*Id.* at 415]
    Thus, the NTE appears to be only a partial answer to the
current problem faced by New York City and other urban
school districts. Under the 45% provision of the New York
Decentralization Law, districts with schools in the lowest 45%
based on citywide reading tests can bypass the Board of Examiners' procedures and select teachers who qualify by alternative routes such as passing the NTE with a score equivalent
to the average passing mark required of teachers during the
prior year by the five largest cities. But using the NTE as a
primary qualification may be dubious and other factors should
clearly enter into selection decisions. The 45% rule, admittedly
a legislative compromise, may nevertheless benefit some city
schools. Dr. Theodore H. Lang, Director of the Personnel Office of the New York City Board of Education, stated, "I hope
that it [the NTE alternative] will bring better qualified teachers,
as well as more Blacks and Puerto Ricans into the system. It
will be closer to the practices of other school systems, giving
the principal more authority in the determination of his staff,
involving the principal in the selection of the teacher and the
principal then having a greater responsibility in the training of
the teacher." [*Id.* at 81]. Dr. Lang's comment points up what
a number of witnesses referred to as the absurdity of the 45%
provision. If the Board of Examiners' procedures really determine "merit and fitness," then why permit schools in the

greatest need of competent staff to bypass those procedures?

Nevertheless, the value of the NTE alternative should and could be assessed by studying those teachers now employed in New York City's schools under this alternative route. They could serve as the basis of comparison to determine how effective this test is in providing school districts with wider sources of personnel and how they compare with those selected by the traditional New York City methods. The NTE in its current form, however, does not seem to provide anything approaching the whole answer to the complex question of selecting the best school personnel.

(c)   A Statewide Examination. A few witnesses at the commission's hearings, mainly those who favored maintenance of the Board of Examiners' system, supported a statewide examination as a satisfactory alternative. Board of Education President Murry Bergtraum testified in favor of elimination of the Board of Examiners as a quasi-independent agency, but recommended a New York State examination ". . . equivalent to the one given for the Bar, not as difficult, I hope, or for other professions" because he considers current state certification, "the accumulation of courses," to be inadequate. [*Id.* at 9]. UFT President Shanker and CSA President Degnan generally concurred. Mr. Shanker would support abolition of the Board of Examiners if a similar statewide examination were in existence. The rationale offered by Mr. Shanker was based on an analogy between teaching and other licensed occupations. He said

> There are literally hundreds of occupations where the state has . . . the responsibility for maintaining particular levels of service and standards in terms of entry into that field, and I think it would be kind of ridiculous if the City of New York or the State of New York says that to drive an automobile and to sell real estate or sell insurance one needs a written examination, but to teach the children of the City of New York, it is not required. . . ." [*Id.* at 340]

A similar view was voiced by Dr. Bernard Friedman, Community Superintendent of District 7 in the Bronx. He said that ". . . no examinations at all . . . show an open contempt for the profession as it is. . . . Society, in a sense, puts its emphasis on a profession to the extent that it examines it." [*Id.* at 467]. In other words, the apparent justification for such an examination is to bolster the image of the teaching profession.

Critics of the current system, however, saw a statewide examination as no real alternative. Dr. Marilyn Gittell, as well as other witnesses, found such an examination another stumbling block for candidates from outside the state. The analogy with other occupations was rejected because, according to Dr. Robert A. Dentler, Director of the Center for Urban Education, it would be ". . . extremely embarrassing to recommend in 1971 that an obsolete system, such as bar examinations, be applied in what is still only a very incompletely emergent profession. . . ." [*Id.* at 527]

David Seeley, Director of the Public Education Association, also considered the analogy of state bar examinations and medical boards irrelevant because a teacher, unlike a doctor or a lawyer, does not set himself up in practice with no checks on his ability. "Teachers are hired by public authorities and, almost invariably, by other professional educators, who work for these public authorities. They have the opportunity and the competence to check into the qualifications of those they hire." [*Id.* at 382]

But even if bar examinations provided an apt analogy, they raise substantial problems of the kind discussed in Chapter 6. This is illustrated by two recent developments. First, a law suit was filed against the New York State Bar Examiners charging the bar examination discriminated against women [*Newark Star-Ledger,* July 20, 1971, p. 8, col. 6]. The case was settled on the basis of changes in the procedures. Second, a Special Committee of the Philadelphia Bar Association, after investigating charges that the Pennsylvania Bar examination was administered in a racially discriminatory manner, reported on December 20, 1970 that certain practices raised "the strongest presumption that Blacks are indeed discriminated against under procedures used by the State Board of Law Examiners." [*See* 44 Temple L.Q. 141 (1971), for the full text of the report, and *Juris Doctor,* vol. 1, no. 3, p. 5 (Mar. 1971).] The findings of the Special Committee contain striking parallels to the Human Rights Commission's conclusions about the Board of Examiners.

The advocates of a statewide examination are aware that such a procedure would not be free of problems. An appropriate test would take time to develop, and Mr. Shanker recognizes it might be opposed by most teachers in the state who now need only course credit for certification. Perhaps the defects of a statewide examination as an alternative were best stated by Dr. Greene when he said that "they [the state] would get the same complaints that the Board of Examiners face. There is nothing that would be magical about their tests that would avoid charges of discrimination. There are states that have tried tests for certification, and they have been accused of discrimination. The tests are too hard and take too long, the same criticisms we face." [*Selection of Teachers,* 1972, p. 147]. In sum, a statewide examination would be imposing on the state that which only two cities in the state now employ and which Buffalo has been moving toward eliminating.

Thus, considerable weight has built up against continued reliance on any *mandatory,* written test for the certification or selection of teachers. (This would not, of course, affect the right of any board of education to choose to use a written test as part of its own selection procedures as long as it met the kinds of standards already discussed.) But this weight must become great enough to move the state legislature. And, as we have seen, this is not an easy task. Formidable political forces are still working for the retention of a written certifying test.

Assemblyman William Passanante of New York City introduced another in the long series of bills designed to abolish the Board of Examiners at the 1971 legislative session. For the first time the bill was reported out of committee after Passanante agreed to modify it to require the New York City Board of Education to establish an alternate examination procedure administered by the chancellor, the State Education Department, or an independent testing service, such as the Educational Testing Service. Nevertheless, the bill was defeated 82 to 59 with black and Puerto Rican New York City legislators favoring adoption and many white New York City legislators opposing it.

New York City continues, therefore, in the unenviable position of being required by state law to carry out its selection procedures through the Board of Examiners. At the same time a federal court has ruled preliminarily that the board's current procedures for supervisory positions are invalid and unlawful. The political impact of that ruling, incidentally, may be substantial. But, the legislature has yet to act.

Interim Measures to Improve Selection Processes

Complete reform of the New York City selection process and others like it is not possible without legislative action. But there are many areas where changes can be made in the interim, changes to better integrate the several parts of the selection process and to make the whole more responsive to the needs of children and the community. Avenues open to the Board of Education could be used to greater effect and the Board of Examiners itself has the power to restructure the content and form of its examination process. A number of these interim measures pertain to special aspects of the New York City school system but many more will undoubtedly be applicable to other school districts as they take steps to improve their selection processes.

Much of the current attention, especially toward increasing

the opportunities for minority personnel, is focused on recruiting. The limited success, thus far, of out-of-town recruiting suggests that substantial problems are created by the complexities and rigidities of the examination process. Those in charge of the Office of Personnel's recruiting programs suggested that attracting outsiders was difficult not only because immediate job offers cannot be made on the spot, but also because New York City has a negative image, a reputation of limited opportunities for minority persons. A vast reservoir of capable manpower remains untapped, both within the city and without, in large part because entry and promotion hinge on a series of separate examinations, each of which can involve substantial pre-examination preparation and expense and substantial post-examination delay. One interim measure for alleviating this problem is the use of simplified examinations—either so-called unassembled examinations, which may consist of review of record without written tests, or one-day walk-in examinations with short-form written tests—especially for those being recruited on campuses outside the New York metropolitan area. There are already precedents within the New York City system for using either type of simplified examination. Alternatively, the National Teacher Examination, which many prospective teachers take as a matter of course, could be used as a part of the selection process instead of a local written test. A simplified procedure could enable New York City to compete on more equal recruiting terms with city school districts such as Detroit whose recruiters are authorized to offer jobs on the spot to applicants who rank in the upper half of their class and who make a favorable impression during the interview.

An interim change in recruiting emphasis might also help. Virtually no effort has been made to recruit candidates for supervisory positions from outside the system. This contributes to New York City's reputation as a closed school system, especially for minority groups. If outside candidates were actively sought (and if the selection process did not make it more difficult for them, as many witnesses testified was the case) the reputation would begin to change.

Further beneficial changes could result from modifying eligibility requirements. The first step in the selection process is the determination of eligibility for examination. The Board of Education has been moving in the direction of changing the qualifications, largely by reducing the number of years that must be served on one job level to be eligible for a promotional examination. Because most minority personnel are relatively new to the system, reducing the time requirements probably will accelerate the rate of their promotion, and there is no evidence that this will adversely affect quality. If the content and form of the examination are unchanged, however, the impact is likely to be limited. Moreover, upgrading remains a lock-step progression through the ranks. What is needed is the determination of qualifications based on skill, demonstrated capacity, and personality, rather than on strict and substantial quantitative measures of time in grade. This approach would be consistent with current developments in educational circles regarding the identification of urban school administrators. For example, Professor Michael Usdan, of the City University of New York and Coordinator of the New York Component of the National Program for Educational Leadership, described that program under which mid-career people, from various professions without the traditional educational or experience background, are being specially trained to lead school districts.

Another area in which reducing the traditional educational and experience requirements may pay great dividends is that of the paraprofessionals. Because the majority of paraprofessionals are minority group members who are mature adults strongly committed to working with children, especially urban ghetto children, and are experienced in working within their communities, they represent a manpower resource that

warrants fuller utilization. If career development were structured to focus on in-service training and development, selection of teachers from among the paraprofessional ranks could
be made with far greater reliability than from among the recent
graduates of teachers' colleges and at a far more rapid rate.

As we saw in Chapter 3, attention should be given to the Puerto
Rican paraprofessional and, for the first time, to the Oriental
paraprofessional, at a time when one of the school
system's most urgent needs is for more bilingual personnel.
Also, more direct efforts should be launched to deal with the
gross shortages and underrepresentation of bilingual teachers
and supervisors. A specific interim reform was suggested by
Dr. Edythe Gaines, then a community superintendent. Speaking of her district, she said, "In a district where close to 60
per cent of the pupils come from Spanish-speaking homes, we
have a talent pool of people who can teach Spanish although
they may not have the other qualifications. . ... We would
not ask that the person be licensed for everything but just be
given a certificate of competency so they can teach Spanish."
[*Selection of Teachers*, 1972, p. 54]. Granting certificates of
competency or exemptions from some of the "normal" requirements for native English-speaking candidates, in favor
of ability to speak Spanish or Chinese and otherwise to communicate with children, is only one of the steps which must
be taken to meet the needs of bilingual children. The alternative to this has been an inexcusable failure to provide even
a minimal education to the tens of thousands of children
who do not speak English well.

Another important facet of the selection process, which
can be the subject of interim change, is the development of
job descriptions. Analyses of functions for all job titles clearly
need updating and refinement. The consensus of testing experts is that a precise job description is a crucial element in
designing an effective selection method. The Board of Examiners, in theory, designs tests to meet job descriptions

given them by the Office of Personnel. For teachers, a new and continually revised job description is an urgent need. According to Dr. Lang, there had not been a new job description for teachers for at least a five-and-a-half-year period. He stated, "I guess we assume we have knowledge of what a teacher does and the Board of Examiners has knowledge of it." [*Id.* at 77] Such an assumption seems unfounded in the face of criticism of the teachers' examinations.

For supervisory and administrative positions, new job descriptions are prepared when a new examination is scheduled, but outside test experts consider them inadequate bases for sound test construction. Dr. Barrett characterized current descriptions of principals' functions as a "skeleton of a job description that does not give the kind of information that is useful for a person who is going to develop a test." [*Id.* at 407] Job analysis is a sensitive and demanding task, one that requires expert skill. Furthermore, community school boards and their superintendents should be involved in the process to assure relevance to local school needs. It is important that where new criteria are being developed, parents and other community representatives, as well as professional educators, make a substantial contribution to the process. The Board of Examiners cannot be faulted entirely, if the tests they design are based on out-of-date and overly broad statements of duties rather than timely and specific skills and qualities.

The next element in the selection process, and the focal issue of the hearings, is the design and administration of tests, written and oral. The most obvious deficiencies result from the limited resources of the Board of Examiners in designing selection instruments, and in assessing their validity. A consensus emerged that far more research is needed into all facets of the examination process. If simplified local examinations or the NTE were used instead of the current, more elaborate examinations, the Board of Examiners would have greater resources for its research efforts. Such an immediate shift in its priorities would be an important first step toward its possible role as a service agency for the city board and community boards.

In any event, the Board of Examiners conducts its examinations only in such licenses and at such times as the Board of Education and chancellor direct. It is certainly within their power to withhold requests for any new examinations until they are satisfied that the examination process has been properly validated. Indeed, they may have a legal responsibility to do so. As we have seen, the State Education Law expressly requires that New York City examinations be periodically validated and the federal courts, largely on federal constitutional grounds, have enjoined the holding of supervisory examinations because of their lack of validity.

The chancellor and community superintendents have yet another way to force the upgrading of the examination process. Temporary examination assistants can be appointed only with the approval of either the chancellor or a community superintendent. The temporary examination assistants are in fact responsible for many of the most sensitive jobs in the examination process—constructing the written test, giving oral interviews, grading the examinations. Yet, virtually everyone concedes that the procedures by which they are selected are wholly inadequate and provide no assurances of ability to carry out these tasks. By itself, this may seriously compromise the validity of the examination process. The fault here does not lie solely with the Board of Examiners. Apparently, the examiners have for some time sought to have the Board of Education establish licenses and an examination process for the position of temporary examination assistant. Moreover, the chancellor testified at the commission's hearings that he has rubber-stamped names of temporary examination assistants sent to him by the Board of Examiners. The chancellor and community superintendents should be able to condition their approval upon the nominees having demonstrated certain expertise and background in test construction and personnel management. In addition, the approval process could be a way to ensure that a more representative number of black and Puerto Rican examination assistants are appointed. Judge Mansfield singled out the disproportionately large number of white assistants as an important source of potential bias in the process.

Ultimate responsibility for the content of the examination rests with the Board of Examiners, though. And many ways have been suggested for the examiners to improve the content and make it more meaningful for today's schools and school children. The board must not be wedded to an elaborate, locally created written test, or for that matter to any written test. During the period beginning in July 1971, when Judge Mansfield's injunction against use of the Board of Examiners' selection process for supervisory positions was in effect, appointments were made on an acting basis under a less formal procedure. By October 1972, it was said that almost one-half of all supervisors had been appointed by that means. This affords the board with a custom-made opportunity to evaluate the results of a selection process without a written test. But, even if the board were to choose to continue to rely on a written test, it must, as a priority matter, react openly and adequately to the charges that the written examinations unduly screen out bilingual and other desperately needed teachers and supervisors.

The final element in selection, the probationary period, also requires careful restructuring. (It will be discussed in more detail in the next chapter.) Optimally, it should serve as a carefully observed internship. Increased local initiative arising from decentralization may focus more attention on the probationary period, but this cannot be left to chance. The Board of Examiners correctly asserts that its tests do not predict performance. Those with the responsibility for rating new personnel must be given the tools for reliable appraisal of performance. Satisfactory use of the probationary period could, in fact, provide significant feedback about the testing process itself.

On balance, the preeminence in professional personnel matters accorded the Board of Examiners results largely from the fact that other elements, intended as important parts of selection, have been neglected. The examiners' apparent autonomy is partially a reflection of inadequate performance by those responsible for preparing job descriptions and for following successful candidates through the probationary period. Even an adequately staffed Board of Examiners can only serve as intended, as a resource to the Board of Education and, therefore, to the schools, if all parts of the selection process are well handled and properly articulated. Until the current system is replaced, it is imperative to close the gaps exposed during the hearings.

Moreover, the Detroit experience indicates that commitment from the top is an essential ingredient. The number of minority group members within the professional staff of any school district can be increased considerably if that is the clear intent of those in charge.

What is required, above all, is the formulation of a positive plan for hiring school personnel, and this can begin even before legislative changes are effected. Many witnesses commented on the lack of guidelines for recruiting, selecting, or evaluating personnel. Such guidelines need to be developed for the system at large, identifying the broad general qualities to be sought and how they can best be measured. In addition, a specific program addressed to increasing minority employment must be carried through. It is not enough to think only in terms of recruiting minority candidates, especially when this amounts to identifying people who become discouraged at the complexity of procedures or for other reasons never materialize as additions to the staff of the school system. Procedures for facilitating their appointment and promotion are the indispensible concomitants. It is time for boards of education everywhere to recognize that problems relating to their selection processes will not simply disappear if they are ignored long enough or if the school system repeatedly vows its good faith. Thoughtful and concerted efforts, following serious analysis of the causes of the problems, are absolutely necessary if children are to be well served. This applies to interim changes no less than to major reform.

CHAPTER 8

ACCOUNTABILITY OF
TEACHERS AND SUPERVISORS

Accountability of school systems and their personnel has become a widely discussed national issue. The concept has many facets. One involves the responsibility of the educational system to provide pupils with a sufficient level of education. In that connection, the New York City school system entered into a contract with the Educational Testing Service for the development of an educational accountability design. The framework proposed by ETS made clear that the design would involve "joint accountability"; that is, the collective responsibility of a school's entire staff rather than the responsibility of individual teachers and supervisors. This aspect of accountability was outside the scope of the commission's hearings and it is beyond the reach of this chapter, but issues of selection, tenure, and promotion are clearly pertinent. And "individual accountability" is part of each of those issues.

Individual accountability takes a number of forms. In most school districts teachers and supervisors serve probationary periods after their appointment to positions. The length of the period varies from state to state and, in some cases, from position to position (a common pattern is a three-year probationary period for teaching positions and a somewhat shorter period for supervisory positions if the appointee had already acquired tenure as a teacher). In New York State the tenure law was modified in 1971 to increase the probationary period for teachers from three to five years and, by entirely eliminating tenure for supervisory personnel, to effectively create a perpetual probationary period for them. Needless to say, this bill was passed over the vigorous opposition of teacher and supervisor organizations. It may reflect a growing legislative concern about the direction of public education and especially about the impact on it of increasing employee security. Interestingly, the latest UFT contract seeks to reduce the probationary period to three years despite the statutory provision.

The probationary period, in theory at least, serves two important and related functions. It is regarded as a potentially vital facet of the selection process. Many witnesses at the commission's hearings spoke of the impossibility of adequately predicting a candidate's potential for being a good teacher without an opportunity to evaluate his or her classroom performance. Regarding the probationary period as a part of the selection process means the *final* decision can be made after a substantial opportunity for performance evaluation. Indeed, many of the suggestions for improvement in state certification focus on greater use of the probationary period as an internship served under a temporary certificate.

The other important role of the probationary period—in a sense the other side of the selection coin—is with respect to the granting of tenure. Only after probationers successfully complete their probationary period can they be given tenure. If they are found unsatisfactory during the probationary period, they can be released without the elaborate panoply of hearings and appeals available to a tenured professional (although through the courts and the collective bargaining process probationary employees are getting increased due process safeguards).

Success or failure during probation for both purposes—selection and tenure—is measured principally by periodic supervisors' ratings. The vast preponderance of the ratings are "satisfactory." If an unsatisfactory rating is given, often the employee has an appeal procedure available and, in any event, the supervisor may be obliged to take certain steps to assist the employee in remedying his or her deficiency within a reasonable time period.

Based on their accumulated ratings, employees are considered for tenure at the end of their probationary periods. Tenure is actually granted by the board of education, acting upon the recommendation of the superintendent of schools. In most larger urban school districts, and certainly in New York City prior to decentralization, the superintendent has typically recommended at one time that tenure be granted to hundreds or even thousands of persons and the board of education, usually without any review of individual records, has approved.

In New York City decentralization appears to be changing this situation. Now the 31 community boards grant tenure to teachers under their jurisdiction. The number of probationers coming before each community board is far more manageable than the thousands which came before the New York City Board toward the end of each school year. Review of individual records is feasible and the community superintendent, who now recommends probationers for tenure, can be expected to have first-hand insights to provide. Recommendations of parent-teacher associations and other community organizations interested in the schools are likely to be considered as well.

A number of community boards have already announced that they are making greater use of the probationary period to screen teachers and supervisors for competency as well as personal characteristics. As a central part of this effort, these boards will expect supervisors' ratings to be more thoughtful and less automatic. Philip Kaplan, Chairman of Community School Board No. 15, said:

> . . . [I] f we start holding the principals accountable for the progress in their schools, they will start weeding out those teachers who cannot teach and meet the levels that they set. [*Selection of Teachers,* 1972, p. 201]

Periodic ratings by supervisors are not limited in their importance to the probationary period. They continue throughout an employee's career in the school system. Effective use of the rating system should be important for promotions as well. Most supervisors come from within the New York City school system. To be eligible for a supervisory examination, an applicant generally must have served a specified number of years as a teacher and, perhaps, as a lower level supervisor also. For some recent examinations, the prior service requirement has been reduced, but even in those cases it is still substantial. Thus, a wealth of information could be available about actual performance of most candidates for supervisory positions. Nevertheless, eligibility for promotion to most supervisory positions has been heavily dependent upon the candidates' success on a centrally administered written test and oral interview. Relatively little weight is given to their record of service in the school system.

Finally, the rating system is pertinent to accountability of tenured personnel. One of the statutory grounds for their removal is incompetence. A careful and detailed rating system could provide the best basis for assessing the competence of tenured personnel, as well as probationers and candidates for promotion. Moreover, for tenured personnel to gain their regular pay increments, they must normally receive satisfactory ratings. From a more positive point of view, if tenured teachers are given meaningful ratings they will be better able to constantly improve their performance.

Unfortunately, practice has not followed theory very closely in the area of performance evaluation. The commission heard much testimony from educators, officials of the Board of Education, community board members, community superintendents, principals and others, to the effect that performance ratings have little meaning. Probationers and tenured personnel alike have been routinely given satisfactory ratings by their supervisors unless they demonstrated extraordinary deficiency. For probationers this means tenure normally has been granted as a matter of course. For tenured personnel this means salary increments have come like clockwork and removal for incompetence has been virtually unheard of. In New York City, for that matter, removal of tenured professionals for any reason is virtually unheard of. During a recent five-year period, a grand total of seven tenured professionals were reportedly removed for all causes including incompetency. And that is from a professional staff of more than 60,000 with a substantial percentage on tenure.

The routineness of the supervisor rating process may reflect the impact of the Board of Examiners. According to many witnesses at the commission hearings, the examination has assumed such awesome proportions in the selection process that once a candidate passes it there is a strong sense that he or she has vanquished the major hurdle along the route to a permanent position in the school system. But others consider the fault to lie with the Board of Education's professional staff which has, over the years, effectively sanctioned a superficial evaluation process.

In any event, it is clear that greatly improved performance evaluation is crucial to reform of school system personnel practices. For on-the-job success will be the key not only to salary increases and tenure but to teacher training and certification and employment as well.

What has caused the shortcomings of the current system? Where should we be looking for improvements in performance evaluation?

To answer these questions, it is necessary to dig deeper into the pertinent testimony at the commission's hearings because, on one level at least, the current system has all the trappings of a thorough and thoughtful evaluation process. It generates enormous quantities of paper—detailed rating sheets which contain evaluations of personnel in innumerable categories. Any educational bureaucrat worth his salt knows how to make his evaluations as formidable and unimpeachable as possible. Yet, despite these trappings and despite the potential usefulness of ratings during the probationary period, there is widespread agreement that the process is largely meaningless.

Dr. Theodore H. Lang, former Deputy Superintendent in charge of personnel, testified, for example, that the probationary period is of critical importance because ". . . the only way to really know whether a teacher is a good teacher is by giving him the opportunity to teach and observing him as he teaches." [*Id.* at 81] Nevertheless, Dr. Lang's view is that ". . . the school system has used the probationary period very little in the past, too little. . . ." [*Id.*]

Dr. Jay E. Greene, a former member of the Board of Examiners, expressed this view also, but from a somewhat different perspective. According to his testimony, a number of changes were made in the examination process, such as omitting the essay questions with respect to teaching techniques, ". . . on the promise that the probationary period would be made use of in a proper way. That utilization of the probationary period never occurred. . . ." [*Id.* at 142]

Murry Bergtraum, President of the City Board at the time of the hearings, also stressed the importance of the probationary period:

> . . . [T]his Board and the Chancellor . . . feel that the real examination process for teachers or for supervisors should be on the job, and that accountability for performance during a probationary period is more important to insure quality of performance than any other method, so that examination processes which go into elaborate systems of trying to forecast performance on the job, might very well not direct themselves to these subjects. . . . [T]he process of being able to direct to another profession persons who do not perform on the job should be looked at because in New York today . . . it is extremely difficult to use the probationary period as a performance period. [*Id.* at 9]

What accounts for this difficulty? According to Mr. Bergtraum, it is the many restrictions and formalities that have been built into the process by rulings of the State Commissioner of Education, by union contract provisions and, to a lesser extent, by statutory provisions. In his words:

> I think that the probationary period must be considered part of the examination process . . .; that a person should be able to be, in a sense, passed or failed . . . based on their superior's assessment of their performance with some minor safeguards but no elaborate process where it becomes an adversary proceeding between attorneys . . . as if they were tenured. If there is a distinction between tenure and nontenure, that's where it should be. That's where we should get rid of people who can't teach and not by constructing examinations which never really test the ability to teach anyway. . . . [*Id.* at 13–14]

Mrs. Blanche Lewis, President of the United Parents Association, shared Mr. Bergtraum's view. She testified, "Our experience indicates that under existing law and regulations, it is almost impossible to separate from service even the most incompetent professional." [*Id.* at 326]

A different explanation for the ineffectiveness of performance evaluation was offered by junior high school principal Irving Flinker. He attributed the difficulty to the fact that ". . . the teacher comes to the school with a license granted by an authoritative body, namely, the Board of Examiners. The principal has greater difficulty validating his objections [in order] to dismiss the teacher when the teacher comes with such a license." [*Selection of Teachers,* 1972, p. 66] Mr. Flinker contrasted the relative ease with which principals can screen out unsatisfactory professionals who have substitute, rather than regular, licenses.

The only testimony which defended, at least in part, the current system of accountability was from UFT President Shanker. He said that although few teachers, probationary or tenured, are formally removed on the basis of poor performance, many are advised informally that they should leave and, if they do, that they will receive good recommendations. "There is nothing wrong with the present procedures," said Mr. Shanker, "if they are used. They aren't used in many cases or, when they are, it is informal procedure that prevails. . . ." [*Id.* at 358]

The conceded failure of the current system in holding professional personnel truly accountable for their performance on the job should make it obvious why parents and taxpayers have become so disgruntled about the public school system. It also raises serious questions about the viability of a total personnel system based upon performance evaluation. But, there are some hints in the testimony about both short-term palliatives for the current system and long-term bases for the creation of a sounder system.

On the theory that in a bureaucracy things filter down almost imperceptibly from the top, an immediate step that could be taken is for the examination process to give much greater weight to supervisor's ratings. This would not apply in the case of a candidate completely new to the school system but it would be pertinent for most candidates for supervisory licenses as well as for candidates for teaching licenses who have been teaching in the school system with a substitute's license or a per diem certificate. Such a change in examination emphasis could be effected by the Board of Examiners without statutory amendment.

Another interim change that could improve the effectiveness of the rating system would be a clear and forceful statement of expectation from the chancellor and Board of Education that the time has come for ratings to be used as a meaningful staff screening and upgrading mechanism. And the upgrading aspect is important. Teachers who are the subjects of superficial ratings are victims of the system as much as the children, their parents, and the taxpayers. If teachers are to continuously improve their performance, they have to be helped. This is especially true of young teachers. What better way to help them than by a meaningful evaluation of their performance.

Yet another immediate step is tied back to the development

of a program for school "joint" accountability. To the extent school staffs are really challenged to perform up to a standard, albeit aggregate, there will be inevitable pressure on every staff member to pull his or her own weight. This is already happening in the schools in some New York City community districts where the staff, through their principal, has been made aware of the community's expectations. These kinds of expectations will quickly work their way down to the level of every supervisor who is responsible for submitting rating forms.

Another effort that can be started immediately is providing those responsible for rating personnel with the tools for reliable appraisal of performance. Effective use of the probationary period, and of performance evaluations generally, requires staff time and planned involvement of colleagues, supervisors, community board members and others, as well as training of all those who take part in the process. Better use of the probationary period could, in fact, provide significant feedback about the examination process itself. If careful performance evaluations reveal little correlation between success on the job and success on the examination, the validity of the examination may be placed in further doubt.

The universities and teacher training institutions should play a major role in this process of improving performance ratings. Boards of education tend to be short of research funds, and this is likely to continue to be the case. But this is an area where the colleges can reasonably be expected to do the work on their own initiative. An essential part of developing meaningful evaluation procedures is determining what good performance is. Until the colleges find this out, they can't be doing a very effective job of training teachers.

As has been suggested, one way for the colleges to begin to explore performance-based criteria is by using paraprofessionals already in the school system as a pilot group. Indeed, experimental teacher training programs have already begun to adopt a paraprofessional model for the first and most important part of training—in-school experience carefully structured to allow for skill development and understanding of teaching problems—with theory and academic subject matter following and related closely to experimental development.

In addition to these efforts, which can be launched in any urban school district immediately, there are a number of other longer range steps requiring legislative or statewide administrative action.

For example, as we have seen, a statewide internship or provisional certification program is being considered or actually developed in a number of states. Its theory is that the initial period of teaching or supervisory service should be a continuation of professional training as well as an evaluation opportunity. To formally recognize it as such would encourage the development of more meaningful in-service training programs and other professionally supportive efforts which are desperately needed. As Wendy Lehrman, an experienced New York City teacher pointed out:.

> ... the answer [to educational shortcomings] must be sought in a
> system which thwarts the potential of its teachers by freezing perform-
> ance standards at the very low level of the granting of the license to
> teach. A system which confers the lifetime title of "teacher" upon
> us before we have had a chance to become teachers, and then slams
> the book shut, has failed in its responsibility to permit us to develop
> beyond second-rate professionals. Many of us do go on trying to pre-
> pare ourselves for teaching long after we have been licensed and given
> tenure. That is when it starts, but that is when the system leaves us.
> ... [T]he Board of Examiners defines us, and by defining us as
> teachers at a certain point and then dropping everybody, that is
> the end. [*Id.* at 232–33]

Structuring the initial period of service as an internship would also encourage more careful evaluation before the granting of permanent status. Tied to that is the fact that the whole institution of tenure, as a "lifetime contract," is being seriously questioned. The fourth annual Gallup poll of "Public

Attitudes Toward Education" revealed that 61% of those
questioned disapproved of lifetime tenure and only 28% supported it. This was so although the public's general opinion of
teachers and teaching as a profession was quite favorable (*i.e.,*
67% said they would like to have a child of theirs adopt teaching as a career). [*See Phi Delta Kappan,* Sept. 1972; *The New
York Times,* Oct. 1, 1972, p. E-11, col. 5.] Perhaps as a result
of this adverse public reaction to tenure, state legislatures have
begun to reduce the scope of tenure laws. The New York
State Legislature has already eliminated tenure for school
supervisors. It is unlikely this absolute step will be taken at
the *teacher* level in New York or elsewhere. But there are
other, more limited efforts to reduce the almost absolute
security of tenured status. New York has increased the probationary period to five years. Other states, such as Minnesota
and New Jersey, are moving toward a system of "reviewable
tenure" under which an employee's broad protection against
removal will lapse after about five years and be renewed only
after a showing of continuing competence. Chancellor Scribner
has recommended such an approach in New York.

These are developments which Albert Shanker, not unex-
pectedly, resists. He has argued that even tenured teachers
can be removed if they are incompetent because "an able
administrator will be able to document the fact in a way that
the courts will sustain." [*The New York Times,* Mar. 12, 1972,
p. E-7, col. 5] The main reason for the "few dismissals" of
tenured teachers is that in schools, as in private industry, the
"vast majority of employees who are called down and told
they are not doing a good job leave quietly, without a
struggle." [*Id.*] Some labor commentators, according to Mr.
Shanker have suggested that "the best response to the attack
on the tenure laws might be to get rid of them entirely, in
the knowledge that teacher unions can negotiate stronger job
protection in their contracts." [*Id.*] But, Mr. Shanker rejected
that view as "only half right." [*Id.*] Strong unions might do

better but weak teacher groups might lose virtually all job security.

But there are positive aspects to restructuring tenure which could overcome the risks. [*See, e.g., The New York Times,* Sept. 24, 1971, p. E-7, col. 1.] Whatever form the restructuring takes, as the scope of tenure protection is reduced, the importance of performance evaluation will be correspondingly increased. If employees serve more or less at the pleasure of their employers, they can be removed much more easily for unsuccessful performance. Hopefully, this greater role for performance evaluation will spur its development along meaningful substantive lines rather than result in its use as a facade for politically or ideologically motivated actions or in abuses of teachers' due process rights.

On the school district level, the development and use of independent observers or observation teams to replace supervisors in the evaluation and rating process may be an important step forward. Supervisors are always torn between their desire to render meaningful evaluations and ratings, and their desire to maintain staff morale. While the ablest supervisors may be able to do both, many can not. Independent evaluation, if sufficiently informed and expert, may solve the problem. Various observation techniques have been developed, and others are being developed, to ensure validity. Of course the observers must be adequately trained in their techniques. In many states the use of these techniques and observers will require modification of state education department rules and regulations, local board of education by-laws, and union contracts. Legal issues may also be raised about improper delegation of authority with respect to certification, employment and tenure decisions but this should not be a serious problem if the state education department and local boards of education maintain the ultimate decision-making power.

Some states are also moving to define a teacher's performance, for accountability purposes, in terms partially of student performance. Under California's new tenure law, for example, all certified personnel including teachers, principals and superintendents will be evaluated periodically on the basis of "standards of expected student progress in each area of study." [*Newark Star-Ledger*, Mar. 19, 1972, p. 43, col. 1] The law, the first of its kind, also requires evaluation of other duties normally performed as part of the professional's regular assignment.

The use of pupil performance raises several problems. How is it to be measured? The use of standardized written tests may pose some of the same problems discussed in Chapter 6, although here they are being used for the narrower purpose of ascertaining specific student knowledge and skills. There is the added risk that teachers will teach to the test, especially if their jobs may depend on the performance of their pupils. The Educational Testing Service is establishing the Center for Statewide Educational Assessment to help states adequately monitor student performance and the effect of the school on it. But even assuming pupil performance can be validly measured, another problem remains: How much is performance actually influenced by the teacher? Experts differ as we saw in the Introduction. To the extent jobs may hang in the balance, the correlation between teacher performance and pupil performance should be treated as a hypothesis to be proven by more definitive research findings.

Another possible advance in accountability procedures is the development of "Teacher Assessment Centers" to which candidates could go for the assessment of their performance capabilities. Experimentation is under way already in Washington, Oregon, and Florida, and guidance about the scope and form of this possibility should be available soon. [*Selection of Teachers*, 1972, p. 736] One potentially important aspect of Teacher Assessment Centers is that they might more visibly and substantially engage teacher professional organizations in the process of determining performance standards and measurement techniques. This is a long overdue step.

The NEA has also recommended a more thoroughgoing involvement of teachers in the accountability process. The Division of Instruction and Professional Development, and other NEA national and state units, have developed a "model teacher standards and licensure act" which would give teachers legal power to govern their own profession. The act provides for a "teacher standards and licensure commission," appointed by the governor of the particular state, to be responsible for accrediting teacher training institutions, issuing four types of teacher licenses, and suspending or revoking licenses. According to an NEA spokesman, "the general idea is that teachers are perfectly willing to be accountable to the public for the results of their teaching but they want the control that should go with it." [*Newark Star-Ledger,* Dec. 20, 1971, p. 12, col. 6] At least 16 state legislatures are considering some of the model act proposals.

Finally, again on the local level, the accountability apparatus will be improved as institutions, such as the New York City Board of Examiners, are entirely eliminated or their energies redirected. For increasingly the written test score is being recognized as, at best, a limited measure of a candidate's promise as a teacher or supervisor. At worst, it is a sham, likely to screen *out* people of imagination, insight, and sensitivity.

At the same time, there is emerging a sense of the real potential of performance-based criteria for holding school professionals accountable and for promoting them, as well as for certifying them and selecting them in the first instance. Many problems will have to be considered and overcome before this potential will be fully realized, but that is hardly a reason for holding back.

EPILOGUE

Since the completion of the manuscript, a development foreshadowed in Chapter 7 has assumed more concrete form. Its potential importance warrants further discussion. The special task force created by the parties to the *Chance* litigation to consider new selection models for the New York City school system has come tantalizingly close to some major breakthroughs.

At its first meeting, the task force's members* agreed that their functions would be to consider simultaneously (1) a model for the best possible selection process for supervisory personnel, whether or not such a process required changes in existing statutes or regulations, and (2) a model for the most effective selection process within the parameters of existing law. At subsequent meetings a number of points of tentative agreement were reached. Among them were the following:

1. The Board of Examiners should function as a service agency for the 31 community boards and the City Board of

---

*Plaintiffs' representatives: Boston Chance, John Hopkins, Rhoda Karpatkin, Luis Mercado and the author; and defendants' representatives: Sylvester King and Nathan Quinones, acting members of the Board of Examiners; Murray Rockowitz, member of the Board of Examiners; and Frederick Williams, then Executive Director of the Board of Education's Office of Personnel and the Chancellor's designee to the Board of Examiners. Counsel for the parties, Elizabeth DuBois and George Cooper for the plaintiffs and Saul Cohen for the defendants, also participated actively.

Education.

2. Duties of positions for all supervisory jobs should be created by the employing board of education, either the City Board or a community board.

3. Elements of assessment based on those "duties of positions," which are common to all school districts, should be jointly arrived at by the community boards, the City Board, the chancellor and the Board of Examiners and the Board of Examiners would use them as a basis for assessing all candidates.

4. Each community board and the appropriate central authority could also develop additional assessment elements which reflected their unique requirements.

5. The Board of Examiners would assess candidates on the basis of those special elements if the community district or central authority requested such service, but there would be no obligation to use the Board of Examiners for this purpose.

6. On the basis of its assessment of the common elements, and whatever special elements it was requested to assess, the Board of Examiners would construct for each candidate a profile which would be made available to the community board or the Chancellor or city board.*

7. The Board of Examiners would attest to the eligibility of all candidates on the basis of health, experience and academic preparation (as determined by statute or by the City Board's or chancellor's policy).

These points reflect an assumption, and it was just that, that a Board of Examiners would be continued in some form. The task force did not engage in any serious discussion about whether the Board should be eliminated, as so many have

---

*The assessment profile approach, commonly used in private industry, may itself represent a significant departure from traditional civil service examination procedures since it usually involves reliance on simulation tests rather than pencil and paper tests.

urged. But there was some feeling that a suitably restructured Board could play a constructive role in school system personnel selection.

Two major questions were left unanswered, however, by the task force's points of tentative agreement—should the restructured Board of Examiners have the power to *disqualify* candidates for reasons other than their failure to meet basic eligibility standards or should its primary function be informational; and should "eligible lists" of candidates have a four-year life as present law requires (*i.e.*, must the list be exhausted or four years pass before a new eligible list can be promulgated for the same job), or should there be an ongoing list which would be added to as additional candidates meet the eligibility requirements?

After the task force had reached these tentative agreements and identified these fundamental questions, it sought the input of community boards, community superindendents, central administrators, and representatives of professional employee organizations and parent organizations. A series of three meetings was held to get reactions to the points of agreement and suggestions about resolving the open questions.

The response was predictably varied. Some community board members and organizational representatives criticized the proposals because they did not urge the elimination of the Board of Examiners, which was seen as a vestigial remnant. Others were critical because of what they saw as the emasculation of the Board. Without clear and independent power to determine who was qualified to teach and supervise in the New York City schools, they said, the Board could not protect against abuses and ensure a uniform level of competency throughout the city system. But the majority of those at the meetings were in basic agreement with the broad outlines of the new system proposed by the task force.

On one of the two critical open questions, there was a surprising consensus. The present four-year list requirement

is undesirable. It was perceived as unfair both to school officials responsible for operating the best possible educational
programs and to the many well-qualified candidates who have
to wait years before they can even be considered for positions.
Ultimately, of course, such a system is unfair to the school
children. The better alternative, according to most of those
present, is some type of continuing list which can be added to
periodically. The precise format and procedures were not discussed in detail but, obviously, a number of significant issues
must be dealt with. Among them is the question of whether
candidates on the continuing list for a certain length of time
must be re-examined to assure that they have maintained
their qualifications.

Responses to the other critical open question—whether the
Board of Examiners should serve an entirely informational
function beyond determining basic eligibility—were more
mixed. A majority of the attendants, especially those representing community boards and organizations of minority
group professionals, favored an informational role. Maximum
discretion belongs in, and could best be exercised by, the
elected community boards and their superintendents, they
said. Without this discretion, it would be more difficult for
these boards to carry out their responsibilities. A strong
minority of the participants, primarily those representing the
central educational authorities and the established professional
employee organizations, argued strongly, however, for the continuation of a "cut-off" function in the Board of Examiners.
Beneath the rhetoric about maintaining uniform educational
and professional standards, the real concerns seemed clear.
Would race be a primary criterion? Would community boards
select "incompetents" if left to their own devices?

But are "incompetents" merely professionals different than
those in the traditional power centers? Are they "incompetent"
because they may have not only a different color but also a
different style and value system? Who is better able to deter-

mine "incompetency," a central testing agency or an elected community board acting on the recommendation of its chief professional, the community superintendent?

At its first meeting after the round of "input meetings," the task force had to deal with some of these questions, as well as the overall issue of whether the points of tentative agreement still seemed to point in a fruitful direction. The prevailing view was that the system outlined was basically sound as a foundation for further development. Also, the task force members were impressed by the near unanimity of responses favoring a continuing list. Even on the informational vs. disqualifying question, a breakthrough seemed near. Indeed, several Board of Examiners members suggested procedures which would give the Board almost entirely an informational role. The issue was not fully resolved but the promise was clearly there.

If agreement can be satisfactorily reached, the further work of the task force should be noteworthy. The door will be open for the development of a genuinely innovative system of professional selection. True, it was opened originally by a court order resulting from an adversary situation, but the real swing of the door will have to come from a collaborative effort carried out in a spirit of cooperation by those administering the system and by those who launched the attack on it. That in itself would be a refreshing breakthrough. It would bode well for the future of urban education.

INDEX

The symbol "(q)" following a page number indicates the appearance in the text of either the written or spoken words of the person named in the index entry.

A

Academy of Educational
   Development, 120
Accountability, 21, 67 ff.
   teachers, 30
Accreditation of teacher educa-
   tion programs, 99 ff.
Acting appointments, 208
Advisory Council of Colleges in
   Teacher Education, 108
AFT, *see* American Federation of
   Teachers
Allen v. City of Mobile, 198
Alloway, James A., 153
American Federation of
   Teachers, 79
   educational policy-making, 88
   merger with National Educa-
     tion Association, 83
*Application of Council of Super-
   visors and Administrators,*
   209
*Armstead v. Starkville Mun. Sep.
   School Dist.,* 195

*Arrington v. Mass. Bay Transp.
   Auth'y.,* 196

B

Bailey, Stephen K., 128
*Baker v. Columbus Mun. Sep.
   School District,* 195, 289
Bar examinations, 226, 292
Barrett, Richard, 204, 228(q),
   247, 298
Barth, Roland, 106
Battle pay, 46
Beginning Teacher Survey, 112
Benson, Charles, 51
Bergtraum, Murry, 121, 174
   291, 308(q)
Bilingual education, 145
   see also, Bilingualism;
     Teachers, bilingual
Bilingualism, 132, 143 222
   discrimination, 230
   paraprofessionals, 297
   see also, Teachers, bilingual;
     Bilingual education